Praise for *Fact, Fiction, and Flying Saucers*

"As a former police detective I am always attracted to UFO researchers who deal in actual facts. People who track down the written documents which confirm fact from fiction, people who establish what the real evidence is. Stanton Friedman and Kathleen Marden are two such people and I defy any rational, intelligent person to read their book and not be impressed by the level of detail on view. An excellent book that deals in hard core facts and leaves the fiction to the sceptics!"

—Gary Heseltine, researcher and editor of *UFO Truth Magazine*
(*www.ufotruthmagazine.co.uk*)

"There is a difference between fact and fiction, and if you have even the slightest open mind about UFOs, you may find yourself getting easily caught up in the material presented by Marden and Friedman. Fact, Fiction, and Flying Saucers pieces together the biggest jigsaw puzzle in history. In the end, we may not have all of the answers, but this book brings us a giant step closer to clarification of the UFO question."

—Lee Speigel, journalist

"Kathleen Marden and Stanton Friedman represent decades of research into the topic of UFOs and alleged alien abduction. This book gives us fascinating insights into their findings and opinions, and makes us examine the motives of those who seem to specialize in debunking the UFO phenomenon. Marden and Friedman demonstrate, although these professional skeptics profess a commitment to scientific rigor, often their research is quite dubious. Why is that? Armed with experience, facts, and informed speculation, Marden and Friedman are in a unique position to respond to this question, and their answer is deserving of serious consideration."

—Alejandro Rojas, editor at OpenMinds.tv

"There is no question in my mind that the critically important subjects Friedman and Marden address in *Fact, Fiction and Flying Saucers* are more timely now than ever. Genuine critical thinking, rigorous research, and dedicated professional investigation are increasingly rare commodities in this age of conspiracies, reality TV, and hyper-sensationalized mass media and internet. The fact that two of the world's most respected author/investigators have again collaborated in the writing of a new book is welcome news anytime. That they chose to take on the subjects they do here makes it even more so. A welcome addition to the world of UFO literature, and a book with the potential to reach a far larger audience than most 'UFO books' can even dream of."

—Peter Robbins, coauthor of the British best-seller *Left a East Gate* and long-time assistant to pioneer UFO abduction researcher Budd Hopkins.

"Why would the world need 'archives' on the subject matter of UFOs, ETs, and the like? Why would it be difficult to gain access to massive amounts of truth? What type of persons would obtain permission to enter these hallowed halls? The answer is Kathleen Marden and Stanton Friedman, two of the top, if not the top, researchers of the truth on these matters.

After reading *Fact, Fiction, and Flying Saucers*, I have no doubt that some groups, whether it be government or big business, have created a genius fun house of smoke and mirrors along with cleverly choreographed and well timed diversionary tactics to obfuscate the truth. Also, the many players involved have manipulated the true facts to draw attention and focus away from the obvious. This has caused many perfectly sane, everyday citizens to question what they have witnessed or experienced. Have our world governments done nothing to disclose the truth to those who deserve the answers? Or on the other hand, are they sharing ideas with others in their arena to create what may possibly be the largest cover up in the world? The arm chair debunkers—debunk only what others have researched. Read this fantastic work of truth for yourself where exposure of cover ups is proven to be fact! You will not be disappointed."

—Denise Stoner coauthor of *The Alien Abduction Files*,
lecturer, researcher

The Truth Behind the Misinformation, Distortion, and Derision by Debunkers, Government Agencies, and Conspiracy Conmen

FACT, FICTION, AND
AND
FLYING SAUCERS

STANTON T. FRIEDMAN
KATHLEEN MARDEN
AUTHORS OF *CAPTURED!*

New Page Books
A division of The Career Press, Inc.
Pompton Plains, N.J.

FACT, FICTION, AND FLYING SAUCERS
EDITED BY JODI BRANDON
TYPESET BY KARA KUMPEL
Cover design by Howard Grossman/12E Design
Printed in the U.S.A.

Images on pages 5, 14, 118, and 140 courtesy of the Marden photo collection. Image on page 31, USAF, no license required, via Wikimedia Commons. Image on page 51 provided by Menzel's daughter, Elizabeth Menzel Davis. "Donald Howard Menzel" by Babette Whipple. CC BY-SA 3.0, via Wikimedia Commons, *https://en.wikimedia.org/wiki/File:Menzel_Portrait.jpg*. Image on page 68 taken in 1977 by Robert Sheaffer. CC BY-SA 3.0, via Wikimedia Commons, *https://en.wikimedia.org/wiki/Philip_J._Klass#media/File:Klass1977.JPG*. Image on page 75, U.S. government photo, no license required, via Wikimedia Commons, *https://en.wikimedia.org/wiki/James_E._McDonald#/media/File:James_E._McDonald_1.gif*. Images on pages 84 and 171 courtesy of the Stanton T. Friedman collection. Image on page 95, U.S. government photo, National Institute of Standards and Technology, no license required, via Wikimedia Commons, *https://en.wikimedia.org/wiki/ File:Edward_U._Condon.jpg*. Image on page 128 of Lonnie Zamora by artist Patrick Richard. Image on page 211, U.S. government photo, no license required, via Wikimedia Commons, *https://commons.wikimedia.org/ wiki/ File:AtomicEffects-Hiroshima.jpg*.

To order this title, please call toll-free 1-800-CAREER-1 (NJ and Canada: 201-848-0310) to order using VISA or MasterCard, or for further information on books from Career Press.

The Career Press, Inc.
12 Parish Drive
Wayne, NJ 07470
www.careerpress.com

Library of Congress Cataloging-in-Publication Data
CIP Data Available Upon Request.

ACKNOWLEDGMENTS

Kathleen Marden, Stanton Friedman, and Jennifer Stein

Kathleen and Stanton wish to thank the following people:

Jennifer W. Stein for her gracious hospitality during our visits to Philadelphia and her research assistance at the American Philosophical Society Research Library. Jennifer is the executive producer and director of the documentary *TRAVIS: The True Story of Travis Walton* (*https://onwingesproductions.com/travis-walton*).

The American Philosophical Society for their assistance during our research visits.

John Schuessler for his assistance with the Cash-Landrum UFO landing case.

Cassidy Nicholas at the Mutual UFO Network for her assistance with photos.

Patrick M. Richard, the extraordinary artist who painted Lonnie Zamora. His original oil painting hangs in the City of Socorro's Visitor Center. Case illustrations, paintings, or project renderings can be discussed with this artist. Please send inquiries to Lunawink@gmail.com.

Lisa Relland, MUFON Canada, for Kathleen's photo.

Robert Sheaffer for his assistance with CSICOP photos.

John Greenewald at theblackvault.com Website for his assistance.

Francis Ridge at NICAP.org for his online archive and the FOIA documents in the Appendix.

Dale Goudie and Jim Klotz from CUFON.org for their online archive.

CONTENTS

INTRODUCTION

The general public, through the mainstream media and as a result of false and misleading claims by debunkers, has for many years
been misinformed on the subject of UFOs despite the many serious
studies conducted by scientists. There have been more than 5,000
reports collected of physical trace cases from 89 countries. UFOs
have not only been observed hovering near the ground, but also
taking off and leaving behind various physical traces. Tests have
been conducted in laboratories of soil beneath where the UFOs were
observed. There are more than 3,500 observations by civilian and
military pilots of nonconventional aircraft in the skies and often
seen by radar as well. These are not merely lights in the sky, but are
clearly manufactured craft behaving in ways that craft originating

on earth cannot. Professional photo analysts have stated that some photographic evidence shows no sign of being hoaxes or computer generated or special effects for simulation. Hundreds of electromagnetic anomalies and elevated radiation readings have been documented in association with UFO close encounters and abductions.

Thousands of people from around the world, whose testimony would be accepted in a court of law about anything else, have reported close-up sightings of unconventional aircraft in the air and on the ground. Some have reported non-human entities in or near the craft. Government documents, often highly redacted, and large-scale studies demonstrate that Earth is being visited by non-humans, despite the failure of the journalistic and scientific communities to examine this evidence.

There is also significant evidence that the U.S. government, civilian and military agencies, has hidden the alien presence through misinformation, distortion, obfuscation, and ridicule. The NSA, CIA, and NRO (National Reconnaissance Office) have all been involved in this cover-up. The efforts included have been supported by politically connected often-prominent scientists, including professional writers and even persons trained as magicians. They have successfully misled the media and the bulk of the scientific community into the belief that the scientists who have carefully examined the evidence, and have positive findings, are unscientific and irrational fanatics and kooks. It is interesting that essentially none of the serious books about extraterrestrial life even reference the scientific UFO evidence.

This book will examine the archival documents that clearly demonstrate the cooperative disinformation effort and will take apart the false claims made by professional naysayers. The authors will set the record straight by examining the often politically motivated misinformation and presenting the compelling evidence that separates fact from fiction. Most people are not aware of this proof that the government is withholding classified information about UFOs, and seem to falsely believe that all data is readily available on the Internet and that no agencies can successfully keep material classified.

We now know enough to plan trips to the stars ourselves if we wished to spend the money. Data from the incredible Kepler satellite and other new instruments gives us an entirely new view of the abundance of planetary systems. Not many years ago it was thought that there might be as many as 8,000 planets in the entire Milky Way Galaxy. Now we know that there are roughly 10,000 planets within a mere 100 light years of Earth.

CHAPTER 1

FACT AND FICTION IN THE UFO WORLD

The authors, because of all the time we have spent at archives and on investigation, understand how difficult it is for people new to the study of UFOs to separate fact from fiction. Much of what has been published is simply not true. An abundance of the literature is deliberate misinformation intended to mislead the public. Throughout UFO history, some individuals have made false claims, for financial gain or media attention, of having worked on ET technology at secret government facilities or of being in direct contact with extraterrestrial beings.

Stanton Friedman and Kathleen Marden at the
American Philosophical Society, Philadelphia, PA

Sometimes diligent researchers discover a false claimant's criminal record. Con men have historically attempted to deceive the UFO community for personal gain. It is reasonable to assume that a slick sociopath might slip through the cracks until exposed, by developing an elaborate scheme and hoaxed evidence. It has occurred in the past, and even careful, scientific researchers have been deceived. Funding for polygraph exams, psychological testing, and the scientific evaluation of evidence has presented a challenge to investigators. Historically, the evidence indicates that only a tiny percentage of UFO reports, even those investigated by the Air Force, have been deemed hoaxes. Yet, debunkers with an anti-UFO agenda have proclaimed that even the best evidence cases are fabrications or misinterpretations. As you will see in this book, a careful analysis of the evidence will refute the debunkers' and disinformants' claims.

Some false claimants are driven by the desire for public recognition and financial gain. Marden has discovered deception for this purpose in a small percentage of the cases she's investigated. The perpetrators are usually immature men or women on the margins of society, who are striving for a modicum of recognition in their otherwise-unproductive lives. Other deceivers have good intentions, but tie together strings of irrelevant information that result in erroneous conclusions. This leads to the unintentional distortion of information as the result of insufficient critical thinking skills. When she discovers evidence of deception, she informs the claimants of her findings and advises them to tell the truth before there false claims are made public by other investigators. This often has a positive outcome. Visits to social media sites will identify attention-seeking researchers and witnesses alike. Be suspicious of those who aggressively promote themselves through photos and sensational claims. Some researchers and witnesses alike are seeking celebrity status and care less about the accuracy of their information than their ascension into the limelight. Witness and researcher credibility is a major factor in the investigation of any UFO-related report, and especially when it involves claims of extraterrestrial (ET) contact.

Periodically, a UFO investigator has been ethically or legally compromised. When this is played out in a public arena, it causes embarrassment for the UFO research community at large. Unfortunately, a few investigators have exaggerated their credentials, claiming to have advanced degrees from colleges that end up being bogus. It has bolstered their credibility and given them more authority than they deserve until they are exposed. Some proponents argue that everyone lies about their credentials, so if someone is exposed for presenting false information about their educational background it should not be held against them. If this is true, we have reached a sad state of affairs, in which ethics and morality are no longer held to a higher standard.

The topic of UFOs is held to a higher standard simply because it has not gained scientific respectability. For this reason, the authors recoil when tenuous evidence causes a huge media stir. Historically, a cloud of suspicion has loomed over claims of UFO evidence when it is played out in the media. For example, in 2015, media attention was given to the sensational claim that a photograph of a tiny mummy was that of an alien body, coined "The Roswell Alien." The news stirred up a huge controversy among UFO researchers, as prominent figures lined up on both sides of the argument. The slides were discovered in 1989, in the home of deceased and childless couple who appeared to be socially and politically well connected. It depicted the mummified body of a small humanoid form inside a glass case. A blurred placard was visible that could not be immediately read. A photo expert confirmed that the slides were from the 1947 period and appeared to be authentic. However, at the end of a great deal of debate, de-blurring software made it clear that the photo depicted the mummified body of a 2-year-old boy. This is one of many unfortunate examples of media hype that has played out before a full investigation of the evidence could deliver a verdict. It will go down in history as one of many black marks on the field of ufology.

Despite the hype that stirs and deflates the public interest, many UFO sightings by credible witnesses cannot be explained. A total of 12,618 sightings were reported to Project Blue Book between 1947 and 1969. Of these 701 remained unidentified, meaning that the description of the object and its maneuvers did not fit into a pattern of any known object or phenomenon. The percentage would have been larger had the Air Force not made the decision to appoint directors who were biased against the possibility that UFOs were extraterrestrial spacecraft. Many of the sightings that were identified as temperature inversions, swamp gas, stars, planets, satellites, and so forth, were made by credible witnesses, such as pilots, scientists, engineers, and even astronomers, and did not conform to the explanation that was assigned to them. Some had substantial evidence that should have eliminated a prosaic explanation.

Of greater importance is the largest study on UFOs ever done for the Air Force (USAF), "Project Blue Book Special Report No. 14," carried out by the Battelle Memorial Institute and completed in 1955. It was found that 21.5 percent of the 3,201 cases investigated could not be explained. A quality evaluation was done and 35 percent of the 308 excellent cases could not be identified. Only 18.3 percent of the 525 poor cases remained unidentified. In addition a cross comparison between KNOWNS and UNKNOWNS determined that, on the basis of 6 different characteristics, the probability that the UNKNOWNS were just missed KNOWNS was less than 1 percent. Also, it should be noted that the UNKNOWNS were completely separate from the 9.3 percent listed as INSUFFICIENT INFORMATION.

The closure of Project Blue Book left the responsibility for investigating UFO reports to civilian UFO organizations that systematically collect and investigate UFO sighting reports. The Aerial Phenomena Research Organization and the National Investigations Committee on Aerial Phenomena have long since closed. This leaves the Mutual UFO Network (MUFON), which has a computerized case management system that collects and investigates UFO reports from around the world. To date thousands of reports have been systematically collected and investigated by trained MUFON volunteers. Each month, MUFON issues a statistical report of UFO sightings from around the world. Monthly reports range from 600 or so, upwards to 1,000. In September 2015, 985 reports were registered on MUFON's case management system: 769 were observed in the United States, 61 in the United Kingdom, and 53 in Canada. The remainder was divided among 49 countries with at least one UFO being reported in each. Of the objects sighted, 296 were reported to have been less than 500 feet away from the witness. One hundred forty-two of these were an estimated distance of less than 100 feet away from the witness. There were 50 landings, hoverings, and takeoffs, and one nonhuman entity was reported to have been observed. In any given month, a significant 10 to 13 percent of the objects sighted are estimated at less than 100 feet from the witness. These are not distant lights in the sky. Yet this information reaches only a small segment of our population. The failure by mainstream media outlets, to report accurate UFO information is a multifaceted problem.

The challenge that careful researchers must confront is the propensity of some well-known researchers to blur the lines between credible and credulous evidence, lumping all cases into the same pot. This type of unscientific thinking casts a cloud of suspicion over the entire UFO research community. It is particularly important to the authors of this book to be impartial, meticulous, and honest in our research and investigations. Extraordinary claims require a thorough analysis of the evidence.

Many scientists and journalists have done their research by proclamation rather than investigation, making the erroneous assumption that all UFO sightings and ET contact claims are misidentifications, hoaxes, or delusions. This failure to examine the evidence has led to declarations of UFO impossibility. Often minimal effort is applied to so-called "scientific" investigations, and this failure to honestly examine the facts results in a rush to false judgment. Sometimes the extraction of tiny bits of information and the omission of factual data are used by disinformants for the purpose of distorting the truth. Speculative arguments pertaining to hypothetical scenarios replace the available facts and a false narrative is created.

Before we deal with the activities of some of the many players over the years, it should be useful to examine two areas that have been the focus of much of the noisy negativist literature. Some of the critical items may have even been well intentioned, but are still grossly misleading or inaccurate. The focus of this book is on the driving force that led to government UFO secrecy and the question of whether certain prominent scientists, journalists, and military leaders conspired to distort the public's knowledge of UFO reality. But first, it is important to discuss the need for secrecy and the government's ability to keep secrets.

Many people have addressed the question of secrecy and concluded that secrets simply can't be kept in today's Internet and social media world. They proclaim that if an extraterrestrial vehicle had crashed near Roswell, New Mexico, in 1947, we surely would have known about it by now. If the government possessed top-secret documents pertaining to the back engineering of ET technology, the scientists involved would surely have produced irrefutable documents to prove it. Dr. Neil deGrasse Tyson, director of the Hayden Planetarium in New York, and the replacement for Dr. Carl Sagan as host on the *Cosmos* TV series, made the following comment at a public lecture at Penn State University in State College, Pennsylvania: "The proof that the government can't keep secrets is how much we know about President Clinton's genitalia." Dr. Seth Shostak, of the SETI Institute, claimed on Larry King's TV show that the public's knowledge of the terrible job done by FEMA, with regard to the Hurricane Katrina disaster, proves the government can't keep secrets. It should be noted that so far as we have been able to determine, neither Tyson nor Shostak has worked under a security clearance. Neither has firsthand experience with the handling and overseeing of classified material. Both have strong academic pedigrees and are accustomed to obtaining information from articles published in the refereed scientific literature. They also apparently believe that the question of extraterrestrial life would be a proper subject for formal scientific literature by academics, not in secret by government agencies. One method for evaluating this notion is to cite some of the many large-scale government research and development programs that have been conducted in secret and whose very existence was kept secret for many, many years. One must also consider the reasons why information about flying saucers would be kept secret by the government.

A good example of government secrecy is that there was no publicity given to the breaking of the German and Japanese military communication codes during World War II until 25 years after the war was over rather than as soon as hostilities ended. There were about 12,000 people at Bletchley Park in England whose job it was to intercept, decode, translate, and carefully distribute the supposedly top-secret German military communications. Extreme care had to be taken to assure that there would be no clue to the Germans that the codes had been broken, because then they would change them, resulting in the deaths of thousands of Allied military people. This, of course, meant that very few Allied military leaders were aware of all the decoded information. The old saying that loose lips sink ships was certainly true. The key concept in keeping secrets is to restrict access to them to people with both an appropriate NEED-TO-KNOW and an appropriate security clearance: typically CONFIDENTIAL, SECRET, TOP SECRET, or TOP SECRET CODEWORD. The codeword could usually be five letters, such as MAJIC, UMBRA, or ULTRA. Contrary to what many believe, having, for example, a Secret clearance, does *not* give one access to all Secret material, only that for which a need-to-know has been established in advance. The clearance used to take months and involved field investigation of where an applicant lived, what organizations he or she belonged to, and if they were missing periods of time when there may have been trips overseas. People who still had family overseas were examined particularly carefully to assure they couldn't be blackmailed for fear of harm to relatives. After WWII was over, the Cold War went in to full swing and Wisconsin Senator Joseph P. McCarthy was claiming there were many communists in the State Department and elsewhere. It is easy to forget that Ethel and Julius Rosenberg were executed as spies in 1953, and there was shock at Russian spies such as Klaus Fuchs having worked at Los Alamos on the atomic bomb.

Another widespread myth is that only scientists need clearances at places like Los Alamos National Laboratory. The fact is that everybody needs a clearance—including janitors, cooks, clerks, and so on—because of the possibility of hearing classified conversations or seeing classified documents on somebody's desk. Therefore, if a claimant submits evidence of employment at Los Alamos as evidence of a degree in physics, without supporting documents, it is worthless. The individual could have been a support staff member or held a custodial position in the facility.

A very important part of the Manhattan Project was the construction and operation of a massive gaseous diffusion plant to enrich uranium in the U-235 isotope. It was only present at a concentration of 0.7 percent in natural uranium ore and, to be useful in an atomic bomb, it had to be about 80 percent. The plant was built at Oak Ridge, Tennessee, and was one mile long. It used 5 percent of all the electricity being produced in the United States to pump uranium hexafluoride gas through tiny holes in nickel barriers, taking advantage of the fact that the lighter isotope, U-235, moves a little faster than U-238. It was operated in secret and many of the people working there had no idea what they were working on, because they didn't have a need-to-know. In 1944, Senator Harry Truman did not know about the Manhattan Project—and was not informed until 13 days after he became president upon the death of President Roosevelt on April 12, 1945. But he had to make the decision to drop the atomic bombs.

As a related example of secrecy, the first atomic bomb was exploded on July 16, 1945, at Trinity Site in New Mexico. It was a great success and released the energy of more than 15,000 tons of dynamite. The fireball was seen from as much as 100 miles away and local sheriffs received many calls about the explosion. A cover story was released saying that an ammunition dump had blown up, but fortunately nobody was injured. Three weeks later an atomic bomb was dropped on Japan. Only then was the public informed that one had been tested at Trinity.

Some have suggested that the men working on the highly classified Majestic 12 committee and other high-security UFO-related projects would have told their wives what they were doing. That is almost certainly untrue. As an example, the wife of General Leslie Groves, who was in overall charge of the Manhattan Project for more than two years, didn't know what her husband had been doing until somebody in his office suggested to her that she would probably be interested in listening to the news on the radio at noon on August 6, 1945. The story was about the bomb dropped on Hiroshima. It was at that moment she discovered that the program had been under the direction of General Groves. Prior to this she did not know about the Manhattan Project or her husband's involvement in it.

Friedman ran into an example of the limits to access regarding classified information when he was working on radiation shielding for the General Electric aircraft nuclear propulsion department. He regularly read the classified edition of Nuclear Science Abstracts. Sometimes there were abstracts about classified shielding research being done by the U.S. Navy for its naval nuclear propulsion systems. He had the required Q clearance for access to secret restricted data. Admiral Rickover's nuclear Navy people would not grant him a need-to-know for the Navy information.

He also had an experience that demonstrated the government's focus on protecting classified information. His slides for a paper to be presented at a Classified Radiation Shielding conference in Texas were not finished in time to be sent with the special courier, who carried classified documents and slides to the conference. Friedman was given a special briefing so that he could carry the slides with him. However, he was required to keep them with him in a briefcase that had to be close to his body at all times. For example, they could not be placed in the trunk of a car while he was driving from the airport. He was told that if the plane crashed special effort would be made to recover the classified information. They were not concerned about his safety. They required his detailed travel itinerary. To say that he was relieved when he turned the material over to the proper authorities would be an understatement.

Another important aspect of security is that information classified as TOP SECRET cannot be included in a document classified only at the SECRET level. Two important examples can be cited. The famous memo from General Nathan F. Twining of September 24, 1947, to USAF Headquarters saying that the phenomenon was real and not imaginary and giving other validation was only classified SECRET and not TOP SECRET because it went to a lot of people. It even contains the totally misleading statement: "Due consideration must be given to the following. The lack of physical evidence in the shape of crash recovered exhibits which would undeniably prove the existence of these objects."[1] This has led some people to think this meant that Twining, supposedly a member of Operation Majestic 12, did not know about the Roswell crash. *Not so.* It meant that high-level secrets could not be included in documents having a lower level of classification. The final report of the famous Robertson Panel, established by the CIA to review government UFO information in the late 1952–53 time frame, was only classified SECRET, not TOP SECRET. It seems certain that information about the crashed saucers recovered at Roswell, the Plains of San Agustin, and Aztec, would have been classified at least TOP SECRET and much more likely at the TOP SECRET CODEWORD level, just as the Majestic 12 documents were classified TOP SECRET MAJIC.

Even within a classified and guarded research facility, classified documents cannot be left out overnight but must be kept in a repository having a combination lock. Guards patrolled the classified area every night. If a classified document was found outside a locked cabinet, the individual to whom the document has been signed out was called at home and required to come in to the classified facility and inventory all his classified documents. More than two such incidents would likely result in dismissal for the careless employee.

Several facts indicate that some of the most important classified information was TOP SECRET CODEWORD. When the National Security Agency finally released a batch of 156 TOP SECRET UMBRA UFO documents because of a Freedom of Information act law suit, they whited out everything except one sentence per page. Obviously anybody receiving a set of the documents received Xerox copies so the white out could not be scraped off to find what was underneath. The CIA originally released about 800 pages of UFO material, but none was classified higher than SECRET. It took more than two years to obtain their TOP SECRET UMBRA UFO documents. Typically everything but a few words per page was blacked out. Again Xerox copies were received, so the black ink could not be scraped off to reveal what was underneath. In addition, a 1948 FBI UFO document obtained by Dr. Bruce Maccabee stated that both the USAF and FBI considered the subject of flying saucers TOP SECRET.

Further definitive proof that the best government UFO information was being withheld was clearly proven beyond any doubt when, in 1979, researcher Robert Todd obtained a copy of the October 20, 1969, memo from USAF General Carroll Bolender pertaining to the closure of Project Blue Book. The USAF Project Blue Book was consistently referred to by government spokesmen as the only USAF group concerned with UFOs. When it was closed as a result of Bolender's memo, the air force claimed there was no national security concern with UFOs. Dr. Edward Condon's people at the University of Colorado echoed this claim. However, the memo contained the following statement: "Reports of unidentified flying objects which could affect national security...are not part of the Blue Book System...and will continue to be investigated when Blue Book is closed."[2] Friedman located Bolender 10 years later and spoke with him by telephone. The general agreed there were two separate communications channels for UFO information. One was public reporting of cases to Project Blue Book. The other was for the reporting of cases that could clearly affect national security, such as UFO flights down the runway of a strategic Air Command Base where nuclear weapons were stored. Clearly these cases would continue to be investigated without any indication of this activity to the public, false air force claims to the contrary notwithstanding.

Another area of concern is the dissemination of disinformation with regard to UFO observers and ET contact experiencers alike. Debunkers have long promoted the hypothesis that fictional accounts UFOs in comic books, science fiction movies, magazine articles, and so forth is a causal factor in the public's belief that UFOs are real. In 1979, Dr. Phillis Fox (Cal. State) tested their speculation by surveying small communities to identify the characteristics of UFO believers and determine the origin of their beliefs.

She discovered that belief in the existence of extraterrestrial intelligence is not generated by fiction in the media. On the contrary, it was knowledge of the space program and unidentified flying objects that could not be explained in prosaic terms that caused people to believe that some UFOs are extraterrestrial craft. Despite Dr. Fox's scientific evidence that debunkers' speculations are wrong, it fell upon deaf ears. They are continuing to disseminate this false and misleading information.

A variety of hypotheses has been developed by social scientists and pseudoscientific debunkers alike, in an attempt to identify conventional causal factors that can account for reports of alien abduction. Personality inventories and psychological experiments have attempted to identify psychological disorders that might be causing delusional thinking among the percipients. Several experimental studies over the past 35 years have attempted to delineate personality traits that separate UFO abduction experiencers from non-experiencers, such as boundary deficit disorder, fantasy proneness, hallucinations, sleep anomalies, confabulation in hypnosis, false memory syndrome, and absorption of cultural mythos. Years of systematic study have indicated that alleged alien abductees exhibit no more psychopathology than the general population. They come from a broad spectrum of societal levels from all over the world, ranging from peasant farmers to professionally prominent individuals. In the absence of a primary psychiatric disorder, experimental psychologists have searched for alternative psychological explanations, but have discovered that most ET contact experiencers who meet the criteria for having experienced a real contact event fall within the normal range of functioning. Yet, the American public has been led to believe that experiencers and UFO observers alike are eccentric kooks. Experiencers who tell their stories often face denigration and harassment by family, friends, and colleagues, and are marginalized in our society. In this book, we'll explore the rationale behind the pervasive policy that dismisses UFOs and abductions. We'll also present case after case of denigration and character assassination by nasty, noisy negativists who appear to be doing the government's work in its most pernicious form. Credible individuals have been viciously attacked for allegedly lodging false claims. Mentally stable people have been publically accused of suffering from a variety of psychological disorders. And sincere witnesses have been called credulous kooks by those who insist upon distorting the public's perception of the UFO phenomenon.

Through extensive archival research and investigation we have discovered a clear pattern of uncertainty, deception, and cover-up at the highest levels of the U.S. government's intelligence community. In *Fact, Fiction, and Flying Saucers* you'll find compelling evidence of a well-orchestrated trail of official lies and deception that has been perpetrated upon the American public for the purpose of disinformation and re-education. But first, let us explore the history of the UFO presence in the 20th century and the decision to conceal its true nature, by the U.S. Air Force, the CIA, government scientists, and media disinformants.

CHAPTER 2

THE AIR FORCE, THE CIA, AND DISINFORMATION BY GOVERNMENT SCIENTISTS: THE EARLY YEARS

A proliferation of reports of unidentified cylindrical or cigar-shaped flying objects sighted in Scandinavia in 1946 alarmed U.S. military forces. If the Russians had been firing rockets developed by the Germans during WWII, it could pose a threat to the United States and its allies. The impending threat was so great that General James H. Doolittle, PhD (1896–1996), who led the raid on Tokyo on April 18, 1942, was sent to Sweden to speak with the Swedish defense officials under the guise of his position as VP of Shell Oil Company. Nearly 1,000 unidentified objects were reported, but many had been identified as possible Russian V-1 rockets, meteors, and misidentifications of conventional phenomena. However, there were reports of flying saucers that could not be explained.

A declassified Top Secret USAF document, dated November 4, 1948, confirms that the USAF was concerned about a flying saucer that had hovered, for 30 minutes, over Neubiberg Air Base in Germany. This was obviously not a rocket. It was one of hundreds of flying saucers to be reported over a wide area. When military officers met with the Swedish Intelligence Service for its assessment of the situation they were informed that reliable, fully qualified technical people had reached the conclusion that the phenomena were too technically advanced to have originated on Earth.[1]

On June 24, 1947, flying saucers generated widespread media attention in the United States. Kenneth Arnold, a highly regarded civilian pilot and businessman, reported observing nine crescent-shaped disks near Mt. Rainier, Washington, weaving in and out between mountain peaks at a high rate of speed. A dozen other nearby witnesses reported their own sightings of similar objects on the same day. The flying crescents were later calculated as racing across the sky at the staggering, impossible speed of approximately 1,700 miles per hour. Media coverage of Arnold's sighting triggered an onslaught of reports across the United States.

Military officers at the Fort Worth Army Air Field were so alarmed by the threat to national security and the danger of public hysteria, that on June 30, Brigadier General Roger M. Ramey and Alfred Kalberer, his chief intelligence officer, held a press conference to allay the public's fear. They said there was nothing to be concerned about; the sightings could be attributed to weather phenomena. But the reports continued to pour in and public concern rose to an all-time high.

On July 8, 1947, a headline in the *Roswell Daily Record* carried the news: "RAAF Captures Saucer on Ranch in Roswell Region." Colonel William Blanchard, the commanding officer at the Roswell Army Air Base had ordered Lieutenant Walter Haut to write the story after rancher Mac Brazel had discovered metallic debris with highly unusual properties and I-beam fragments scattered over a wide area about 70 miles from Roswell. Intelligence officer Jesse

Marcel, of the 509th bomb group, and Captain Sheridan Cavitt, senior counterintelligence agent, had inspected the site and collected samples of the debris. There was an area gouged out of the soil approximately three-quarters of a mile long.

The news was carried to the Associated Press and two radio stations before the lid clamped shut. Samples of the debris were transported by Major Jesse Marcel, an intelligence officer for the 509th bomb group, to Brigadier General Roger M. Ramey, commanding officer of the 8th Air Force in Fort Worth, Texas. Marcel later stated that he had placed the debris on Ramey's desk and walked down the hall to the map room to show Ramey the crash site location. When he returned to the general's office, he discovered that the debris was missing. It had been replaced by remnants of a common weather balloon. Photographs were taken of Marcel and Ramey with the weather balloon and the public was informed that Major Marcel was mistaken. Later that day a press release rescinded the original story and replaced it with "General Ramey Empties Roswell Saucer." The public was not informed that Marcel was very familiar with the appearance of weather balloons and could easily distinguish between metallic debris with highly unusual properties and a weather balloon array.

The Pentagon had already been evaluating the flying disk problem to determine if it posed a threat to national security. Did it represent hardware from Russia? Could it cause public hysteria? Was it illusionary? Lieutenant Colonel George Garrett, from the Army Air Force Intelligence Collections Division at the Pentagon, issued the first estimate of the situation on July 30, 1947. It was based upon the analysis of 16 cases and sent to military technology leaders, who reported that no such technological device existed. The Draft Estimate stated "This 'flying saucer' situation is not all imaginary or seeing too much in some natural phenomenon. Something is really flying around."[2] Garrett suspected that a domestic project was responsible for the sightings. Yet no such project was discovered. The unique aerial vehicles were described as metallic, elliptical objects that oscillated during flight, flat on the bottom and slightly domed on top, and as large as a C-54.

The second Estimate of the Situation was delivered on September 23, 1947. Known as the Twining Memo, it was actually written by Air Materiel Command Intelligence Chief Colonel Howard McCoy. The estimate was not one man's opinion; McCoy was expressing the conclusions drawn from a panel of experts, including the chiefs of the Engineering Division, the Air Institute of Technology, several laboratories, and Colonel William Clingerman, executive officer for Material Command Intelligence. The three-page "AMC Opinion Concerning 'Flying Disks" was sent to Brigadier General George Schulgren, assistant Pentagon director of intelligence. It was classified SECRET and therefore could not include information that was classified TOP SECRET or TOP SECRET CODEWORD. It stated as follows:

2. It is the opinion that:

The phenomenon reported is something real and not visionary or fictitious.

These are objects probably approximating the shape of a disk, of such appreciable size as to appear to be as large as man-made aircraft.

There is a possibility that some of the incidents may be caused by natural phenomena, such as meteors.

The reported operating characteristics, such as extreme rates of climb, maneuverability (particularly in a roll), and action which must be considered <u>evasive</u> when sighted or contacted by friendly aircraft and radar, lend belief to the possibility that some of the objects are controlled manually, automatically or remotely.

The apparent common description of the objects is as follows:

Metallic or light reflecting surface.

Absence of trail, except in a few instances when the object apparently was operating under high performance conditions.

Circular or elliptical in shape, flat on bottom and domed on top.

Several reports of well kept, formation flights varying from three to nine objects.

Normally no associated sound, except in three instances a substantial rumbling roar was noted.

Level flight speeds normally above 300 knots are estimated.[3] (See the Appendix for the entire FOIA document.)

General Nathan Twining

In response to the Twining Memo and a number of highly credible reports of unidentified aerial objects, Major General L.C. Craigie, director of research and development and Commanding General of the Air Material Command, issued a directive dated December 30, 1947, that established a project to collect, collate, and evaluate all sightings that could affect national security. It was given the code name Project Sign (also known as Project Saucer) and was classified SECRET and RESTRICTED. On February 11, 1948, it was assigned to the Air Technical Developmental Center. Within the year Project Sign analyzed and evaluated 243 cases. In his Estimate of the Situation Robert Sneider, director of Project Sign, and his team favored an extraterrestrial hypothesis, concluding that flying saucers were probably extraterrestrial craft under intelligent control, capable of out-flying and out-maneuvering U.S. and Russian aircraft. USAF chief of staff General Hoyt Vandenberg refused to sign this Estimate of the Situation, claiming an absence of physical proof, such as a piece of hardware that would confirm these disks were of extraterrestrial origin. (It is important to note that a piece of hardware such as was retrieved in the Roswell crash would have been classified TOP SECRET or TOP SECRET CODEWORD and could not have been mentioned by Vandenberg.) This led to the closure of Project Sign. The approved report stated that no conclusive evidence was available to prove or disprove the existence of unconventional structured craft and only the examination of the remains of crashed objects would provide the proof they were looking for.

Project Sign was replaced by Project Grudge in February 1949. All but two of Project Sign's lowest ranking officers were reassigned to other duties, leaving the two remaining officers to work with the U.S. Weather Service and a few college professors. Their mission was to assign simple scientific explanations to the reports that Project Sign had evaluated and could not explain. Approximately a quarter of the reports defied explanation, so the psychology branch of the Air Force's Aeromedical Laboratory attributed them to psychological causes. Project Grudge ascribed the "Unknowns" to conventional objects, mass hysteria, hoaxes, and mental illness, concluding that there was no evidence of a threat to national security except for the dangers that mass hysteria posed. A secret Grudge report was issued, but remained classified until it was declassified and released by Captain Edward Ruppelt three years later.

In 1951, Captain Edward Ruppelt was assigned the task of reorganizing Project Grudge. By March 1952 he changed the debunking focus of Project Grudge and issued a directive to all U.S. Air Force facilities worldwide to immediately begin sending information on UFO sightings to the Air Technical Intelligence Center (ATIC). The larger, more structured investigative group, now known as Project Blue Book, systematically collected and cross-referenced an increasing number of reports. Ruppelt examined the reports in Project Grudge's files with a skeptical eye. In his book *The Report on Unidentified Flying Objects*, published in 1956, he wrote, "It doesn't take a great deal of study of the old UFO files to see that standard intelligence procedures were no longer being used by Project Grudge. Everything was being evaluated on the premise that UFOs couldn't exist. No matter what you see or hear, don't believe it."[4]

By 1952 the ATIC had received about 4,400 UFO reports, 1,593 of which were considered worthy of analysis. Of these 18.51 percent had been identified as "Balloons," 11.76 percent as "Aircraft," 14.2 percent as "Astronomical Bodies," 4.21 percent as "Other," 1.66 percent as "Hoaxes," 22.72 percent as having "Insufficient Data," and a highly significant 26.94 percent as "Unknowns." Pilots and air crews had reported 17.1 percent of the UFO sightings; 5.7 percent were made by scientists and engineers; 1.0 percent were made by air traffic control tower operators; 12.5 percent were radar reports; and 63.7 percent were made by military and civilian witnesses.[5]

Project Blue Book files indicate that during early spring 1952, radar sightings, mostly from the Air Defense Command, had increased rapidly. In June, 149 reports had been submitted to the Air Technical Intelligence Command. On July 1, 2 F-94s were scrambled to intercept two UFOs over Boston. They didn't spot the UFOs, but moments later, a report came in of a silvery cigar-shaped craft, six times as long as it was wide, passing over Boston. It was reported by three people, including an Air Force captain. Two hours later, 12 student radar operators and three instructors at Fort Monmouth, New Jersey, saw two UFOs on their SCR 584 radar scope. An instructor and several of the students went outside and sighted the objects. They were hovering in the exact location as was seen on the radar scope. Moments later, they zipped off toward Washington, DC.

A physics professor at George Washington University reported that he and approximately 500 other witnesses watched a dull, smoke-gray-colored object half the size of a quarter at arm's length, north–northwest of Washington. (Note: The moon can be covered by an aspirin at arm's length.) It hovered and moved in a back and forth arcing motion for eight minutes before it descended behind tall buildings.

On July 10, 13, and 14, airline crews reported the observation UFOs that they said could not have been lighted balloons or conventional aircraft. The objects hovered, moved slowly, and took off at an incredibly rapid rate of speed. Two nights later, a high-ranking civilian aerodynamicist at Langley Air Force Base and another man reported two amber-colored lights much too large to be aircraft lights. They traveled silently toward the north and made a 180-degree turn back to their original position. The silent objects were joined by several more as they traveled south. An investigation by the Air Force concluded that no conventional aircraft was in the exact location at the time of the sighting. If it had been a jet, it would have been in close proximity to the witnesses, yet it was completely silent.

On the night of July 19, at 11:40 p.m., short- and long-range radar scopes at Washington National Airport detected eight unidentified targets east and south of Andrews Air Force Base. Records from Andrews AFB indicate that a series of three sets of targets were observed on two radar scopes at Washington National Airport and on one at Andrews Air Force Base. National had detected 10–12 targets on the first radar scope at 8:54 p.m. The second radar scope displayed the 10–12 targets at 8:57 p.m. They remained in the Washington area in excess of an hour. A third set of four targets was observed from National and Andrews AFB near Beltsville, Maryland, and Herndon, Virginia, at 10:23 p.m.

The targets moved at speeds of 100 to 130 miles per hour until suddenly two of them accelerated to extremely high speeds and left the area. One was clocked at 7,000 miles per hour. Night crews from several airliners and tower operators visually observed mysterious lights in the location where they had been picked up on radar. Air Force jet interceptors were scrambled but could see nothing even though visibility was excellent. A few minutes later, after the F-94s had left the area, the targets were back on the radar scopes. The F-94s returned to the area and made visual contact with the lights, which blinked out when the interceptors approached them. Finally they locked on to three targets, but each lock-on was broken when the objects sped away. Finally, one remained steady and the jet pilot locked onto it. He made visual contact, but as he sped in its direction it disappeared.

On July 25, Major C.P. Carlson, Post Chaplain at the Edgewood Arsenal, Maryland, at 10:30 PM, observed a flying object in the vicinity of Annapolis that appeared to be travelling at the speed of a jet, in a northwest direction, at approximately 10,000 feet. He described it as a large, silent fireball that travelled on a steady course for six seconds and then vanished.

On July 26, all hell broke loose when unidentified flying objects were observed on the radar scopes at the Air Traffic Control Centers at Washington National Airport and the Approach Control Radar at Andrews Air Force Base. It was a clear, humid night with a south wind measuring 10 mph. Visual observations were reported to Andrews and Bolling AFBs, and to the Air Route Traffic Control (ARTC) Center by pilots of a commercial aircraft and one Civil Air Command Aircraft. ARTC personnel reported up to 12 returns simultaneously on their radar scope starting at 9:20 p.m. They appeared as solid aircraft only moving at a slower than usual rate of speed.

At 10:00 p.m. Andrews Approach Control confirmed that they had been tracking the same targets. The Washington National Radar crew reported one strong target that moved across the radar scope at a speed of 30–40 mph. At 10:46 p.m. a CAA flight visually spotted five objects that glowed from orange to white, and commercial pilots reported observing a red-yellow glowing object. Two F-94s were scrambled at 11:00 p.m. Both pilots observed lights, but were not able to close in on them before the lights blinked out.

At 10:30 p.m., a USAF B-25 vectored on numerous targets over a period of one hour and 20 minutes. This time Major Dewey Fournet, project officer for UFOs in Washington, DC, and Lieutenant John Holcomb, a Navy electronics specialist assigned to the Air Force Directorate of Intelligence, were dispatched to the ARTC center. Holcomb observed "seven good, solid targets"[6] He made a quick check with the Airport Weather Station and was informed that there was a slight temperature inversion at about 1,000 feet. He advised the Command Post that he felt the targets could not have been the result of a temperature inversion and requested a second intercept flight. A jet interceptor was dispatched, but the objects were no longer visible when it arrived at the site.

The ARTC crew at National Airport emphatically reported that the targets on July 26 were solid. They did not follow aircraft or cross the scope consistently in the same general heading, as a spurious target would. They were observed dropping out of the pattern, as if they were intelligently controlled. The crew described them as having a "creeping appearance."[7] One crew member commented that one object disappeared from the scope when it was being pursued by the F-94.

The Civil Aeronautics Control Center's senior air traffic controller, Harry Barnes, asked Capitol Airlines pilot S.C. Pierman, whose plane was in the air, to look for the objects he saw as unidentified blips on the radar screen. Pierman made visual contact with six white, tailless, fast-moving lights over a 14-minute period. Over the next four hours he directed several airline pilots toward the targets.

They and USAF interceptors made visual contact with glowing white lights.

During his Project Blue Book investigation of the Washington event, Captain Edward J. Ruppelt interviewed Major Dewey Fournet and Lieutenant John Holcomb. They had seen the radar targets and heard the radio conversations with the jet intercept pilots at National Airport. Major Fournet stated that everyone in the radar room saw both weak weather-related targets on the scope that night, caused by a temperature inversion, and *solid* targets that could not have been radar ghosts. They were experienced professionals who knew the difference between a spurious blip and a solid object. These anomalous propagation events were common in the Washington area, having occurred almost every night that summer, and the radar operators were experienced at identifying them. However, on the night of July 26, into the early morning hours of July 27, the radar tower operators observed not only radar blips caused by a temperature inversion, but also targets that had the characteristics of solid, metallic objects that were not caused by atmospheric conditions. These targets not only appeared on radar screens, they were sighted visually from the air by aircraft crew members and by witnesses on the ground.

There was so much public interest in the Washington, DC, events that Major General John A. Samford called a press conference at the Pentagon on July 29, 1952, at 4:00 p.m. It was the largest press conference since World War II and lasted for one and a half hours. Major General Samford, Air Force chief of intelligence; Major General Roger Ramey, director of operations and commander of the 8th Air Force during the July 1947 Roswell crashed saucer event; Colonel Donald Bower, Technical Analysis Division, ATIC; Captain Roy James, Air Technical Intelligence Center; Captain Edward J. Ruppelt, Project Blue Book Director, ATIC; and Mr. Burgoyne L Griffing, electronics branch, ATIC met an enthusiastic press.

Major General Samford informed the crowd that the U.S. Air Force has been monitoring U.S. air space since 1947, through Project

Saucer, and in 1952, through a more integrated, stable program. Between 1,000 and 2,000 reports had been analyzed and identified as friendly aircraft, hoaxes, electronic or meteorological phenomena, light aberrations, and so forth. However, approximately 20 percent of the reports came from "credible observers of relatively incredible things."[8] The unexplained reports, he told the press, are what keeps the Air Force concerned. The problem, he explained, is that scientists require evidence that is substantial and can be measured precisely. So far, the measurements had not been precise. His goal was to attempt to acquire the measurement value on the UFOs to make them "amenable to real analysis."[9]

He reassured the press that the objects did not appear to be a menace to the United States, adding, "Reports like this go back to Biblical times. There have been flurries of them in various centuries."[10] He mentioned reports of inexplicable aerial objects in 1896, and a current flurry of reports that began in Sweden in 1946. He advised the press that the Air Force was giving it adequate attention, but not frantic attention.

The UFO report that General Samford was referring to was observed by hundreds of people in the San Francisco Bay area as they were going home from work on November 22, 1896. They described a large, dark, cigar-shaped object with stubby wings. Hours later it was seen traveling north over what is now the Golden Gate Bridge. It was later reported over Santa Rosa, Sacramento, Chico, and Red Bluff, by thousands of people. On November 30, it was seen again moving against the wind.

After making a brief statement, Major General Samford opened the floor to the press. In response to an inquiry Samford replied, "On the order of sixty percent (of the reports) come from the civilian population...eight percent from civil airline pilots...and twenty five percent from military pilots."[11] Samford gave examples of sightings that caused concern but had prosaic explanations such as two military jets locking in on each other or locking in on a ground target.

The majority of the questions asked by the press centered on possible alternative explanations for the radar returns. This atmospheric affect, he explained, causes spurious ghosts to appear on radar screens that sometimes creates confusion, especially for inexperienced radar operators. Samford explained that the radar blips on July 26 were different. "They saw good returns," he stated, but added that this did not necessarily mean they were solid objects.[12] He said a very close bird can cause a large blip on the radar screen, but experienced radar operators know the difference.

Captain James stood up and reassured the press that there could be a prosaic explanation for the radar sightings. Like Samford, he brought up the possibility that the radar targets were caused by freak atmospheric conditions, such as temperature inversions that caused false radar echoes. Major General Samford added, "I don't think that we are quite sure that the Menzel [Dr. Donald Menzel, an astrophysicist with close ties to the CIA and NSA] theory of temperature inversion or that scientists are sure that is a good theory. It is supported by some people. Other people who have equal competence, it would appear, discredit it. So, the gamble as to whether that is the cause or not is a fifty-fifty proposition."[13] He stated, "We're not trying to discredit the observers. That's the reason that I said that we have many reports from credible observers of incredible things. They also say they're incredible.... There is nothing else known in the world that can do these things except phenomena!"[14]

Earlier that year, in May, Dr. Donald Menzel had met with Air Force Project Blue Book's chief, Captain Edward Ruppelt; Stefan Possony, a psychological warfare expert and acting chief of the directorate of Intelligence Special Study Group under Major General Samford; Colonel Frank Dunn, ATIC chief; Brigadier General William Garland; and Possony's assistant Leslie Rosenzweig, at Possony's office in the Pentagon. Menzel informed the military officers that he had solved the Air Force's UFO problem through a few elementary experiments using liquids of different densities. According to Ruppelt, Menzel acted authoritatively, as if he were giving the USAF an order to comply with his debunking agenda. He asked the officers if they had any comments, to which Possony asked Menzel why he thought his few very elementary and simple experiments proved anything. According to Ruppelt, Menzel evaded his question and switched the topic to hoaxes. He informed the group that hoaxes played a large part in UFO sightings. Not true. Only 2 percent of sighting reports had been deemed hoaxes by the USAF. Next, Menzel asked the men to support his anti-UFO statements in two magazines: *Time* and *Look*. When General Garland and his cohorts informed Menzel they needed to know more before they could offer him a blind endorsement, Menzel blew his stack.

In order to ease the situation, Ruppelt suggested that Menzel leave a copy of his work to be reviewed by ATIC consultants, scientists at the Battelle Memorial Institute, a physicist at UCLA, and Dr. J. Allen Hynek, consultant to Project Blue Book. Menzel refused, but later proposed that he be an unpaid consultant to Project Blue Book. Blue Book declined his offer, but later Project Blue Book welcomed Menzel's debunking explanations.

The UFOs over Washington caused such a stir that the Federal Aviation Administration (FAA) asked the Technical Development and Evaluation Center of the Civil Aeronautics Administration CAA, in Indianapolis, Indiana, to investigate the unidentified targets observed on air traffic control radars. The Civil Aeronautics Administration Technical Development and Evaluation Center (TDEC) published its report in May 1953. It concluded that temperature inversions had been present in *almost* every instance when unidentified radar targets or visual objects had been reported during the month of July 1952. The scientists *believed* that the correlation of the appearance of radar targets with visual reports of "flying saucers" was due to mirages caused by abrupt temperature inversions. They failed to acknowledge the strong, solid returns and fast-moving targets noted by the Washington National *senior* controller and the USAF during the significant events of July 19–20 and 26–27, 1952. Nor did they acknowledge the testimony of visual reports by the jet intercept pilots, nor the ground visual observations. The great disappointment with their report lies in the fact that they failed to conduct a thorough analysis of the factual data. Their so called "scientific" explanation was based upon a fraction of the evidence, but was touted by journalists such as Philip J. Klass of *Aviation Weekly* magazine. Simple scientific explanations for complex evidence had long been a pattern in the Air Force's cover-up of UFO evidence. But another government agency, the CIA, asserted itself into the mix.

CIA records indicate that it had been secretly monitoring UFO reports since 1951. It had been incorrectly informed by the Air Force that UFOs were sighted only in the United States, when in fact reports had been received from around the world. The Air Force had been sending selected cases directly to the CIA, but the information contained within the files was sometimes incomplete. On August 1, 1952, Edward Tauss, acting chief of the Weapon and Equipment Division, Office of Scientific Intelligence (OSI), wrote an informal report on an overall evaluation of flying saucers in preparation for a comprehensive briefing on the subject, scheduled for August 8, 1952, with the commanding officer at ATIC, Wright Patterson AFB. He stated that most of the 1,000 to 2,000 UFO reports received by the ATIC could be easily explained. However:

> ...so long as a series of reports remains "unexplainable" (interplanetary aspect and alien origin not being thoroughly excluded from consideration) caution requires that intelligence continue coverage of the subject. It is recommended that CIA surveillance of the subject matter, in coordination with proper authorities of primary operational concern at ATIC be continued. It is strongly urged, however, that no indication of CIA interest or concern reach the public, in view their probably alarmist tendencies...[15]

On August 20, 1952, CIA director Walter Bedell Smith, after being briefed on the situation, ordered his staff to prepare a memorandum for the National Security Council to establish a multi-agency investigative body to study UFOs. His primary concern was the threat of psychological warfare.

Two days later, a briefing document by Ralph Clark, deputy assistant director to the CIA's Office of Scientific Intelligence and based upon a visit to the Air Force's Air Technical Intelligence Center, stated that the Air Force denied that flying saucers were U.S. or Soviet secret weapons or extraterrestrial visitors. The document stated that all reports were probably due to conventional aircraft, natural phenomena, and atmospheric conditions. The evidence clearly indicates that this information was false.

Due to the fact that the saucers were most often seen in the vicinity of atomic energy installations, it was suggested that they might be byproducts of atomic fission that acted as a catalyst to produce them. No weight was given to the idea that ETs might be concerned about our destructive use of nuclear weapons or the potential problem that our warlike behavior posed should we develop the capability to travel into space. The Project Blue Book personnel had not told the CIA that 30 percent of its reports, made by commercial and Air Force pilots, could not be identified as known phenomena. Nor did they state that serious interest had been aroused among some top level officials who suspected that UFOs might be of extraterrestrial origin.

On September 7, 1952, Dr. H. Marshall Chadwell, assistant director of the CIA's Office of Scientific Intelligence sent a lengthy memo to CIA director Walter B. Smith outlining the "UFO Problem, Facts Bearing on the Problem, Discussion, Conclusion and Recommendations." He outlined the Air Force's investigating structure and stated that a worldwide reporting system had been initiated and major USAF bases had been ordered to "make interceptions of unidentified flying objects."[16]

The ATIC had contracted the Battelle Memorial Institute to establish a machine indexing system for official UFO reports. Of the approximately 1,500 reports the Air Force had received since 1947, 20 percent remained unexplained. However, the ATIC had made no attempt to make a definite determination of the phenomena that had been causing the sightings. The recommendation was made to analyze and systematize the information, identify the fields of science equipped to investigate the various phenomena, and make recommendations for the appropriate research. Dr. Julius Stratton, vice president of MIT, had proposed a special study group through Project Lincoln, the USAF's air defense project at MIT. In conclusion, he stated that the flying saucer situation posed two dangers: psychological (mass hysteria and panic) and air vulnerability (identification of visual and electronic phenomena). He proposed taking steps to assess psychological warfare risks and plan for defenses; set a national policy with regard to UFOs through the National Security Council (in order to minimize the risk of panic); elevate the level of cognizance and action to the National Security Council; and cooperate with the Psychological Strategy Board with regard to psychological warfare weapons.

Clearly, the CIA's primary concern was the threat of psychological warfare by the Soviets against the United States during an attack. They feared that Soviet sympathizers in the United States might report UFO sightings during a Soviet attack, diverting air defense jets away from Soviet attacking aircraft and toward a fictitious target. Additionally, if the public reported UFOs during an attack, it could clog defense communication lines and seriously impede the U.S. military's defensive efforts. To counter this possibility, CIA director Walter B. Smith approved a National Security Intelligence directive that became national policy in the intelligence community, establishing a pervasive federal attitude toward UFO reports and reporters.

The Scientific Advisory Panel on Unidentified Flying Objects (Robertson Panel) convened January 14–18, 1953, to review and appraise evidence that the United States might have been visited by extraterrestrials in light of pertinent scientific theories. It was funded by the CIA's Office of Scientific Intelligence and classified SECRET, not TOP SECRET. The CIA enlisted the services of *selected* scientists to review the best Project Blue Book data on record.

One concern was the potential danger to national security posed by public concern over UFOs.

The CIA's Robertson Panel Scientific Review Board, a whittled-down version of the proposed scientific review panel, without OSI personnel and Lincoln Labs engineers, discussed UFOs for four days starting on January 14, 1953. The panel was given only 15 reports for detailed study out of several hundred that were available, although it quickly reviewed a few additional reports. Dr. Allen Hynek, the Project Blue Book astronomical consultant, stated, "This was akin to asking Madame Curie to examine a small fraction of the pitchblende she distilled and still expecting her to come out with radium."[17]

Dr. H.P. Robertson, a distinguished mathematical physicist formerly of Princeton and the California Institute of Technology, and chief science consultant to the CIA, was appointed as the panel chairman. Dr. Donald Menzel, his friend, wrote that Robertson thought the subject of UFOs was preposterous and the panel was stacked with four scientists ignorant of UFOs and a biased administrator. Every member of the panel held a TOP SECRET security clearance.

They were Dr. Thornton Page, an astrophysicist and expert on military intelligence, who had left the University of Chicago in 1951, for government service as deputy director of the Operations Research Office in the Department of the Army (He admitted that he knew almost nothing about UFOs); Dr. Lloyd Berkner, a well-known intelligence consultant and prominent physicist and engineer from the Carnegie Institution and then–acting assistant to the Secretary of State (he was conspicuously absent until the afternoon of the third day of the sessions); Dr. Samuel Goudsmit, an atmospheric physicist and chief scientist at Brookhaven National Labs; and Dr. Luis Alvarez, a radiation physicist from the University of California, Berkeley (he had worked at MIT's Radiation Laboratory and on the plutonium bomb at Los Alamos; in 1968, he was awarded the Nobel Prize in physics). Also present were the leaders of the CIA's Project Team from the Office of Scientific Intelligence, deputy assistant director Ralph Clark, Colonel Frederic Oder, Physics and Electronics Division, and David Stevenson, Weapons and Equipment Division.

Panel members were advised of the dangers that publicity pertaining to UFOs might pose to national security, including mass hysteria, the clogging of communications channels, and the danger of reduced military vigilance caused by hoaxed sightings, especially by Soviet sympathizers. Dr. Robertson informed the closed-session Panel that their job was to reduce public concern by assigning prosaic explanations to UFO reports. Later, four representatives from the USAF were invited into the session: Project Blue Book director Edward Ruppelt, Blue Book astronomical consultant Dr. Allen Hynek, CIA Office of Scientific Intelligence officer Frederick Durant, and Pentagon UFO chief Dewey Fournet. The remainder of the morning seemed haphazard at best with discussions on psychology; a presentation of the ATIC's month-by-month statistics on the summer's UFO flap; and two movies of suspected UFOs in flight.

One movie showed compelling film of suspected UFOs in flight in Tremonton, Utah. On July 2, 1952, at about 11:00 a.m., Navy warrant officer Delbert Clement Newhouse was driving from Washington, DC, to Portland, Oregon, before reporting for duty at the Aviation Supply Depot, Naval Supply Center, Oakland, California. He was accompanied by his wife, Norma, and their 12- and 14-year-old children, Delbert and Anne. Seven miles north of Tremonton, on U.S. Highway 30 South, Norma alerted husband to a group of strange objects in the sky. Newhouse, a chief photographer with 21 years in the Navy and 2,000 hours' flying time as an aerial photographer, realized that he had never seen anything like the dozen or so disk-shaped craft that reminded him of two pie pans, one inverted on top of the other. He pulled to the side of the road and watched approximately a dozen shiny, disk-like objects moving around in the sky. They were nearly overhead when he first observed them, but had moved away before he started to film them with his Bell and Howell 16 mm motion picture camera. His 3-inch telephoto lens was set on infinity.

The objects, viewed from an estimated distance of 5 miles, appeared to be internally illuminated and were completely silent. Newhouse estimated the size of the objects as that of B-29s at 10,000 feet. Some hovered motionless whereas others made abrupt changes in their flight path. All of the UFOs had remained together in a group, circling and darting in the cloudless blue sky, from the time the Newhouse family spotted them until they began to disappear over the western horizon. This is when one object left the main group and headed east.

Two of the country's best photo labs, the USAF's lab at Wright Field and the U.S. Navy's lab at Anacostia, Maryland, analyzed the film, attempting to prove the objects were balloons, aircraft, atmospheric mirages, or birds in flight. The Air Force photo analysts determined that the objects could not have been airplanes, balloons, or birds in flight. The Navy analysts made a frame-by-frame analysis of the motion of the lights and the changes in the lights' intensity, concluding that the UFOs were intelligently controlled vehicles that were *not* airplanes or birds in flight. All possible prosaic explanations were eliminated by both branches of the military. The objects captured on film by Newhouse defied explanation. That is, until they were viewed by the Robertson Panel.

One scientist stated that he thought the UFOs could be sea gulls riding on a thermal current much like ones he'd seen near his home on Berkeley, California, on San Francisco Bay. He had not analyzed the film. The U.S. Air Force and U.S. Navy photo analysts had considered this possibility, but the velocity of the one UFO that had left the main group and traveled east eliminated the gull explanation. Undeterred by the military experts' analysis, the Robertson Panel's scientists ignored the scientific evidence and concluded that the objects might have been sea gulls in flight.

In the end, citing the lack of sound data in most cases and the slow follow-up caused by the modest size and limited facilities of the ATIC, the panel decided there was no evidence of a direct threat to national security by the objects sighted. Their exact words were: "We firmly believe there is no residuum of cases which indicate phenomena which are attributable to foreign artifacts capable of hostile acts, and that there is no evidence that the phenomena indicated a need for revision of scientific concepts."[18] It seems preposterous that the Robertson Panel could examine 15 cases in detail, in which scientific evidence was ignored and other evidence was omitted, and come to "a firm belief" that there was no evidence of phenomena outside their scientific understanding.

However, the Panel was clearly concerned about the threat of psychological warfare. If public hysteria caused an overload of false UFO reports, it could threaten national security. This led to an official policy change that directed the national security agencies to "take immediate steps to strip the Unidentified Flying Objects of the special status they have been given and the aura of mystery they have unfortunately acquired."[19] A re-education program was recommended to reduce the public's interest in the possibility of extraterrestrial visitation through television, motion pictures, and popular articles. It proposed the use of astronomers, psychiatrists, and assorted celebrities to reduce public interest in UFOs. The plan was to present UFO cases, reported by credible witnesses, and to debunk them by offering speculative alternative explanations. The embarrassment to the witnesses would surely cause others to clam up if the plan worked. In addition to this, the Panel recommended that UFO-related organizations should be considered potentially subversive and *observed* by national security agencies.

The official policy change brought about a new Air Force regulation. In August 1953, Air Force Regulation 200-2 created the Air Intelligence Squadron of the Air Defense Command. The new policy directed Project Blue Book to inform news media representatives on UFOs only when they had been positively identified as a familiar object. The names of the principals, intercept and investigation procedures, and classified radar data could not be revealed. In an effort to remove them from the public eye, all unsolved cases were classified.

Initially, the 4602d Air Intelligence Service Squadron was assigned the role of supporting the Air Defense Command intelligence function through the collection of evidence, limited field analysis, and rapid reporting of air combat intelligence. The 4602d's responsibilities grew over the following several months. In June 1953, under the subheading "Unidentified Flying Objects," in a document classified SECRET, we find a statement that the investigation of unidentified flying objects is not part of their mission and field units are not authorized to make investigations of this type without prior approval by Headquarters. It further states that when Headquarters has issued approval and a field team reaches the scene of a crash, they should immediately send a report of what they have found.

In December 1953, Joint Army-Navy-Air Force Regulation number 146 (JANAP-146) made it a crime for military personnel to discuss classified UFO reports with unauthorized persons. Violators faced up to two years in prison and/or fines of up to $10,000.

By August 1954, AFR-2 regulations made the Air Defense Command responsible for conducting all field investigations within the Zone of the Interior to determine the identity of any UFOB, "any airborne object which by performance, aerodynamic characteristics, or unusual features, does not conform to any presently known aircraft or missile type, or which cannot be positively identified as a familiar object."[20] The Air Technical Intelligence Center at Wright Patterson UFO Base, Dayton, Ohio, would analyze and evaluate all reports only after the Air Defense Command had exhausted all efforts to identify the UFOB and all information and evidence collected. Citing a personnel shortage at Project Blue Book Headquarters, the reports that could affect national security were siphoned away from Blue Book, leaving Blue Book to deal with the more trivial reports. AFR 200-2 again stated that Blue Book could discuss UFO cases with the media only if they were regarded as having a conventional explanation. If they were unidentified, the media was to be told only that the situation was being analyzed. Blue Book was also ordered to reduce the number of unidentified cases to a minimum.

The CIA's debunking directive and the Air Defense Command's directives opened the door to closely connected government scientists, such as Dr. Donald Menzel, who was secretly on the NSA's payroll, to wage a disinformation campaign against the Air Force's Project Blue Book and the American public. His first book was published in 1953. We'll discuss Dr. Menzel's anti-UFO propaganda activities in the next chapter.

CHAPTER 3

DR. DONALD HOWARD MENZEL

Dr. Donald Howard Menzel (1901–1976) was probably the best-known and most influential UFO debunker in the 1950s and 1960s. He was a professor of astronomy at Harvard University, generally conceded to be the top American university. Born in Florence, Colorado, and brought up in Leadville and Denver, Menzel was a precocious student with strong interests in chemistry, the Morse code, science fiction, and the study of information systems. He earned an AB degree in chemistry and AM in mathematics and astronomy from the University of Denver before entering Princeton in fall 1921, where he earned AM and PhD degrees in astrophysics. Between 1924 and 1931 he worked successively at the University of

Iowa, Ohio State University, and the University of California Lick Observatory.

In 1931, he accepted an offer from Harvard, where theoretical astrophysics was valued and supported. The ensuing nine years were the most scientifically productive in his career. But his work in astronomy was interrupted by World War II. During WWII he served as lieutenant commander in the U.S. Navy, specializing in cryptanalysis through the Office of Naval Communications. He was an expert on radio wave propagation. Through his work in naval intelligence, he tackled such problems as how to deal with Japanese fighter planes diving with the sun at the pilot's back. He made a major contribution to determining ways of continuing radio transmissions even when solar storms occurred, and used his knowledge of the solar prominences (Corona) to help in both problems. After the war, he played a leading role in establishing the Central Radio Propagation Laboratory of the National Bureau of Standards.

In 1954, Menzel assumed the position of director of the Harvard College Observatory and Paine Professor of Practical Astronomy and Professor of Astrophysics. Through his association with Harvard and his entrepreneurial spirit, he was able to establish the Smithsonian Astrophysical Observatory on the grounds at Harvard Observatory, to replace the underfunded, understaffed, and dilapidated observatory, and provide a permanent source of financial support for the institution. He later obtained Navy funding for a major expansion of the solar astronomy facilities at Climax, Colorado, and the establishment by the USAF of a new solar observatory at Sacramento Peak, New Mexico, for the study of solar-ionospheric influences on radio transmissions. When solar storms occur, charged particles from the sun hit the ionosphere and interfere with radio transmission from one point to another on the earth. His work resulted in great improvement in military communications.

Menzel also had interests in private industry performing services for 40 different companies. His major contracts included Hughes

Aircraft Company, North American, Thompson Ramo Wooldridge Systems, and Martin Marietta.

Dr. Donald Menzel by Babette Whipple

Menzel was a prolific writer of science fiction articles under a variety of pseudonyms. He enjoyed doodling sketches of Martians and other extraterrestrial creatures and writing articles to debunk claims of extraterrestrial visitation. One of his three very negative books about UFOs was translated into Russian and was even favorably reviewed by Dr. J. Allen Hynek, the Air Force scientific consultant to Project Blue Book, despite its entirely negative tone.

Menzel's approach to UFO investigations was to proclaim possible explanations for cases based on theoretical possibilities that seemed reasonable only when one ignored the facts. He rarely talked to witnesses. Often his focus was on faulty human perception, pointing out what poor observers UFO witnesses supposedly are. Never once did he suggest that the reason most UFO sightings could be explained as relatively conventional phenomena is because observers are actually pretty good witnesses. We know that they saw Venus, for example, because they were looking in the right direction at the right time, even if they didn't know it was Venus.

Menzel attempted to influence Barry Goldwater when NICAP members were advocating for a Congressional hearing on UFOs. He warned Goldwater, "An active minority group can often be dangerous. I am, therefore, sending you under separate cover, a copy of a full analysis of the flying saucer phenomenon, from the standpoint of a trained and, I hope, competent scientist. I have had full access to the Air Force files and the Air Force officials have themselves spoken in favor of the authenticity of the work."[1] He then requested a statement from Goldwater on his position on the subject of UFOs.

Menzel was asked at the last minute to submit a written paper to the UFO Symposium held on July 29, 1968, by the Committee on Science and Astronautics of the U.S. House of Representatives. Six other scientists made in-person presentations to the committee. They were Dr. J. Allen Hynek, scientific consultant to Project Blue Book and chairman of the astronomy department at Northwestern University; Dr. James Harder, professor of engineering at the University of California, Berkeley; Dr. James E. McDonald, co-chairman and professor of the department of atmospheric physics at the University of Arizona; Dr. Carl Sagan, Cornell University astronomer; Dr. Robert M.L. Baker of the Computer Sciences Corporation; and Dr. Robert L. Hall of the department of sociology at the University of Illinois in Chicago. McDonald had been the primary instigator of the hearings. He was one of the few scientists who took Menzel's unscientific explanations to task. Stanton Friedman, the youngest scientist to present a written presentation to the committee, may be the only one still alive.

Menzel's seven-page paper characterizes flying saucers as a modern myth and compares the phenomenon to ghosts, spirits, witches, elves, hobgoblins, and the devil. This demonstrates his desire to strengthen the scientific taboo on the subject. He considered himself a scientist, but labeled pro-UFO scientists as "believers," "UFO buffs," and "UFO addicts"[2], with faulty reasoning and sloppy science. This was a gross exaggeration and a misstatement of fact. The physical scientists on the panel had a history of excellent investigation leaving no stone unturned. Conventional phenomena had to be carefully considered and methodically eliminated as possible explanations. Menzel charged that all UFOs are only misidentified conventional phenomena. Hynek stated that it does not matter if 100 or 100,000 people mistake conventional phenomena for UFOs. What matters are the reports that continue to defy explanation after all prosaic explanations have been eliminated. Friedman stated, "The purpose of science is to sort data and focus on that which is relevant to the search at hand.... Eye witnesses and photographic and radar reports from all over the earth by competent witnesses of definite objects whose characteristics such as maneuverability, high speed, and hovering, along with definite shape, texture, and surface features rule out terrestrial explanation."[3]

Menzel presented several hypothetical situations in which trained observers might mistake atmospheric phenomena for UFOs, such as ice crystals and temperature inversions, but did not speak of events where conventional explanations had been ruled out. He offered explanations, such as balloons, kites, birds, and spider webs, but insisted that arguments in favor of the interplanetary explanation of UFOs are fallacious, stating again that UFOs are a matter of faith, not science. His statement "I know of no reliable case of simultaneous visual and radar sightings"[4] clearly demonstrates his negative bias and failure to accept the scholarship of scientists such as Dr. James McDonald, J. Allen Hynek, and Stanton T. Friedman. He was most certainly aware of radar-visual sightings. The trick was in the word *reliable.*

McDonald presented his investigation of the July 19, 1952, Washington, DC, radar visual case that received widespread publicity and spurred the longest press conference since WWII. He had interviewed five of the CAA people and four of the pilots. McDonald wrote:

I have gone over the quantitative aspects of the official explanation that this was ducting or trapping of the radar beams. That is quite untenable. I have gone over the radiosonde data, computed the radar refractive index gradient, and it is nowhere near the ducting gradient. Also, it is very important that at one time three different radars, two CAA and one Andrews Air Force Base radar all got compatible echoes. This is extremely important.... I must express for the record my very strong disagreement with Dr. Donald H. Menzel...whose two books on the subject of UFOs lean very heavily on meteorological explanations. I have checked case after case of his, and his explanations are very, very far removed from what are well-known principles of quantitative aspects of meteorological optic objects.[5]

(See Chapter 4 for a more detailed account of this case.)

Menzel's unpublished autobiography, discovered by Friedman in his archival collection, tells of his many experiences evaluating problems for the navy concerning anomalous propagation, clear air turbulence, and a variety of atmospheric conditions. Menzel wrote of his evaluation of the July 1952, visual-radar sightings in Washington, DC: "Major General Samford, whom I know very well from my Navy days, was by now in charge of the agency [NSA] that had succeeded to the type of work I'd undertaken for Naval Communications, made an announcement supporting my evaluation."[6] Menzel's evaluation ignored the expert witnesses' testimony with regard to the radar and visual sightings of an unknown target and dismissed this major event as nothing more than anomalous propagation caused by a temperature inversion.

He provided an invaluable debunking service to the USAF from 1960 to 1968, as a consultant analyzing UFO reports. Most of the cases sent to him were the ones that Hynek was unable to solve—the true Unknowns. Menzel solved the cases by providing explanations for the majority of the cases, even when the solution was untenable. This required total disregard for witness credibility and the perplexing evidence that caused Hynek to list them as Unknowns. The Air Force then removed the case from the Unknown category and assigned it a conventional case disposition.

Friedman's paper pointed out that Edward Ruppelt, former head of Project Blue Book, the Air Force's official UFO investigative effort, makes specific mention of not only Unknowns observed on radar, but of combined visual and radar Unknowns. In addition to this, Friedman cited Dr. J. Allen Hynek's discussion of radar-visual sightings in the December 17, 1966, issue of the *Saturday Evening Post*.

At a time when the scientific community was feeling a squeeze on government funding, Menzel used this opportunity to dissuade Congress from allotting additional funds to UFO research. Marden discovered correspondence between debunker Philip J. Klass and Menzel at the American Philosophical Society that reveals that, days before the symposium, Klass had warned each member of the Committee on Science and Astronautics, "McDonald called for a program which would begin with an international scientific study of UFOS, at a cost of 'a few tens of millions of dollars."[7] According to Klass, a global network of UFO sensors would cost the United States billions of dollars per year. He ended by writing, "If UFOs are explainable as hoaxes, misidentifications, and freak atmospheric phenomena, McDonald's proposed multi-billion dollar per year program will be history's most ridiculous and expensive boondoggle." He added that McDonald has "repeatedly and bitterly attacked the US Air Force."[8] In a letter from Menzel to Klass dated August 20, 1968, Menzel expressed the sentiment, "I want to do everything I can to scuttle the boat to Hynek and McDonald for money to be spent on UFO studies." (Menzel sent enclosures to Markowitz, Condon, Quintanilla, and Boyd.) This raises questions with regard to Menzel's association with Hector Quintanilla, Project Blue

Book's chief from 1963 to 1969. Hector Quintanilla, wrote in his manuscript "UFOs: An Air Force Dilemma," "Dr. Donald Menzel, who authored 'The World of Flying Saucers' has helped me on some very ticklish cases. I consider Menzel to be a true scientist and not a publicity grabbing charlatan" and added, "Philip Klass, who wrote 'UFO's—IDENTIFIED' offered the project office a number of UFO cases that turned out to be beauties."[9]

Menzel made the bold proclamation that the nearest possible aliens would have been hundreds of light years away, stating, "I think it is very possible that intelligent Life—perhaps more intelligent than we—may exist somewhere in the vast reaches of outer space. But it is the very vastness of this space that complicates the problem. The distances are almost inconceivable. The time required to reach the earth—even at speeds comparable with that of light—range in hundreds if not thousands of years for our nearest neighbors."[10] Surely he knew there were loads of stars within 50 light years, but he could not imagine that alien science and technology might be more highly developed than mid-20th-century earth science or that intelligent life might exist in our region of space.

Menzel was unquestionably an expert at the scientific observation of eclipses, having observed many in different parts of the world. But there is an enormous difference between being prepared with sophisticated equipment to observe a precisely predictable phenomenon and the sudden observation of one or more UFOs, usually without any instrumentation available, and where the behavior of the UFO often includes rapid or highly maneuvered flight and sudden starts and stops.

There are no references in the seven-page paper that Menzel submitted to the Science and Astronautics Committee. In contrast, Friedman's paper has 65 references in the primary paper and an additional 17 in an appendix, many from scientific journals and from two to Menzel's books *Flying Saucers* (Harvard University Press, 1953) and *The World of Flying Saucers* (Doubleday, 1963). His third book was published posthumously with Dr. Ernest Taves in 1977.

Friedman has commented that if he had read Menzel's book first instead of Edward Ruppelt's *The Report on Unidentified Flying Objects*, he would never have read another, because it was so biased. The shocking aspect was that Menzel had an outstanding background as an astronomer and had served three years in the U.S. Navy despite his age. Harvard was considered to be at the peak of academia. It appears that Menzel had an agenda that included making every effort to dissuade colleagues worldwide from investigating UFOs. He claimed all sightings had prosaic explanations. In an item in *Physics Today* he proclaimed that all UFO witnesses are poor observers. No source is given for this extraordinary false claim. Friedman had trouble understanding why such a high-ranking physical scientist would issue such unscientific psychological explanations. Why was he so negative? He had written quite a bit of science fiction, usually under pseudonyms, even earning part of his college expenses in graduate school at Princeton through his creative imagination and excellent writing skills.

Friedman did have one puzzling close encounter with Menzel at Harvard. He had telephoned in the morning to invite Menzel to a lecture he was presenting that evening to the Harvard Engineering Alumni Association. The conversation went as follows.

Friedman: "Dr. Menzel, this is nuclear physicist Stanton Friedman."

Menzel: "Oh, I know all about you."

Friedman: "Did you read my congressional testimony next to yours in the Congressional UFO Symposium Proceedings?"

Menzel: "No. I have seen memos and letters about you. You can't be a scientist and believe in flying saucers."

Friedman laughed and Menzel started to rant. Friedman stated that he hadn't called to argue, only out of courtesy to invite

Dr. Menzel, because he was speaking at Harvard at 8 p.m. and had no idea if there had been any external publicity. Menzel retorted, of course, that he wouldn't attend.

There was a very good response at the lecture and Friedman told of asking Dr. Menzel to attend. He certainly didn't know what Menzel meant by memos and letters until Marden, in 2014, discovered copies, at the American Philosophical Society, of letters from Friedman to Dr. Condon at the University of Colorado in 1969. They were strongly worded. Condon had obviously sent copies to Menzel. Condon and Menzel's UFO correspondence is there, as well as Klass papers. Surprisingly there is no Friedman file in the Klass papers despite the fact they had corresponded for 20+ years.

The story of Menzel and UFOs took a very strange turn in late 1984 when Jaime Shandera, a TV producer in Southern California, received a roll of exposed 35mm film in an envelope with no return address, though postmarked Albuquerque. Jaime had been introduced by Friedman to William Moore, with whom Friedman had worked to research the Roswell UFO Incident starting in 1978, when Friedman lived in California. They found 62 witnesses in a year and a half, as described in the book *The Roswell Incident* by Moore and Charles Berlitz (Friedman received a percentage of Moore's royalties), and in the book *Crash at Corona* by Friedman and aviation writer Donald Berliner. (Friedman had moved to Fredericton, New Brunswick, Canada, in 1980, not because the FBI chased him, as is noted in some rumors that circulated, but because his wife's parents, five of her siblings, and numerous nieces and nephews lived there.) Moore developed the film. It had two sets of eight pictures of the so-called TOP SECRET MAJIC Eisenhower Briefing Document dated November 24, 1952. Also included was a September 24, 1947, memo from Harry Truman to then–Secretary of Defense James Forrestal establishing a group called Operation Majestic 12 (MJ-12), to deal with the Roswell crash and the bodies and wreckage from it. The group included six military people, five scientists, and Forrestal. Most shocking was the extraordinary claim that

Dr. Donald Menzel was a member of this group! The other names made sense, and it was easy to establish they all had very high level security clearances. (See the table of members of the MJ-12 group in the Appendix.) But surely Menzel didn't need a clearance to teach astronomy. They were certainly unwilling to publish the briefing without doing a lot of research, especially with regard to Menzel. His papers were at the Harvard University Archives. Clearly they needed to be reviewed.

It was no surprise that Dr. Vannevar Bush was listed. He had been head of the Office of Scientific Research and Development during World War II, which developed the proximity fuse, the atomic bomb, and dozens of other high-tech devices. Also, a Canadian memo dated November 21, 1950, from Wilbert Smith, who had headed the Canadian Government Group investigating UFOs, had stated that "...their modus operandi is as yet unknown, but there's a small group working under Dr. Vannevar Bush."[11] While Friedman and Moore were researching the various MJ-12 members, Friedman noted a 1950 letter in the Bush papers at the Library of Congress Manuscript Division. It was addressed to Bush from a Boston attorney, Robert Proctor, thanking Bush for his assistance in getting Menzel cleared by an Air Force Loyalty Board trying to take away Menzel's USAF secret security clearance! Why did Menzel have a clearance, and why were they trying to take it away? It was during the heyday of Senator Joseph McCarthy, who saw communists under every bed. Friedman called Proctor and was told there were more than 1,000 pages of testimony about the loyalty hearing located in Menzel's papers at the Harvard University Archives.

At about this time the Washington-based Fund for UFO Research had sent out a list of possible research project topics to its associates asking them for their favorites. The vote was for Operation Majestic 12, and Friedman was asked to submit and cost out a proposal. He quickly did so and they awarded him $16,000, a princely sum for UFO research. Friedman's first goal was to check out Menzel's papers at Harvard. The Archives indicated he needed written permission to do so from two Harvard officials and from Mrs. Menzel to view an unpublished autobiography. He obtained them.

At Harvard there really weren't any UFO folders, so he selected one labeled "John F. Kennedy," wondering what the connection was between Menzel and Kennedy. That was actually a very fortunate choice. It turned out that Senator Kennedy had been on the Board of Overseers at Harvard, and had chosen the astronomy department and its observatories as his area of interest. Friedman found out that Menzel greatly admired Kennedy. They had even had breakfast together on walks from Kennedy's office to the campus. Menzel was impressed because JFK wrote his own reports rather than asking Menzel to do it, as had been the case with Kennedy's predecessor. Menzel had joined a group "Scientists for Kennedy" during the 1960 presidential election. There was a letter from Menzel to Kennedy offering to help JFK with regard to the National Security Agency. He told Jack (they were on a first-name basis) that he had a longer continuous relationship with the NSA and its Navy predecessor, more than 30 years, than had anybody. Menzel added, "When we are properly cleared to each other, I can tell you more."[12] Menzel's unpublished autobiography said that the loyalty hearing was the worst experience of his life. He couldn't bring up his TOP SECRET U.S. Navy clearance, and his accusers weren't even present. Many prominent scientists went to his defense, including Dr. Bush and a number of other big names. The basis for the charge that he was disloyal were strange things like having headed an eclipse expedition to Siberia in 1936, having brought a pair of nylon stockings to a Soviet astronomer for his wife, and having said friendly things about the Soviets at a Russian American Friendship dinner in 1942, at which everybody expressed gratitude for the Russians holding back Hitler's horde. Also, the then-head of the astronomy department was Dr. Harlow Shapley (1885–1972), who was opposed to Harvard doing government research and was thought to be a communist sympathizer. Menzel was guilty by association. He was finally cleared after a massive effort by his colleagues. Friedman was surprised that he could find nothing about the hearings in the *New York Times* or *Washington Post*.

A gold mine of information about Menzel's many government connections was his then-unpublished autobiography. Menzel taught cryptography, and helped train a number of woman cryptographers at Radcliffe (Harvard's women's college) and six other women's colleges in the area. He did classified consulting work for various civilian and government agencies. He was commander of the Naval Reserve Communications Unit No. 1 in Cambridge for many years. None of this multitude of post-war classified work was mentioned in two special issues of *Sky and Telescope* dedicated to Menzel: one at the time of his death (1976), and the other at the 100th anniversary of his birth (2001). Friedman published an article, "The Secret Life of Donald Menzel" in the *International UFO Reporter* (Jan/Feb. 1988, pp. 20–24). Predictably some readers were in denial, declaring that Menzel couldn't have led a double life knowing full well that Roswell had really happened and there was a highly classified group monitoring the situation. Friedman pointed out that every spy leads a double life. Three prominent ones were Kim Philby, Guy Burgess and Donald McLean, who worked for British Intelligence, but were finally found out to be Soviet spies.

Menzel was in the best possible position to help the intelligence community. For example, his specialized knowledge would be useful in reviewing the strange symbols on Roswell wreckage; evaluating messages from other countries about UFO sightings as picked up by the National Security Agency; and discouraging Soviet and Chinese spies from thinking the United States was doing anything scientific about UFOs. As pointed out by Air Force General Carroll Bolender's October 20, 1969, memo, sightings that could affect national Security were *not* part of the USAF Blue Book system. They were instead reported in accordance with JANAP 146 or Air Force Manual 55-11. Those files have never been released. In the Eisenhower Briefing Document there is a fascinating line saying that many thought that the origin of flying saucers might be other planets in our solar system, but that Dr. Menzel thought they must come from other solar systems. An excellent cover for that notion was a strange comment in his congressional testimony that the nearest source for alien visitors must be hundreds of light years away. The fact is there are 2,000 stars within 54 light years.

The Betty Hill star map discussed in *Captured! The Betty and Barney Hill UFO Experience* by Friedman and Marden points to Zeta 1 and Zeta 2 Reticuli two stars in the southern sky constellation of Reticulum (The Net) only 39.3 light years from the sun and only an eighth of a light year apart.

It is very important to recognize the historical context of the times preceding the Roswell Incident, which happened during the first week of July 1947. The most destructive war in humankind's history ended in August 1945, with the dropping on Japan of two atomic bombs, each releasing the energy of about 17,000 tons of TNT. They had been developed in total secrecy despite the expenditure of billions of dollars. In total 50 million people had been killed during the war, and 1,700 cities had been destroyed. The Cold War had begun with the Allies being certain that the next enemy would be the Soviet Union, which had lost more than 20 million people during the war. Surely they and others would try to develop the new atomic weaponry. There were discussions in the Manhattan Engineering District, which developed the atomic bomb, concerning the development of a truly even more horrifying weapon: the hydrogen bomb (H-bomb), which would use the nuclear fusion process that produces the energy of the sun and of all stars. The first H-bomb was detonated in 1952, in the Pacific, by the United States, and released the energy of 10 million tons of TNT. A big chemical bomb in 1944 released the energy of only 10 tons of TNT. The largest H-bomb was exploded later by the Soviets and released the energy of 57 million tons of TNT!

General Leslie Groves, who had directed the Manhattan Engineering District, was asked, in 1948, how long it would take for the Russians to develop a nuclear weapon. He remarked that it would be about eight years and that they still didn't have a means for delivering them. The United States had developed the B-29 bomber primarily for that purpose. As it happened, the Russians exploded their first atomic bomb in August 1949, years earlier than anticipated. A declassified memo from 1951, found in the files of the National Security Council at the Truman Library, reported that the Soviets had made more progress in developing atomic bombs and methods for delivering them in the prior 18 months than had been expected for five more years. As it happens the United States had left a B-29 behind and the Soviets had made copies. Because of the United States underestimating Soviet capabilities and the penetration of U.S. nuclear weapons labs by spies, there wasn't even an all-encompassing system of radar stations to monitor the skies for incoming Soviet bombers. The Ground Observer Corps had people posted at the tops of buildings keeping an eye on the sky. Former German scientists were aiding both sides in the development of intercontinental ballistic missiles and then orbiting rockets. The joke in the 1950s was that the Russians' ex-German scientists were ahead of the U.S. ex-German scientists.

This was certainly demonstrated when the Soviets launched Earth's first satellite (Sputnik) in 1957, followed by the first animal, the first man, and the first rocket to go around the moon. The first U.S. attempt at launching a satellite blew up on the launch pad. Worldwide the U.S. reputation as the big, powerful, innovative country was in tatters. U.S. researchers were certainly working in secret on trying to learn from saucer wreckage, from all the scientific evidence being gained from radar measurements, from the ground, and from military planes and equipment, including cameras and spectrometers on board military aircraft and naval vessels.

Surely after learning how useful disinformation was in WWII, to deceive both the Japanese and Germans, it would have been prudent to carry disinformation about the presence of extraterrestrial spacecraft to the Russians and Chinese, as well as the U.S. public. Donald Menzel, after all, was not just an outstanding and highly respected astrophysicist, but very experienced in the intelligence field both during and after the war. At least as important were his skills at writing science fiction dating back to the 1920s and even being offered editorships of science fiction publications. Nobody would have been better qualified. After all, there were very few uncleared scientists involved in ufology to argue with him. He would be the champion of the astronomical community, most of whose members didn't dare to take UFOs seriously and still don't.

In a conversation with a Harvard colleague who knew Menzel very well, Friedman asked how the colleague thought Menzel would feel about publishing noisy negativism while knowing full well that aliens were visiting, that their vehicles had crashed, that the government had loads of classified data. His response surprised Friedman: "He would have loved it. He always knew he was smarter than almost everybody else." He could be sure that no "outsider" knew as much as he did about the topic. He was very patriotic judging by all his wartime and postwar efforts for the Navy.

It is clear that both sides in the Cold War were intent on developing more powerful aircraft and rockets for both offensive and defensive purposes. Satellites offered the best technique for monitoring the activities of one's enemies and being able to spy on their activities. Flying saucers certainly had developed the ability to be very maneuverable and much faster than American and Russian aircraft. It was normal during WWII for both sides to evaluate crashed enemy aircraft for new and better technology. Not surprisingly, the recovered crashed saucers from outside Roswell and in the Plains of San Agustin, New Mexico, in July 1947, and at Aztec in March 1948, would have been prime targets for examination.

Several Roswell debunkers have said that if crashed vehicles had been recovered, half the physicists in universities would have been required to dig into the technology. That notion is ludicrous, as there was already in existence a very highly competent group of industrial scientists with high-level security clearances. There was a huge infrastructure set up to develop nuclear and other highly advanced weapon systems. There were several large laboratories such as Los Alamos, Oak Ridge, Sandia, Livermore, and Hanford devoted to nuclear technology. Each had thousands of employees, and high security clearances. The government didn't need uncleared college professors. All of these labs are still in place. When working on classified projects, in the national labs and industry, the goal is *not* "publish or perish," as it is in academia, but, rather try to get the program objectives accomplished.

Menzel certainly was, with his scientific reputation (he was voted a member of the National Academy of Sciences in 1948), and fictional writing skills, in the best position of all the MJ 12 members to provide anti-UFO propaganda especially to the scientific community and the press. He was an outstanding astronomer. For reasons unknown, astronomers were and often are still expected, by the press, to be knowledgeable about UFOs, star travel, and life in the universe, despite a total absence of knowledge about advanced technology, high-level security, and the motivation of Earthlings, no less aliens. The book *Science Was Wrong* by Friedman and Marden has a number of examples of astronomers' ignorance about these topics. One glaring example was the claim by Dr. J.W. Campbell, a Canadian astronomer, in his 1941 article in *Philosophical Magazine*, "Rocket Flight to the Moon," that a rocket able to get a man to the moon and back would have to weigh a million tons at launch. The Apollo system weighed a mere 3,000 tons at launch in 1969. Campbell had made every possible wrong assumption about going to the moon.

Menzel also traveled a great deal both overseas and in the United States. Friedman found, through a Minnesota member of *MUFON*, that a colleague of Menzel recalled that Menzel had left in a hurry from a lucrative consulting effort with Engineering Research Associates in Minnesota, headed by Menzel's WWII boss, to deal with a classified problem in New Mexico, in July 1947.

He certainly would have been highly qualified to render an opinion about the strange symbols on Roswell crashed saucer I-beams. It should be stressed that there is no way to disinform Soviet scientists and military researchers without also disinforming Allied colleagues. On page 4 of the Eisenhower Briefing Document, the statement is made that "Since it is virtually certain that these craft do not originate in any country on earth, considerable speculation has centered around what their point of origin might be and how they get here. Mars was and remains a possibility, although some scientists, most notably Dr. Menzel, consider it more likely that we are dealing with beings from another solar system entirely."[13]

One way to develop a much fuller appreciation of Dr. Menzel's contributions to cryptography is to read the 33-page article by Craig Bauer and John Ulrich of York College of Pennsylvania, "The Cryptological Contributions of Dr. Donald Menzel" (*Cryptologia* 30(2006): 306–39). It should be stressed that, although there have been several books published about academics contributing to the Allied effort during WWII, such as Robin Wink's *Cloak and Gown: Scholars in the Secret War 1939–1961* (1996), none have noted Menzel's very highly classified contributions.

It must also be noted that the major reason many classified projects had been declassified is that the projects no longer required being hidden. For example, President Eisenhower in 1953 set up three separate, highly classified groups to each consider a method for containment of the Soviet Union by other-than-military responses. The results of "Operation Solarium" were not declassified until the mid-1980s. It is perfectly clear that the lid is being kept on the question of flying saucers and the activities of Operation Majestic 12 (undoubtedly re-titled). The NSA has barely touched declassification of all its UFO-related intercepts. The CIA has also long kept classified old TOP SECRET UMBRA UFO materials. There really is a Cosmic Watergate, and Donald Menzel was right in the middle of it.

CHAPTER 4

PHILIP J. KLASS

Philip Julian Klass (1919–2005) burst onto the UFO scene in 1966 with the fervor of a man with a mission to complete. Public interest in UFOs had reached an all-time high, and U.S. citizens were clamoring for a Congressional investigation of the evidence. An unbiased scientific inquiry could potentially lead to disclosure of the UFO presence and demonstrate the complete vulnerability of our national defense system against a technologically advanced force. That year two new bestselling books had stirred widespread public interest. *Incident at Exeter* and *The Interrupted Journey* by John G. Fuller, a respected author and journalist, were receiving widespread publicity. Both books contained information that threatened to arouse public hysteria unless a simple, scientific explanation could be offered to explain the perplexing events detailed in the books. *Incident at Exeter* sensationalized a terrifying close encounter by an 18-year-old man and two police officers in Kensington, New Hampshire, and several additional sighting accounts in the Granite state. *The Interrupted Journey* told the story of a credible New Hampshire couple's shocking close encounter with a hovering, silent craft and their subsequent abduction by nonhumans. It was the first of its kind. (See Marden and Friedman's *Captured! The Betty and Barney Hill UFO Experience* for a comprehensive case study.)

Avionics journalist and prominent UFO skeptic Philip Klass, taken in 1977.

Although prior to 1966 Klass, a mainstream journalist for *Aviation Week and Space Technology* magazine, had focused little attention upon UFO reports, a professional organization of which he was a member, the Institute of Electrical and Electronics Engineers, was planning a three-day technical conference in Washington, D.C., in early October. The planning committee had proposed a public symposium on UFOs. Klass wrote of his indignation in *UFO's— Identified*, "UFOs seemed to me to be a subject best left to fanatics and cultists...I feared that the good name of this respected society would be used to dignify a subject of no real concern to science."[1] It is apparent that although he had limited knowledge of the scientific investigation of UFOs, he had formed an intractable bias against UFO reality. Because of his strong opinion on the subject he was asked to be a member of the panel of speakers at the session. About half the committee members were moderately interested in UFOs, whereas the rest shared his concern. Although Klass had little knowledge of the subject matter, he stated that he was one speaker who "could argue against the fanatics."[2]

He had derived his limited knowledge on UFOs primarily from newspaper articles. The one column he had written on the topic was his *Aviation Week* debunking article on the significant July 1952 radar-visual UFO sightings over Washington, D.C. His information had come from the Civil Aeronautics Administration's report that had ignored the radar-visual sightings by military pilots and military and civilian radar operators. Reiterating the CAA's claim that there was no scientific evidence to support the contention that extraterrestrial craft had over flown the United States, he wrote that the alleged invasion by space aliens was only ghosts on the radar screen caused by a temperature inversion.

In preparation for his anti-UFO position on the Institute of Electrical and Electronics Engineers panel, he purchased his first book on the topic: *Incident at Exeter*. This began Klass's passion for debunking UFOs. *Incident at Exeter* detailed a flurry of UFO sightings, often near power lines, in the state of New Hampshire, and highlighted a close encounter by an 18-year-old man, Norman Muscarello, and two Exeter, New Hampshire, police officers, Eugene Bertrand and David Hunt. The close encounter occurred after midnight on September 3, 1965, when Muscarello was hitchhiking from his girlfriend's home in Amesbury, Massachusetts, to his residence in Exeter. Traffic was light so he was forced to walk most of the 8 or so miles along Route 150. As he moved along the rural route in Kensington, his attention was drawn to a row of five extremely bright red lights behind a farmhouse. They were so bright that he was unable to detect the object's form. However, he was able to determine that they were connected to an object, because they were arranged in a row and moved in unison. The lights flashed in rapid succession (1-2-3-4-5-4-3-2-1) and bathed the woods and the farmhouse in a red glow. The object was completely silent and moved erratically, like a falling leaf. At one point it approached Muscarello at such a close range that he took cover in a ditch, behind a stone wall. Finally, the object moved toward the woods, and this gave Muscarello the opportunity to knock on the farmhouse door. But his knocks went unanswered. Finally, he flagged down a passing car and asked to be taken to the Exeter Police Department. He arrived at approximately 1:45 a.m.

A terrified Muscarello reported the incident to Officer Reginald Toland, who, in turn, made a radio call to Patrolman Eugene Bertrand. Bertrand had been busy attempting to calm a distressed woman who was too upset to drive. He had found her vehicle parked on the side of the road in Exeter at approximately 1:00 a.m. She stated that a huge, silent object, with red lights, had followed her car from Epping east toward Exeter and at one point had stopped directly above her vehicle.

Bertrand accompanied Muscarello to the Kensington site in search of the UFO. Suddenly, it rose up from behind two tall pine trees, wobbling in the distance about 100 feet above them and 100 yards away. The lights were in a line at about a 60-degree angle, and a large, dark form was visible behind it. It moved in their direction barely clearing a 60- to 70-foot tree and stopped approximately 100 feet in the distance. At this point, Officer Bertrand dropped to the ground and started to draw his gun. Concerned for their safety, the two men took cover in the patrol car. Soon Patrolman David Hunt arrived. His attention was drawn to horses kicking in the barn and dogs howling in the distance. Finally, the object moved behind the farmhouse over the field approximately one-half mile away from the men, at an altitude of approximately 100 feet, and departed in a southeasterly direction toward the coast.

At 3:00 a.m., shortly after the craft had departed Kensington, a man phoned the Exeter Police Station to report a UFO near the Hampton, New Hampshire, toll booth. Officer Toland alerted the Hampton police and they made a report to Pease Air Force Base.

Pease Air Force Base had five B-47s in the area on the night of September 2-3 on Operation Big Blast "Coco," a SAC/NORAD training mission, but it had terminated by 03/0430Z (12:43 a.m.), nearly an hour before Muscarello and Bertrand arrived at the field, and jets were en route to the home stations.[3] (See the letter in the Appendix.)

Despite the fact that the Air Force could find no reasonable explanation for the close encounter, the Pentagon explained the sightings as high-altitude aircraft, stars, or planets that were magnified by a weather inversion. (There was a small, five-degree inversion from the surface to 5,000 feet. But one should note that the object was only 100 feet away from the witnesses.) Officer Bertrand had served in the Air Force for four years, on refueling missions, and argued that it was impossible for him to have mistaken a military operation for the object he saw. He'd observed an unconventional object at close range, not distant craft, planets, or stars. He considered himself and Officer Hunt competent observers who would not exaggerate their sighting. He added that the temperature inversion explanation was not acceptable, as there was no inversion in Kensington, New Hampshire, that night. Officers Hunt and Bertrand sent a strong rebuttal to the Major Hector Quintanilla, chief officer at Project Blue Book, stating:

It is important to remember that this craft we saw was no more than 100 feet in the air, and it was absolutely silent, with no rush of air from jets or chopper blades whatsoever. It lit up the entire field, and two nearby houses completely turned red. It stopped, hovered, and turned on a dime.... What bothers us most is the many people are thinking that we are either lying or not intelligent enough to tell the difference between what we saw and something ordinary. Three other people saw this same thing on September 3, and two of them appeared to be in shock from it. This was absolutely not a case of mistaken identity."[4]

In February 1966, John P. Spaulding, Lieutenant Colonel USAF, advised the police officers that the UFO Investigation Officer at Project Blue Book had been unable to identify the object they observed. Major David H. Griffin, Base Disaster Control Officer, Command Pilot, stated, "At this time I have been unable to arrive at a probable cause of the sighting. The three observers seem reliable persons, especially the two patrolmen. I viewed the area of the sighting and found nothing in the area that could be the probable cause. Pease AFB had 5 B-47 aircraft flying in the area during this period but do not believe they had any connection with this sighting."[5]

Skeptics have argued that the witnesses observed a refueling operation that night. However, the Project Blue Book files clearly state, "Records were checked and revealed that no refueling operations were conducted on the nights of 2-3 Sep and 6 Sep.... *There were no refueling operations in the New England area during the time in question.* [emphasis added]"[6]

The facts didn't matter to Philip Klass. Following the modus operandi of Dr. Donald Menzel, he was resolute in his decision to find a mundane explanation for the Kensington sightings. In this case, he could not write the police officers off as kooks and cranks.

They were respectable, competent witnesses. To discredit this case he would have use his bachelor of engineering degree and his 10 years' experience as an aviation electronics engineer to develop a hypothetical explanation that would dissuade those who were ignorant of the facts from giving credence to the UFO presence.

He conjectured that freak atmospheric electrical phenomena (plasma) that occur under unusual conditions were a plausible explanation for the Kensington event. Plasma is a small glowing cloud of electrified air. Because coronal plasma can be generated on high tension power lines under unusual conditions, such as when dust or salt deposits on the lines in a dry season, Klass, by ignoring the important information in the case, was able to develop a hypothetical explanation that might appeal to those who were unfamiliar with the facts.

He knew that under certain rare conditions, insects can alight upon the power lines and create a high electrical field concentration. This would potentially spark a short coronal discharge causing tiny short-loved plasma balls to form on power lines when a thunderstorm is nearby. Klass speculated that under certain rare conditions ball lightening, whose average size is 30 cm (11.81 inches), with a range from 5 cm (1.97 inches) to 80 cm (31.50 inches) could grow to massive proportions and be mistaken for an alien spacecraft. He said that although plasma physicists report that the average lifespan of ball lighting is only four seconds, some plasmas have been reported to last up to several minutes.

But this did not explain the huge silent object with red pulsing lights that bathed the woods and houses in red light and hovered near credible witnesses. Nor does it explain the close encounter that was observed by competent witnesses over an extended period of time and the reports by additional witnesses on the same night. By ignoring the facts and building a new scenario, Klass, in the August 1966 edition of *Aviation Week and Space Technology* magazine, explained away the Exeter UFO sighting as nothing more than plasma on high tension lines in the distant woods behind a Kensington,

New Hampshire, farmhouse. Klass failed to explain why a seasoned police officer dropped to his knee and nearly drew his gun to fire at a distant flickering light. Nor did he mention that the craft hovered in close proximity to the witnesses. Nor did he explain the discrepancy between the object's huge size and the fact that his explanation did not fit the data. When nothing else worked he relied upon human psychology, proclaiming that errors in human perception were responsible for the faulty reporting. He speculated that all of the witnesses had been viewing tiny, short-lived, flickering lights and only imagined that they were huge red lights that bathed the woods and a farmhouse in red. To the uninformed public, it sounded reasonable. But scientists who had done their homework weren't buying it.

One of these scientists was Dr. James E. McDonald, a highly respected atmospheric physicist from the University of Arizona. He took Klass to task in a private communiqué, dated September 28, 1966, stating, "The most obvious difficulty with the ball lightening hypothesis is that there is no evidence to suggest that any plasmoids of that type can be naturally generated in absence of intense electrical storms.... You might seem to be sidestepping that difficulty; but you fail to confront the fact that hundreds of credible observers have reported UFO phenomena without any involvement of powerlines."[7]

McDonald's comments did not deter Klass. He was convinced that if his theory could be confirmed scientifically, the public's interest in UFOs would diminish. When observers reported an object the size of a house, he argued that human misperception accounted for the enormous size. When UFO witnesses reported observing lighted windows divided by struts or structures, he dismissed them as dark spots in plasma. Metallic, structured disks became nothing more than misinterpreted glowing plasma orbs. Reports of non-human entities were said to be nothing more than the projection of past experiences, beliefs, and emotions, similar to a Rorschach Inkblot test. Intelligent, credible witnesses were transformed into

74

Dr. James E. McDonald

fanatical kooks who didn't know the difference between a huge silent craft, hovering only 100 feet in the distance, and a twinkling light miles in the distance. No amount of available evidence mattered and no degree of witness credibility was acceptable.

His plasma hypothesis led to months of lobbying powerful, politically connected people to his cause. His mantra carried prosaic explanations to all UFO reports, because interplanetary travel was, in his mind, *impossible*. If we Earthlings hadn't made the technological advancements necessary for safe interplanetary travel, certainly no one else could have.

Late in 1966, Klass introduced himself to Robert Low, project coordinator for the Air Force–funded Scientific Investigation of UFOs. Through a series of carefully crafted letters he gained Low's trust and began to influence both Low and project director Dr. Edward Condon. Klass was so successful that he persuaded Low to convince Condon to fund a symposium of plasma physicists to examine his plasma theory. But when the plasma physicists convened on October 27 and 28, 1968, in Boulder, Colorado, to review Klass's plasma UFO cases, they unanimously agreed that he had presented insufficient data for a definitive scientific conclusion and refuted many of his cases as being scientifically unlikely or impossible.

Dr. James McDonald announced that Klass's plasma theory was "quantitatively absurd...when one used elementary computations"[8] and criticized Klass for his failure to understand basic electrical concepts and undergraduate physics, a scathing criticism of a man who'd earned his undergraduate degree in electrical engineering and worked as an electrical engineer for 10 years. McDonald demolished Klass's thesis, stating that by stringing together vaguely related chains of information, his deductive reasoning was not only dangerous, but ludicrous. Equally absurd was Klass's failure to mention the benefits of having plasmas around vehicles in the atmosphere. Using electric and magnetic fields, to control the plasmas, can have a major impact on lift, drag, heating, radar profile, and sonic boom production. These are all very important to flight.

Klass's temper flared into a bitter personal vendetta against McDonald that raged until the latter's death in 1971. Over the next several years, he issued a series of White Papers that questioned McDonald's credibility and honesty, and succeeded in garnering politically connected authority figures to his position. His cordial exchanges with project director Edward U. Condon and Robert Low resulted in offers of support in his attempts to discredit McDonald. He attended some of McDonald's lectures and reported damaging information to Condon and Low. Condon rewarded Klass by writing a letter of recommendation to his employer, Joseph H. Allen, president of McGraw-Hill, Inc., the parent company of *Aviation Week and Space Technology* magazine. Dated May 24, 1968, it read as follows:

Assuming that you will want to inform yourself about the UFO situation, I mention that you have an excellent resource in your own organization in Mr. Philip J. Klass of the Washington editorial staff of *Aviation Week*. He is very knowledgeable, not only about flying saucers, but also about the foibles of flying saucer buffs, in particular Prof. James McDonald of the University of Arizona. He has been most helpful to our project in the last year and a half and I commend him to your attention.[9]

Klass's archival collection at the American Philosophical Society documents a concerted effort between the Condon Committee's top bosses and Klass to defeat McDonald. In reference to statements McDonald had made about the Northeast power failure, Low wrote, "That's just what I needed. You've been—as usual—a great help... I'm glad to see that McD seems to be moving out onto some rather slender limbs."[10]

With an intractable passion to destroy James E. McDonald, Klass waged a letter-writing campaign to the Office of Naval Research, McDonald's major source of cloud research funding, questioning his integrity and accusing him of the misuse of public funds. McDonald had received a grant from the ONR to do cloud research in Australia and had investigated UFOs while there. On December 20, 1967, Klass attempted to interfere with McDonald's UFO research when he contacted Russ Greenbaum at the Office of Naval Research to report that he'd tape-recorded McDonald statements at two lectures and was prepared to loan them to the ONR. Klass charged that the ONR might be funding UFO research under the guise of cloud physics.

With information provided by Klass, newspaper columnist Jack Anderson had written of McDonald's alleged misuse of Navy funds in his "Washington Merry-Go-Round" column at the *Washington Post*, on September 14, 1968. In a letter dated September 25, 1968, McDonald informed Dr. Robert A. Frosch, assistant secretary to the

Navy for research and development, that Anderson had guardedly informed him that "Klass had apparently approached him or his colleague, Mr. Pearson, with charges that I (*JEM) was misspending Navy funds on UFO studies."[11] The ONR knew of McDonald's UFO interests and had no objections to his personal hobbies. Klass then upped the ante. In a scathing letter to Dr. Robert A. Frosch, dated September 16, 1968, he wrote:

> The shocking mis-use of Navy research funds cited in the enclosed article is not only true but was condoned (if not encouraged) by the Office of Naval Research contract monitor who was responsible for protecting Navy/taxpayer interests. Furthermore, the situation was allowed to continue on many months after it was brought to the attention of ONR officials. I am prepared to document these charges if your interest warrants.[12]

Klass's no-holds-barred campaign against McDonald led to a harrowing investigation, in which McDonald was exonerated of wrongdoing, but resulted at least indirectly in the revocation of his ONR cloud research funding, and finally, funding from the National Science Foundation. Although the ONR determined that he had not misused public funds, the damage had already been done. Once again, Klass's manipulation of the facts and intractable hostility toward the scientific investigation of UFOs succeeded in suppressing scientific inquiry and academic freedom.

Klass mailed a memo to Donald Menzel on July 19, 1968, stating that he had distributed an anti-McDonald letter to the House Science and Astronautics Committee, and requested that he distribute it to his associates. The enclosure stated that McDonald "called for a program that would begin with an international scientific study of UFOs, at a cost of "a few tens of millions of dollars." And if McDonald's plan succeeded it would become "history's most ridiculous and expensive boondoggle!"[13]

The evidence that Edward Condon buttressed Klass's efforts is unambiguous. In an October 31, 1969 letter to Klass, Condon wrote, "If you hear of serious efforts to try to get additional federal money for UFO study, such as McDonald advocates, I would appreciate being tipped off so I can oppose them."[14]

Klass had predicted in 1969 that McDonald might end up on a psychiatrist's couch. This would not be surprising considering Klass's relentless campaign to destroy his career. On June 7, 1971, after McDonald's attempted suicide, he wrote to Condon, "I know you will share in my hope that the rumor/report is not true, for it would merely compound the tragedy of what Jim has done to his career as a result of his UFO obsession. But frankly having watched Jim and heard him speak on numerous occasions, and having seen him become increasingly frantic over his failure to convert the world, I had two years ago predicted that he might soon have a nervous breakdown."[15] One has to ponder the degree to which Klass's attacks contributed to the feelings of despair that led to McDonald's suicide in 1971. His estrangement from his wife certainly contributed to his demise. But Klass's constant personal attacks upon him, his loss of funding, and the subsequent scorn by his peers most assuredly played into his feelings of despondency.

Philip Klass often presented himself as an authority figure to warn government agencies of the danger that certain UFO researchers posed. His next high-level attack was upon J. Allen Hynek, PhD (1910–1986). Hynek held a doctorate in astrophysics from the University of Chicago. He joined the physics and astronomy department at Ohio State University in 1936, advancing to full professor in 1950. In 1947, he joined the Air Force's Project Sign as its scientific advisor on UFOs and then Project Grudge until it closed in 1952. He held the position as chief astronomical consultant for the Air Force's Project Blue Book from 1952 to 1969. In 1956, he joined the staff at the Smithsonian Astrophysical Observatory in Cambridge, Massachusetts, as associate director, where he directed the American Space Satellite Tracking Program. In 1960, he became chairman of the astronomy department at Northwestern University and director of the Lindheimer Astronomical Research Center. Initially he was highly skeptical of UFO reports and debunked many cases. Over time, however, it became clear to him that UFO sightings deserved scientific scrutiny, not ridicule and debunking. In 1973, he established the Center for UFO Studies, an organization committed to the scientific study of UFOs.

Hynek had written "The UFO Mystery" in the February 1975 issue of the *FBI Law Enforcement Bulletin*. His article advised the FBI that police officers from many different countries have observed unidentified flying objects at close range. Yet despite testimony by credible officers in a position of authority, UFOs had been a subject of ridicule. However, after a quarter century of laughing them off, Hynek wrote, the scientific world was slowly awakening to the fact that something real was going on.

Hynek went on to state that there are three popular misconceptions about UFOs:

1. UFO reports are made mainly by crackpots.
2. Reporters have over active imaginations.
3. Observers interpret conventional craft as UFOs due to their emotional desire to see something exotic.

Of course, none of these is true. Hynek's article disputed every anti-UFO argument that Klass had been promoting in the popular media. It is no wonder he was furious.

In strong terms laced with sarcasm, Klass rebuked the FBI for publishing Hynek's article and referred to Hynek as "the spiritual leader of the vocal group of "believers" and "kooks" who claim that we are being visited by extraterrestrial spaceships."[16] Klass accused the FBI of giving its endorsement to a hoax (UFOs are extraterrestrial in origin) and a fraud (Dr. Hynek). The FBI informed Klass that Hynek was a widely respected scientist, recognized by all creditable professionals in his field of expertise and associated with a leading university. To this statement Klass retorted, "He won't be for long!"[17] The FBI investigation that followed cited Hynek's impeccable credentials, but was less than complimentary toward Klass. The FBI file states, "Hynek has been associated professorially with some of finest universities in this country and is recognized in the most prestigious scientific circles. On the other hand, Klass has no such sterling reputation and has twice been under FBI investigation in connection with the unauthorized publication of classified information."[18]

In addition to this, the FBI concluded that Hynek had presented an objective and scientific view of the UFO phenomenon. Citing Klass's intemperate criticism and often-irrational statements to support them, the FBI made the decision to be circumspect in any future contacts with him. Later, the FBI believed that Klass was prone to using acerbic language to get his point across, but was probably not a kook as was previously suspected.

Klass's FBI records divulge that he was twice investigated for the unauthorized publication of classified military information. He again came to the FBI's attention in 1964, when he befriended official Soviet personnel and socialized at the USSR embassy. After being questioned by agents at the Washington Field Office, Klass notified the FBI whenever he had conversations with Soviet personnel that he deemed significant.

There is evidence that Klass waged a character assassination campaign against a third scientist: this book's coauthor Stanton T. Friedman. A highly regarded UFO researcher known for his meticulous, scientific methodology, Friedman earned his MSc in physics from the University of Chicago in 1956, and worked for 14 years on highly advanced fission and fusion rockets and various compact nuclear power plants for space application. He became interested in UFOs in 1958 and since 1967 has lectured about them at more than 700 colleges, professional groups, and UFO conferences in all 50 states, 10 Canadian provinces, and in 18 foreign countries. He has provided written testimony to congressional hearings and has spoken twice at the United Nations.

In an egregious attempt at character assassination, on August 15, 1980, Klass notified A.G. McNamara, Herzberg Institute of Astrophysics, National Research Council (NRC), Ottawa, Canada, that he should take steps to prepare for Friedman's impending move to Canada. The letter went undiscovered for years until UFO historian Richard Dolan found it at Canada's Public Archives. It began:

> I have reason to believe that Canada will soon gain a new full-time UFO lecturer of the "snake-oil salesman" variety...who will soon move to Canada to become its chief UFO Guru...I can assure you that you and your associates will be accused of a UFO-Cover-up (or "Cosmic Cover-up," as he is prone to say) that "dwarfs the Watergate scandal."... His one-hour lecture is so filled with half-truths and falsehoods that it would take me several hours to offer a rebuttal. And like wrestling with an octopus, when you manage to pin down one leg, the other seven are still thrashing about.[19]

He further warned the NRC that Friedman's decision to move to Canada was prompted by his failing UFO lecture business in the United States—another lie. The truth is that he had already received a great many enthusiastic letters from colleges and universities on his lectures across the continent, including Harvard, Berkeley, McGill, and the University of New Mexico, and various engineering societies. In fact, his lecture schedule was so demanding that he was often away from home, thus contributing to his wife and children's desire to be near their family in Fredericton, New Brunswick, where her parents, five of her siblings, and extended family lived.

Klass enclosed a scathing white paper he had written on Friedman that he said demonstrated his modus operandi and his distortion of facts. The authors will present a plethora of evidence later in this book that will clearly demonstrate it was Klass who distorted the facts. And it was Klass that had serious character flaws.

In response to Klass's false and inflammatory letter, the NRC alerted its staff that they could ill afford the publicity that Friedman might generate for them. Stating that there was no science in the subject of UFOs, they turned their UFO files over to the Public Archives of Canada, with the additional recommendation that UFO witnesses' identifying information be expunged from the reports.

Friedman and Klass engaged in antagonistic correspondence over a period of many years. Given their long association, one would expect to find a Friedman file at the American Philosophic Society, alongside Klass's correspondence with other prominent UFO researchers. Yet Friedman's correspondence file is conspicuously missing. However, Klass's false and damaging remarks about Friedman can be found in his correspondence with his anti-UFO associates. He paints a carefully crafted, but fabricated image of an ethically compromised scientist who conveys false tales to the public for financial gain. It appears that Klass considered Friedman his nemesis and was embarrassed over Friedman's confrontational style with regard to Klass's false information. For example, in a letter dated December 18, 1987, Friedman wrote:

> Yes, history will probably judge us both to some extent on our activity with regard to the MJ-12 documents. You will be found to be a liar, to be guilty of blatant and intentional misrepresentation, libel, and consistently inadequate and inaccurate so called research which is actually typical of the propagandist not legitimate journalist and certainly not related to the scientific method. I will be found to have done far more research, more carefully more objectively and with great concern for accuracy and truth.[20]

Later, Friedman embarrassed Klass by publicizing a bet that he'd won over the typeface on government documents and by displaying Klass's check to him for $1,000. Klass was furious and threatened to sue Friedman, but lacked the grounds to do so, because Friedman had concealed Klass's personal information. It is apparent that Klass built the record at the APS with the intention of defaming Friedman.

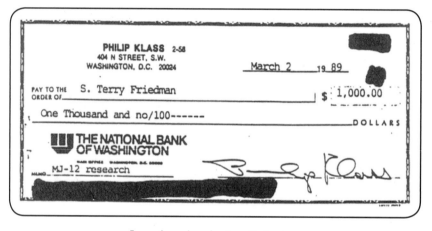

Klass's check to Friedman

When Klass wasn't bashing UFO researchers in white papers and letters to scientists and political figures, he was admonishing media sources and college presidents for giving credence to UFO reality. In a deceptive ploy he offered the sum of $10,000. to anyone who could prove that UFOs were real, based upon his criteria. In order to qualify for the prize, one had to submit a certified extraterrestrial artifact comprised of elements not found on Earth to the National Academy of Sciences. Any combination of earth elements in ratios not manufactured on Earth did not meet Klass's criteria for acceptability. A second option was to present a bona fide alien being to the United Nations General Assembly. Anyone who accepted Klass's offer, without first reading his impossible requirements, was expected to pay Klass $100 per year, for a maximum of 10 years.

It was an impossible order to fill, but Klass boasted widely that the absence of evidence proved the Earth has never been visited by an extraterrestrial civilization.

In a letter dated December 18, 1987, Friedman criticized Klass by writing, "Your ridiculous money offers further demonstrate the lack of reality in your approach...There will be, I suppose, one historical question—why has Philip Julian Klass done such a grossly inept job of 'research'? I will let the psychiatrists worry about that one."[21]

It is clear that Klass's research was sometimes grossly inept, yet when he investigated a case for the purpose of launching an ad hominem attack on a witness, he left no stone unturned. His files contain confidential medical and psychological reports that he intended to use to damage witnesses, if necessary. When there were multiple witnesses, he pursued the most vulnerable. He had lengthy phone conversations with witnesses that he transcribed, oftentimes inaccurately and in his favor. To Klass every credible witness was his opponent, and it was his job to fabricate a scenario in which they appeared to be involved in criminal activity. Upstanding members of the community were maligned in public attacks, credible witnesses with evidence were called kooks or liars, and innocent victims of alien abduction were subjected to increased trauma by his incessant mistreatment. (This will be discussed in more detail in Chapter 7 and Chapter 8.)

Questions pertaining to Klass's undercover operations have been raised over and over again. Could he have been an USAF, CIA, or NSA disinformant? We have evidence that he debunked UFOs for Project Blue Book Director Hector Quintanilla. It is no secret that the CIA made widespread use of journalists, especially those who made frequent trips overseas. Klass's correspondence files indicated that he made regular trips to Europe for business and pleasure. Carl Bernstein's cover story for *Rolling Stone* magazine, "The CIA and the Media," states that newspapers, magazines, and broadcasting companies such as the *New York Times*, the Associated Press, *Newsweek* magazine, the American Broadcasting Company, the National

Broadcasting Company, CBS, and Time Inc., cooperated with the CIA. Journalists were not necessarily on the CIA's payroll. Many received favors that would advance their careers or were handed cash in exchange for their work. Others had less-structured relationships with the CIA. McGraw-Hill and *Aviation Week and Space Technology* magazine were not mentioned in Bernstein's journal article. Therefore, we have no solid evidence that Klass worked for the CIA or NSA. We can only speculate that he might have. Otherwise, we would have to examine the underlying psychological issues that drove his sociopathic desire to destroy those he viewed as his opponents in a war against the scientific study of UFOs and the witnesses who report them.

Klass waged a campaign against the scientific investigation of UFOs that extended beyond witnesses and adult researchers to young people. Although he traveled frequently to Europe for work vacations he found time to correspond with school children. In a typical letter that he repeated over and over again, he wrote:

> If you are now in high-school, you have reached the age where you ought not believe in flying saucer stories—UNLESS YOU ALSO STILL BELIEVE IN SANTA CLAUS, THE EASTER BUNNY AND THE TOOTH FAIRY.... The problem is that newspapers, radio and TV only report the original claims made by liars such as Travis Walton and Charlie Hickson. When the case is later exposed as a hoax, the news media is too embarrassed (usually) to report that the case is a hoax—and so many people go on believing that the case has never been exposed.[22]

Serious UFO investigators, after a thorough investigation, had not concluded that Walton and Hickson were liars. It was Klass, through his dishonest, contrived investigation of their cases and his manipulation of the facts that distorted the public's view.

Periodically, Klass's correspondents accused him of being an intelligence operative for the USAF, CIA, or NSA. When this occurred, he met the challenge creatively. He offered to pay challengers $10,000 if they could prove he had ever been paid a dime by any agency. The trick was in the details. Klass insisted upon sending copies of his federal income tax filings for a period of 10 years as long as his challenger would reciprocate. In one case, he promised to pay his accuser $25,000 if he could find evidence in his tax reports proving that he was on the USAF, CIA, or other intelligence agency's payroll *and declared it.* The accuser backed down, not wanting to send his personal information to Klass. Klass used this retraction to promote his innocence. A key piece of information that was not mentioned concerns journalists who worked for the CIA in exchange for cash or favors.

In 1976, Klass became a founding member of the Committee for the Scientific Investigation of the Paranormal, currently the Committee for Skeptical Inquiry, for which he served on the executive council and chaired the UFO subcommittee. The organization had been established by philosophy professor Dr. Paul Kurtz to serve as a watchdog group to dissuade the media from lending credibility to phenomena that its members considered unscientific.

It was criticized from within by CSICOP (Committee for the Scientific Investigation of the Paranormal) co-chairman, Marcello Truzzi, PhD (1935–2003). Truzzi was a professor of sociology at Eastern Michigan University and founded the Society for Scientific Exploration. He was director of the Center for Scientific Anomalies Research. Truzzi resigned from the CSICOP after receiving a vote of no confidence from the executive committee because he wanted to present a balanced viewpoint in the organization's journal. Charging that its goal was to block honest inquiry and refute claims of the paranormal through deceptive practices, Truzzi railed at CSICOP's intractable position. He popularized the term *pseudo-skeptic* to describe members, such as Klass, who clearly conveyed an unscientific debunking attitude toward claims of the paranormal. He wrote of pseudo-skeptics, "Since 'skepticism' properly refers to doubt rather than denial—nonbelief rather than belief—critics who take the negative rather than an agnostic position, but still call themselves 'skeptics', are actually pseudo-skeptics and have, I believe, gained a false advantage by usurping that label."[24]

Philip Klass, due to his position as a mainstream journalist for McGraw-Hill Publishing Company and his work for Dr. Edward Condon of the Scientific Study of UFOs, carried pseudo-skepticism to numerous television talk shows and documentaries, purporting to present a scientific point of view, when in fact he was usually presenting misinformation and hypothetical arguments without satisfying the burden of proof. He and other members of CSICOP were exposed by Truzzi for raising the bar when evidence suggested that some paranormal claims might be real. They liberally applied the terms *true believer, promoter,* and *unscientific* to scientific UFO researchers, while they frequently had no such scientific credentials. Thus, a nuclear physicist was cast as a UFO promoter who lacked a basic knowledge of science. A photo analyst with a PhD in optical physics was falsely transformed into a gullible promoter who would uncritically accept almost any UFO photo as genuine. UFO witnesses were portrayed as liars, kooks, hoaxers, and people with perceptual problems. Every UFO investigator immediately became suspect of falsifying evidence or ignoring the facts.

Phil Klass's fanatical obsession continued until late in life. Letters in his archival collection at the American Philosophical Society speak of his 18 to 20 hours a day spent on his job at *Aviation Week and Space Technology* magazine and his UFO-debunking work. He specialized in distorting the facts in cases that were supported by convincing evidence and inventing new imaginative scenarios that were devoured by the unsuspecting media. False information replaced facts and good, reputable people were dishonored, all in the name of divesting ourselves of the UFO problem. He was prolific, unyielding, cunning, and deceptive.

He was employed at *Aviation Week and Space Technology* magazine for 34 years, wrote seven books, and published a bimonthly *Skeptics UFO Newsletter*. After his retirement in 1986, he worked from his home as a contributing editor while he continued to promote anti-UFO propaganda in the mainstream media. Philip Julian Klass died in Florida on August 9, 2005, and is buried at Merritt Island.

CHAPTER 5

DR. EDWARD UHLER CONDON

Dr. Edward U. Condon (1902–1974) is most often remembered for his role as the scientific director of the Scientific Study of Unidentified Flying Objects. Born in Alamogordo, New Mexico, he spent his childhood in nearly every state west of Colorado. His father was a civil engineer for the Southern Pacific Railroad, a job that did not give the family time to put down roots until he reached his teenage years. He and his family then settled in Oakland, California. He went to work as a reporter for the *Oakland Daily Post* while completing the one course he needed to graduate from high school. He'd set his sights on earning a liberal arts degree at the University of California, Berkeley, but dropped out after only six weeks, due to disinterest in the curriculum.

Less than two years later, he returned to Berkeley where he earned his AB (1924) and his PhD in physics (1926). Then he studied the new quantum physics for a year on a post-doctoral fellowship in Gottingen University in Germany. While there, he became friends with Dr. J. Robert Oppenheimer, a developer of the world's first nuclear bomb. Early in his professional career, he taught physics at Columbia, Princeton, and the University of Minnesota. But Westinghouse drew Condon to private industry in 1937. He worked for Westinghouse, and briefly on the Manhattan Project. In 1940, he was appointed as a consultant to the National Defense Research Committee. Shortly thereafter, he worked to develop the radiation laboratory at MIT, the lab where America's radar development began. When his work was completed, Condon returned to Westinghouse to work on its radar development program.

He was elected by Army General Leslie R. Groves to the top secret S-1 Committee at the National Bureau of Standards. In 1943, he moved to Los Alamos to work under Oppenheimer as deputy director on a phase of the Manhattan Project. He believed strongly that the military should not control scientific research and development. His failure to recognize military compartmentalization rules that dictated you can't tell your friends without telling your enemies got him into trouble that plagued him for many years. His opinion that security at Los Alamos was "stifling and unnecessary"[1] and hindered development so angered General Groves that he transferred Condon to the Radiation Laboratory at Berkeley, where he worked on the theoretical aspects of the bomb's development. From there, he returned to Westinghouse and set up its nuclear program. In 1944 he was inducted into the National Academy of Sciences (NAS).

In 1945, he was offered a job that he couldn't refuse: director of the National Bureau of Standards, a job that he kept until 1951. In 1946, President Harry Truman appointed him to evaluate the national atomic bomb tests in the South Pacific and to the National Advisory Committee on Aeronautics (now NASA). The same year, he was elected president of the American Physical Society. Very few scientists had been honored by their peers by being elected president of the American Physical Society and the American Association for the Advancement of Science. New leaders get elected each year.

Condon was an important scientist as a pioneer in quantum mechanics, which is very far removed from dealing with non-laboratory phenomena observed unexpectedly by often-untrained individuals without access to scientific instrumentation. Theoretical quantum mechanics is very far removed from the real world. But Condon left a real physics legacy through private industry.

Condon worked with Donald H. Menzel and Howard Dellinger to outline a proposal for a multimillion-dollar-a-year civilian Central Radio Propagation Laboratory, an agency that could provide systematic services, which included a worldwide network for ionospheric and weather data gathering through the National Bureau of Standards. When Dellinger retired as director of the Interservice Radio Propagation Laboratory, Condon offered the job to Menzel, but Menzel declined the offer.

Condon was an outspoken advocate of placing atomic energy under civilian, rather than military, control and international cooperation among scientists. This led to challenges to his security clearance and disloyalty charges by the House Committee on Un-American Activities. He and other scientists were committed to having the Atomic Energy Commission placed under civilian control, an unpopular opinion among conservatives. He'd undergone intermittent harassment for several years primarily because he didn't agree with the military's highly secretive, compartmentalized stance on classified science projects. He thought that it was an impediment to scientific development. The charges leveled against Condon were completely without merit and fortunately for him he was quickly cleared. This left a clear path for his work at the Bureau of Standards. But in April 1951, the House Un-American Activities Committee leveled a new attack against Condon. Four months later, disheartened by the constant political maneuvering, he tendered his resignation stating that the financial sacrifice was too great to continue on his current path.

He returned to private industry at Corning Glass as director of research and development. But his political problems continued to dog him. In 1952, he was charged with associating with Communists. This created an obstacle to his ability to perform his job at Corning, when his security clearance was denied. He was later granted a limited access clearance. But it was revoked in 1954, by Richard Nixon, one of Condon's long-term adversaries. This latest slap on the face was the last straw. It led to Condon's angry resignation. For the ensuing year he worked as president of the American Association for the Advancement of Science, but he left that post in 1955. He was offered a position on the faculty of two major universities, but the trustees refused to confirm his appointment due to pressure from Washington. Completely disheartened by his government's vindictive revocations, Condon accepted a job at the University of Pennsylvania for the 1955–56 terms and then moved to Washington University in St. Louis, as chairman of the physics department, where he remained until 1964, when he joined the University of Colorado. His security clearance was once again reinstated in 1965, in order to work on a government project: the Air Force–funded Scientific Study of Unidentified Flying Objects. His work began in 1966 and continued until the project's conclusion in 1968.

The Condon Project was the outcome of controversy that had had brought charges by politicians, UFO groups, newspaper reporters, scientists, and the public at large of a cover-up by the Air Force. Simultaneously, Project Blue Book Head Hector Quintanilla was disenchanted with the Air Force's collection of UFO data, calling it a waste of time and money. The National Investigations Committee on Aerial Phenomena and its director, Major Donald Keyhoe, USMC (retired), undertook efforts to initiate Congressional Investigations on UFOs. The privately funded Washington UFO organization was highly critical of the Air Force's dismissive attitude toward UFOs and its inadequate investigations. On the other side, the Air Force considered Keyhoe and private UFO clubs a thorn in its side, perpetuating the aura of mystery about a topic that could not be addressed scientifically. Lieutenant Colonel Hector Quintanilla was growing

Dr. Edward U. Condon, physicist and director
of the National Bureau of Standards (NBS;
now NSIT [National Institute of Standards
and Technology]) from 1945 to 1951

impatient with Keyhoe's constant lobbying effort. He wrote, "Every time he or one of his members writes a letter to a Congressman, the Air Force, the DOD, or the President, one of us has to drop whatever we are doing and react immediately...During the period from October 1966 through March 1967, SAFOI processed 9,265 pieces of UFO correspondence which included 108 Congressional referrals and 123 letters addressed to the President."[2] Quintanilla was clearly irritated by what he termed harassment by NICAP (National Investigations Committee on Aerial Phenomena) of the Air Force, Congress, Project Blue Book, and the SAFOI. Quintanilla expressed his frustration in his manuscript "UFOs: An Air Force Dilemma," stating that his office staff was overworked and he was nearing a nervous breakdown from worry about the politics in the program. But this ended when General E.B. LeBailly, from the Secretary of the Air Force Office of Information, requested that a Scientific Advisory Board to be appointed to evaluate Project Blue Book. The board of six prominent scientists came to be known as the O'Brien Committee after its chairman, Dr. Brian O'Brien, a consulting physicist. Additional members were Dr. Willis H. Ware from the Rand Corporation, Dr. Launor F. Carter from the Systems Development Corporation, Dr. Jesse Orlansky from the ODA, Dr. Carl Sagan from Harvard and Cornell, and Dr. Richard Porter. The committee prepared a position paper dated March 1966 that outlined its priorities. Their stated goal was to advise the Air Force of improvements that could be made in the program to "enhance the Air Force's capability in carrying out its responsibility."[3]

The committee paid special attention to the Robertson Panel, the CIA-funded committee that in 1953 recommended a program to remove the aura of mystery around UFOs. The panel, headed by Dr. H.P. Robertson, received 75 case histories, of which eight were reviewed in detail and 15 more in less detail. Citing the lack of sound data in most cases, and the slow follow- up caused by the modest size and limited facilities of the ATIC, the panel determined that UFOs did not pose a direct threat to national security except in cases where public hysteria caused an overload of false UFO reports. The panel recommended a reeducation program to reduce the public's interest in UFOs through television, motion pictures, and popular articles, and monitoring of UFO related organizations by national security agencies. The committee recommended that contracts be negotiated with a few universities to investigate in depth "certain selected UFO sightings."[4] No statement was made about the possible termination of Project Blue Book, but it was a milestone to that end. The record shows that Quintanilla and others were definitely in favor of ending the controversy about UFOs once and for all.

Northwestern University, through J. Allen Hynek, lobbied the Air Force for the project, but by that time Hector Quintanilla was angry with Hynek, who did not lockstep to Quintanilla's mindset. Quintanilla had requested the dissolution of Hynek's contract as Project Blue Book consultant, due to his public comments in favor of the serious study of UFOs, a position to which Quintanilla objected. Given the political tension between the two, he certainly did not favor placing Hynek in the position of project director. Two dozen universities were given consideration at preliminary meetings, but many refused to entertain the idea of studying a taboo topic, such as UFOs. Finally, the University of Colorado (Boulder) signed the Air Force contract. The university's proximity to the National Center for Atmospheric Research and the research headquarters for the Environmental Science Services Administration made UC a natural choice.

The Office of Scientific Research of the Air Force had to choose a project director that they considered suitable for the job, one who would work toward the Air Force objectives of the study. Dr. Edward Condon fit the bill. But he accepted the position in an incautious moment, not fully aware of the controversy his personal opinions would bring with regard to what constituted scientific evidence. He insisted that a favorable finding on the ET hypothesis would require an extraterrestrial spacecraft and/or the body of a being clearly not of this earth, for laboratory analysis. Photographic evidence, radar evidence, and eyewitness testimony by hundreds of credible witnesses mattered not. In the end, he garnered bitter criticism by his opponents who accused him of a cover-up.

David Saunders, the co-principal investigator of the Condon Committee, wrote in his book *UFOs? Yes! Where the Condon Committee Went Wrong* that no one could pin Condon down to his reason for accepting the Air Force's contract. He is known to have stated that he took the job because he liked a mystery. Others thought that it was his patriotic duty. He told one reporter that he wouldn't believe in flying saucers until he could get one into a laboratory and find competent scientists to examine it with him. Saunders wrote that he believed Condon was honoring his pledge to bring federal and private research projects to the university. The $313,000 allocated to the project by the Air Force promised to give a financial boost to the university. Cost overruns pushed the final price tag into the half-million-dollar range. The introduction to the complete report on the *Scientific Study of Unidentified Flying Objects* states that Condon was elected to serve as the scientific director of the project because of his eminence as a scientist, his independence, and his positions as president of the American Association for the Advancement of Science and the American Physical Society, and director of the National Bureau of Standards. His purpose for accepting the job was stated to be of public service to the U.S. Air Force's Office of Scientific Research.

One should not assume that Condon's belief in the idea that science should not come under military control is an indicator that he had no loyalty to his government or that the outcome of the Condon Project was determined without bias. He was accused of bias throughout the Project, due to his focus upon crackpot cases. Most observers agree that he had a negative agenda early on in the Project. This is borne out by a letter to the editor of the *Denver Post* in October 1966. He wrote, "What can be learned from the UFO project can make valuable contributions to knowledge of atmospheric effects and of people's behavior when observing them under unusual conditions.... Therefore, we will be doing a great public service if we can by teaching improve public understanding to the point where many of the things now seen and reported as UFOs become as fully understood as eclipses."[5] In January 1967, Condon addressed two science societies in Corning, New York: the Corning section of the American Chemical Society and the Corning Glass Works chapter of Sigma XI. In front of a full house he issued this statement: "It is my inclination right now to recommend that the government get out of this business. My attitude right now is that there is nothing to it. But I'm not supposed to reach a conclusion for another year."[6]

Condon relegated the day-to-day operation to Robert Low, a man he could depend upon to build the record to present the image that the Project was unbiased when in reality it had little expectation of finding a saucer. Robert Low, graduate school dean and Condon's Project coordinator was no neophyte at political glad-handing. His former position as executive officer at the National Center for Atmospheric Research at the joint University of Colorado–Harvard High Altitude Observatory was an asset to the Project. He was a natural choice to for the day-to-day operation of the UFO study. Dr. Franklin E. Roach, an astrophysicist with the Environmental Science Services Administration, was named co-principal investigator. Both organizations researched man's natural environment, specializing in the physical characteristics of the atmosphere and near space. Dr. Stuart W. Cook, chairman of the university's psychology department, rounded out the team as co-principal investigator. Initially, four out of five Project investigators were psychologists, but physical scientists were added over time.

The Air Force's contract called for the selection of more than 100 scientists from various universities to take part in the research. Project Blue Book and NICAP made their files available to the scientific team. Organizational procedures presented a challenge initially, but over time protocols were established. The Air Force expected the scientists to be neither pro-UFO or to hold a negative bias, but inevitably some scientists held personal biases. Quintanilla was most concerned with scientists who'd been swayed by the evidence in favor of the ET hypothesis, referring to them as "charlatans, phonies and mediocre" individuals who attempted to undermine Condon's efforts.[7] Quintanilla and NORAD (North American Aerospace Defense Command) gave Condon a complete briefing of unclassified material to the highest security classification. If he entered the Project without a personal bias toward UFOs, which is doubtful, Condon acquired one somewhere along the line.

It has been suggested that Condon knew the final outcome of the Project before its inception. But his statements indicate that he had not participated in the infamous "Trick Memo," an internal document penned by Robert Low for James Archer, dean of the graduate school, and Thurston Manning, dean of faculties and vice president for academic affairs, in August 1966. Witnesses agree on Condon's reaction when he learned that the memo had been discovered and passed to Dr. James McDonald, who then gave it to NICAP: His blood boiled. John Fuller's article in the May 14, 1968, edition of *Look* magazine told of a half-million-dollar trick to make Americans believe the Condon Committee was conducting an objective investigation when in fact it was anything but objective.

It was the second time that Low had caused turbulence in the Project. Low's first embarrassment occurred in October 1966, in a statement he made to the *Denver Post* asserting that the UFO Project came pretty close to the university's criteria of non-acceptability. Low's memo addressed the concerns of three staff members who were opposed to taking on the Project because the University of Colorado would lose prestige in the scientific community. Low continued:

Our study would be conducted almost exclusively by nonbelievers, who, although they couldn't possibly *prove* a negative result, could and probably would add an impressive body of evidence that there is no reality to the observations. The trick would be, I think, to describe the project so that, to the public, it would appear a totally objective study but, to the scientific community, would present the image of a group of nonbelievers trying their best to be objective but having an almost zero expectation of finding a saucer. One way to do this would be to stress investigation, not of the physical phenomena, but rather of the people who do the observing—the psychology and sociology of persons and groups who report seeing UFOs. If the emphasis were put here, rather than on examination of the old question of the physical reality of the saucer, I think the scientific community would quickly get the message.[8]

Yet, despite the evidence that Low knew the Project's outcome from the very beginning, the documented evidence leads one to believe that he was truly curious and scientific early on in the Project. This contradictory information is perplexing. However, the record shows a clear shift toward a more negative conclusion with each passing meeting with the Air Force brass and through communication with debunkers.

David Saunders wrote that Low spent much of his time building the record, and this is borne out by researchers who've read Condon's files at the University of Colorado. What is not evident is Low's increasingly close association with arch debunker Philip J. Klass. Late in 1966, Klass introduced himself to Low, and through a series of carefully crafted letters fell into Low's good graces. Initially, he stated that he was not attempting to influence the jury, but in fact the record confirms this was precisely his intent. Klass had frequent, lengthy telephone discussions with committee members and sent voluminous debunking correspondence to the project. He penned a constant flow of letters to Robert Low. Although he had only recently completed his first UFO investigation, Klass passed himself off as an expert. He proclaimed the significant case of a landed craft and beings by Lonnie Zamora, a law enforcement officer in Socorro, New Mexico, was a hoax. More experienced investigators had reached the opposite conclusion, but Low was "very interested" in Klass's new information.[9] In another letter, Low, warming up to Klass, stated that the team would love to have a copy of his tape of Chavez, Zamora, and Moore. But it won't serve as a substitute for a discussion with Klass. Klass's copious notes about the meeting indicate that Low was being influenced toward Klass's mindset and now considered the Lonnie Zamora Socorro incident a hoax. This despite the abundance of evidence that Zamora and others witnessed an unconventional flaming craft that left physical trace evidence on the ground that defied conventional explanation even after a thorough investigation had been conducted by credentialed military and scientific personnel.

The record is clear that over time Klass ingratiated himself into the hearts and minds of the Project's two most influential men, director Edward U. Condon and project coordinator Robert Low. They became less tolerant of highly credentialed scientists such as Allen Hynek, James McDonald, and David Saunders, who pushed for an investigation of the evidence in highly significant historical cases. Condon and Low shifted their focus toward newer, less-significant cases that they could explain away as plasma, atmospheric anomalies, hoaxes, and mistakes in human perception.

It appears that Lieutenant Colonel Robert Hippler, Science Division, Directorate of Science and Technology, of the USAF in Washington, D.C., influenced Condon and Low's approach to the Project and its final outcome more significantly than Klass. At an Air Force Advisory Panel Briefing on January 12, 1967, Condon pushed for a focus on those who report seeing UFOs, rather than on the investigation of evidence itself. Hippler voiced his opposition, explaining that he didn't want the Project and Air Force to be accused of not taking reports seriously. Condon's approach would certainly support that end. The record shows that his fascination with crackpot cases *did* result in a public outcry of foul play. Hippler's clever idea was to obfuscate the Project's real focus through a series of protocols that would give the appearance of scientific objectivity, but would produce the results he desired: to end the expenditure of public funds on UFO investigations. He stressed the importance of placing the focus upon current cases instead of giving consideration to the older, highly significant UFO cases. Cases that defied explanation, such as the Zamora Socorro, New Mexico, sighting, came along only occasionally, so if older cases were eliminated there wouldn't be many residual cases with strong evidence. It would serve the Air Force's hidden agenda well. If the emphasis was placed upon physical hypotheses, such as ball lightening, temperature inversions, comets, and so forth, the case for saucer reality would quickly fall apart. Those that remained, after all skeptical avenues had been explored, would simply be ignored. Good science, right? The expense of continuing the Air Force's UFO reporting system was a huge priority that weighed heavily on the major players' minds.

Low initially objected to the exclusion of perplexing historical cases from the study, but later placed his emphasis on new cases, just as Hippler had recommended. This change might have been affected by Hippler's letter to Condon dated January 27, 1967. He wrote, "When you have looked into some sightings and examined the Blue Book records and become acquainted with the true state of affairs, you might consider the cost of the Air Force program on UFOs, and determine if the taxpayer should support this for the next decade. It will be at least that long before another independent study can be mounted to see if the Air Force can get out from under this program."[10] The decision not to investigate older cases was strategically made in order to facilitate the debunking process.

By August 1967, Low was beginning to voice a biased opinion. He met with Philip Klass at Klass's Washington, D.C., apartment on August 3. Klass's notes indicate Low admitted it was sometimes hard to keep an open mind to the possibility of extraterrestrial visitation, and sometimes caught himself leaping to conclusions and asking leading questions. Correspondence between the two men indicates that over time Klass persuaded Low that not one truly anomalous object had ever entered the Earth's atmosphere or been observed by the thousands of witnesses who reported them.

In October 1967, Klass proposed a plan to simulate alleged UFO photos taken by 17-year-old James Lucci, the son of a professional photographer for the Air National Guard, in Beaver County, Pennsylvania, on August 8, 1965. He offered to pay the project the sum of $500 for its consulting work. His goal was to promote the idea that all photos that could be easily reproduced were hoaxes. This plan would make it possible to debunk all UFO photos by demonstrating that photos could be simulated. It would also create a problem for future researchers, who might experience confusion about which photo was the original and which was simulated.

The Lucci photo was on the cover of the *Incident at Exeter* by John Fuller (1966), the first UFO book that Klass had ever read. It had sparked his curiosity and natural tendency to debunk anything that was purported to be of extraterrestrial origin. The photo was taken at approximately 11:30 p.m. when James and his brother John, 23, were outside taking time exposure photographs of the full moon. They claimed that the glowing disk-shaped object with a hazy radiance beneath its underside appeared from behind a hill. James stated that he captured two shots of the object before it rose out of sight. His neighbor from across the street confirmed that he had also observed the object. Three professional photographers from the *Beaver County Times* analyzed the photos and declared them authentic. They stated that the photos, in their opinion, were not the result of photographic or physical faking or camera anomalies such as lens flares, reflections, developing process problems, and so forth. It was also reported to Project Blue Book and NICAP. Later, the Air Force admitted to the press that a UFO was reported near Pittsburgh at approximately this time. NICAP investigators spent five days interviewing the witnesses, investigating the case, and recording technical photographic evidence.

Low informed Klass that it was inappropriate and unethical to offer money to simulate the photos, but Project funds could be allocated for the purpose if they thought it would contribute something important to their knowledge and understanding of the UFO problem. Klass's idea was deemed important and the simulation study was carried out by William Hartmann, an astronomer from the University of Arizona, as Case #53. A simulated photo was made by taping a handle to a small plate, illuminating it with a flashlight and moving the arm during time-exposure photography. The simulated photo was more out of focus than the original, but had some of the same qualities. Hartmann concluded that the out-of-focus, saucer-like object with an alleged gaseous discharge from its lower side could be easily simulated. Thus the case was given no probative value. To this day, the Lucci photo remains controversial.

Klass continued to spoon-feed debunking information to Low and Condon throughout the Project, supplying his personally biased sometimes false information to them, and offering tape recordings of statements made by their perceived enemies and on the biggest crackpot cases he could find. He consistently stirred up negative feelings for scientists who saw value in continuing the scientific study of UFOs. One of these scientists was Dr. James McDonald.

Dr. James McDonald was an outspoken opponent of Edward Condon's laissez faire attitude toward the scientific study of UFOs. He charged Condon with failing to vigorously scrutinize the important class of very strong evidence cases and was highly critical of Condon's focus upon the amusing anecdotal tales found in his best crackpot cases, often brought to his attention by Philip J. Klass. Condon's continuing fascination with "kooks" led him to accept an invitation from UFO rabble rouser, the late James Moseley, to attend his Congress of Scientific Ufologists conference at the Commodore Hotel in New York, June 21–25, 1967. Despite the title of the conference, the speakers were largely unscientific. Only one scientist was on the speaker list, and there were three contactees who reportedly fit into the kook category. Condon's scientific team had strongly objected to his attendance at the conference and it is easy to understand why. He returned to Colorado with a new library of amusing kook reports to share with the public.

In a letter to Robert Low, dated January 31, 1968, McDonald wrote:

> I see a picture in which so very much pivots on what Dr. Condon himself says and believes, yet a picture in which Dr. Condon does not evince any keen scientific interest in digging into those types of UFO cases that created the very Air Force problem which he agreed to try to clarify.... It is not crackpots from the Third Sphere, or women who claim to have had five affairs with men from Venus, or

persons who predict Venusians landings in Utah, or persons who claim relations from a planet in Andromeda who have created the UFO problem you people took on... but the pilots, law enforcement officers, and other seemingly credible observers whose UFO reports have kept the pot boiling.[11]

Klass noted in his archival records that Low had reached his limit regarding "McDonald's attempt to dictate...the way the U. of Colorado should conduct investigation" and was driving Low "away from his point of view with his insistence and criticism."[12] According to Klass's notes, Low was "very unhappy" with Dr. James McDonald, professor of atmospheric physics at the University of Arizona. McDonald was a senior physicist at the Institute of Atmospheric Physics and a consultant to numerous federal agencies, including the National Science Foundation, the National Academy of Sciences, and the Office of Naval Research. After 10 years of research he had concluded that UFOs are "something from outside our atmosphere."[13]

Klass spied on McDonald and delivered damaging information with regard to his statements to Low and Condon. In return, Condon was exceedingly grateful for Klass's favors and support and, as mentioned in Chapter 4, endorsed him as a highly knowledgeable go to guy on the topic of flying saucers and the shortcomings of so called "flying saucer buffs"[14] such as Dr. James McDonald, a highly qualified meteorological physicist, who had in fact devoted considerable time and effort to the scientific study of UFOs. The truth is that Klass was not an expert on the topic of UFOs, having been active in the field for less than two years and entering the field with the preconceived notion that all UFOs had viable prosaic explanations.

In a letter dated February 27, 1968, Low informed Klass that he and Condon were "very grateful" for the assistance he gave to them on the project, adding, "You were a constant source of assistance and encouragement...by keeping us informed of late developments and by warning us of events about to take place, performed an invaluable service."[15]

McDonald is one of several scientists that Klass had under covert surveillance for the benefit of Condon and Low. A complete discussion of these activities will be presented in Chapter 6. And so the carefully designed and orchestrated fraud continued to its final goal.

The 11-member National Academy of Sciences Review Panel was appointed in the later part of October and early November 1968 to provide an independent assessment of the scope, methodology, and findings of the University of Colorado's final report. The report was presented to them by fellow NAS member in good standing Edward U. Condon. Condon had concluded, "Travel of men over interstellar distances in the foreseeable future seems now to be quite out of the question. It is safe to assume that no intelligent life outside our solar system has any possibility of visiting Earth any time in the next 10,000 years."[16] Of course no basis is given for this remarkable statement by Dr. Condon.

The panel reviewed papers written by the technically trained scientists, such as Markowitz, McDonald, and Menzel. It convened on December 2 for a discussion of the members' initial assessments and met again on January 6, 1969, to conclude its deliberations and prepare its findings. In all, 59 UFO reports were investigated, 10 of which were historical reports. Ten chapters were devoted to the technical and psychological issues that pertain to UFO reports. All sightings were of short duration. A few events remained unexplained after all other categories were excluded. Of the 35 photos examined, nine were deemed probably fabrications and seven as natural or manmade phenomena, 12 were classified in the "insufficient data" category, and seven were considered possible fabrications. Not one was placed in the "unknown" category despite compelling evidence.

Not one was deemed to have a shred of scientific credibility. The "Trick Memo" was not presented as evidence that the project was biased from its inception. Nor were the letters or statements presented above given consideration. The NAS committee concluded that there was no basis for the idea that the subject of UFOs was shrouded in official secrecy. Nor was there evidence that UFOs present a defense hazard. It concluded that there was no basis for special reporting and study of UFOs such as Project Blue Book, as there is no convincing evidence that UFOs are extraterrestrial. However, study of important areas of atmospheric optics, such as radio wave propagation and atmospheric electricity should be continued. In addition to this, funds should be allocated for the study of UFO reports and beliefs in the areas of social science and communications. It concluded that the "least likely explanation of UFOs is the hypothesis of extraterrestrial visitations."[17] The sham was complete. The Air Force closed Project Blue Book in December 1969. To this day, the cover-up continues and mainstream science has declared the scientific study of UFOs taboo.

CHAPTER 6

DARE WE CALL IT CONSPIRACY!

The U.S. government's involvement in the study of unidentified flying objects has at times been serious and productive. More often, however, political expediency in the interest of national security has concealed the evidence and dissuaded the media and the American public from giving it serious consideration. Friedman and Marden have uncovered evidence of a carefully orchestrated conspiracy by key players, such as Dr. Donald Menzel, Dr. Edward Condon, Robert Low, Philip Klass, Hector Quintanilla, and others to demolish scientific interest in the study of this most important phenomenon. Prominent scientific researchers have been effectively slandered or reduced to laughing stocks. Funding for the scientific evaluation of physical evidence has been withdrawn, whereas funding has been allocated for academic studies designed to identify the psychological causes of the public's alleged misperception. In this chapter, the authors will present the evidence that certain politically connected scientists and journalists conspired among themselves, and with government agencies to debunk UFO reports and eradicate public funding for the scientific study of UFOs.

In Chapter 2, we spoke of Dr. Donald Menzel's meeting with military officers at the Pentagon in May 1952, to discuss his plan for debunking UFOs by offering a few elementary scientific explanations to the gullible public. Menzel acted authoritatively, as if he had already been appointed to enforce a preexisting decision. His long association with the NSA's predecessors, the Signal Security Agency and the Armed Forces Security Agency, placed him in a position to carry out the government's plan. Despite the Air Force's statistical evidence that only 2 percent of the sighting reports were hoaxes, Menzel had disseminated false information stating that hoaxes played a large part in UFO sightings. Based upon what we know it seems clear that the Air Force and CIA were developing an orchestrated plan to lie to the American public. Menzel had already written debunking articles for *Time* and *Look*. His experience as a science fiction writer and his education as an astrophysicist were two useful assets for the intelligence community's campaign to promote false propaganda.

When the Office of Scientific Intelligence, Central Intelligence Agency, convened on January 14–18, 1953, it developed a plan that would effectively dampen the public's interest in UFOs. The "Durant Report of the Robertson Panel" recommended a broad educational program that would effectively re-educate the American public and debunk UFOs. This sweeping policy would protect the United States from public hysteria that might clog communications channels and cause a threat to national security. The proposed education program offered various prosaic explanations that could explain UFO sightings as conventional aircraft, balloons, meteors, fireballs, and so forth, to remove the aura of mystery surrounding the topic. The orchestrated plan called for ridicule of prominent cases and credible observers with the goal of suppressing UFO reports. It would teach radar operators, ground observer corps personnel, pilots, and others that prosaic explanations can be effectively employed to explain UFO sightings. This education plan has been carried out through television programs, motion pictures, and popular magazine articles. (See Chapter 10 for details.)

The Battelle Memorial Institute's work on Special Report #14 for Project Blue Book had begun in March 1952 and had not been completed when the Robertson Panel met in January 1953. Without the Battelle Memorial Institute's assessment of its 3,201 Air Force UFO reports, it was up to Project Blue Book to supply its files to the CIA's UFO study group. Edward Ruppelt, Project Blue Book director, later wrote that the CIA's secrecy led to reluctance by Blue Book staff to give its operatives complete access to its files. Therefore, the Robertson Panel was working with incomplete information when it convened in January 1953. One has to consider that the final outcome might have been different if Navy Warrant Officer Delbert Clement Newhouse's statement that he observed internally lighted, disk-shaped craft, not birds in flight, had been available. Without this key evidence, and after the panel of scientists viewed video of reflective seagulls in flight, they quickly identified the UFOs on Newhouse's film as birds in flight. It is important to note, however, that they dismissed the military's scientific evaluation of his video. This begs the question: Was it a well-orchestrated CIA sham?

Dr. Allen Hynek, the astronomical consultant to Project Blue Book and associate member of the Robertson Panel, who for years assisted the Air Force in its cover-up, wrote of the Robertson Panel in *The UFO Experience: A Scientific Inquiry*, "No explanation was made of or explanations offered for the great many 'Unidentified' cases already in the Blue Book files. Since the cases had been selected for them by Blue Book, which had already stated views on the subject of UFOs, the prejudicial nature of the 'trial of UFOs' is obvious.... The panel was not given access to any of the truly puzzling cases."[1]

Hynek continued, "The Robertson Panel did get someplace: they made the subject of UFOs scientifically unrespectable, and for nearly 20 years not enough attention was paid to the subject to acquire the kind of data needed even to decide the nature of the UFO phenomenon. Air Force public relations in this area were egregious and the public was left with its own decisions to make: was the Air Force attitude the result of 'cover-up' or of foul up and confusion?"[2] The historical record reveals the answer to Hynek's question. The Air Force had obfuscated the UFO evidence and the CIA was more than happy to follow suit.

The CIA's plan encouraged scientists to debunk UFOs through deductive reasoning, offering prosaic scientific explanations rather than the unbiased assessment of the evidence, just as Dr. Donald Menzel had proposed in May 1952. The panel recommended the use of compelling cases raising the public's interest in the mystery, followed by rational explanations that would demolish the public's interest in the case. The National Security Agencies were instructed to "take immediate steps to strip Unidentified Flying Objects of the special status they have been given and the unfortunate aura of mystery they have acquired."[3] Thereafter, federally appointed scientists used deduction and speculation to dispense with the UFO cases they evaluated.

Project Blue Book's chief, Captain Edward Ruppelt, was replaced, in March 1954, by a less-objective USAF officer, Captain Charles Hardin. Hardin made it known that he was bored by the topic of UFOs and believed that anyone who had an interest in UFOs was crazy. During his tenure "Unidentifieds" were drastically reduced from 8.25 percent in 1953 to 0.2 percent by 1956. In 1957, that figure dropped to 0.14 percent.[4]

Menzel responded to H.P. Robertson's report on Unidentified Flying Objects, on April 9, 1958, in a critical letter that admonished Robertson for using "language capable of misinterpretation by the very people who are trying to make something out of the aura of mystery."[5] He warned Robertson that "the saucer boys" would surely argue that UFOs posed an indirect threat to the national security after they read his statement that UFOs do not constitute a "direct" threat to national security. He suggested rewording phrases that the public might not understand, such as "current scientific concepts," "foreign artifacts," and "inimical forces." Menzel urged Robertson to state that he favored an "integrated program designed to reassure the public that flying saucers can be completely explained in terms of natural phenomena in the earth's atmosphere or reflections from material objects of terrestrial origin," adding "even go further than that and state that none of the evidence in anyway substantiates the suggestion that flying saucers are manned vehicles from outer space." He offered to cooperate with Robertson or "any agency desiring information in an effort to clear up this 'aura of mystery.'"[6]

Some UFO researchers believe that the Durant Report's recommendations were never carried out. The authors disagree. Evidence indicates that the media began to take UFO reporting less seriously and military and government authorities no longer commented on UFO reports. A splendid example of the massive misrepresentation on the part of the United States Air Force about UFOs is provided by the October 25, 1955, Air Force press release entitled "Air Force Releases Study on Unidentified Flying Objects." The report itself was not distributed. It was only through the major effort made by Dr. Leon Davidson, a scientist at the Los Alamos Scientific Laboratory, that some copies were made available. The first thing to notice is that the report title, "Blue Book Special Report No. 14 (BBSR 14)," is not included! If it had been, presumably some newsman would have asked what happened to reports 1 to 13. (They were classified.) The second is that no mention is made of the organization that did the work—namely Battelle Memorial Institute in Columbus, Ohio. The third missing element is the name of the person or persons doing the work. Fourth, not one piece of data from the more than 100 charts, tables, and maps in the report was given.

Furthermore, the statement by the Secretary of the Air Force, Donald Quarles, is absolutely false. He said, "On the basis of this study we believe that no objects such as those popularly described as flying saucers have over flown the United States. I feel certain that even the Unknown 3 percent could have been explained as conventional phenomena or illusion if more complete observational data had been available."[7] Note that the 3 percent only applies to the 131 sightings of the first four months of 1955.

Another misrepresentation in subsequent years was to automatically label a case with one witness as "Insufficient Information" no matter the quality. In addition the annual press releases automatically listed cases which had no explanation at the end of the year as "Insufficient Information." If these two groups had been included, as they should have been, the percentage of UNKNOWNS would again have been around 20 percent. Because the press was unaware of these facts, it is not surprising that newsmen paid little attention to UFOs.

It is of interest that Friedman found information in Donald Menzel's files indicating that he had a copy of BBSR 14 but Menzel never referred to it in his three books. The Condon Report talked about Project Blue Book but never mentioned BBSR 14 though it covered more than 20 times as many cases as Condon's people did. Friedman had sent Condon details about it. Perhaps surprising to most people is the simple fact that according to a special UFO subcommittee established by the American Institute of Aeronautics and Astronautics, one could come to the opposite conclusions from Condon's as 30 percent of the 117 cases studied in detail could not be identified. As a side fact it turns out gold is worth mining if there is an ounce of gold in a ton of ore. With regard to uranium one finds that only 0.7 percent of uranium atoms are fissionable (the U-235). But that is what is fissioned in nuclear reactors and atomic bombs.

We must recall that, according to USAF General Carroll Bolender's memo of 1969, reports of UFOs that could affect National Security were not part of the Blue Book System. From the government's concerns with national defense, these should have been the most important.

There is evidence to confirm the Durant Report's recommendation for the surveillance of UFO groups. It was carried out when Major Donald Keyhoe, director of the National Investigations Committee on Aerial Phenomena, was monitored by the intelligence community. His name is mentioned frequently by disinformants in private communiqués in archival collections. Jim and Coral Lorenzen, directors of the Aerial Phenomena Research Organization, wrote in their book *UFOs Over the Americas* (1968) that Coral was visited by Project Blue Book consultant Dr. Allen Hynek and Captain Edward Ruppelt's assistant, Lieutenant Robert Olsson, in June 1953. They urged her to diminish the public's interest in UFO sighting reports by publishing information about the misidentification of conventional objects. Government figureheads seldom commented on UFOs, and when they did, they reassured the public that all UFOs could be explained.

In a fine example of media censorship, on January 22, 1958, NICAP director Major Donald Keyhoe, appeared on CBS television's *Armstrong Circle Theater* in a show titled "UFOs: Enigma in the Skies." The Air Force had carefully scripted Keyhoe in order to censor his comments for security reasons. But Keyhoe departed from the script announcing that NICAP had been secretly working with a U.S. Senate committee to investigate UFO secrecy. The audio was immediately cut off in mid-sentence. For the next 45 minutes CBS was deluged with thousands of complaints from the public accusing it of censorship. To this CBS replied, "This program had been carefully cleared for security reasons...public interest was served by the action taken by CBS."[8] Keyhoe wrote to NICAP members that he had attempted to state, "In the last six months, we have been working with a Senate committee investigating official secrecy on Unidentified Flying Objects. If open hearings are held, I feel it will prove beyond doubt that the flying saucers are real machines under intelligent control."[9]

115

Several individuals have stated that government officials approached them claiming that they wanted to fund cartoons and documentaries that would show clear photos of UFOs and/or alien bodies. Ward Kimball, a Disney animator famous for creating Jiminy Cricket, the Mad Hatter, and the Cheshire Cat, testified that in the mid-1950s Walt Disney was contacted by the Air Force to make a UFO documentary to familiarize the American public with the UFO presence, in which official photographs of UFOs would be shown. According to Kimball, Disney began to work on the project but was later informed that the Air Force had no intention of providing official photos of UFOs. Friedman spoke with Kimball, who confirmed that he had met with an Air Force colonel. The colonel had informed Kimball that "There indeed was plenty of UFO footage, but that neither Ward, nor anyone else, was going to get access to it."[10]

In 1982, Linda Moulton Howe, an Emmy Award–winning TV producer, investigative reporter for radio and internet, and author, was approached with an offer from the Air Force to show official evidence for a film she was producing for HBO (*www.earthfiles.com*). The film was to be titled "UFOs—The ET Factor." Attorney Peter Gersten had informed her that Sergeant Richard Doty might be willing to do an on-camera interview with Howe for the HBO production. Shortly thereafter, Howe flew to Albuquerque to meet with Doty. When he did not show up at the airport, she called Jerry Miller, chief of Reality Weapons Testing at Kirtland AFB and former Project Blue Book investigator, for a ride. He phoned Doty and the three drove to Kirtland AFB, where Doty escorted Howe to an office. He handed Howe a plain black and white document titled "A Briefing Paper for the President of the United States on the Subject of Unidentified Flying Vehicles." The document spoke of UFO crash retrievals and the bodies of hairless, gray-skinned aliens with oversized heads, large eyes with vertical pupils, and no protruding noses or ears. It also stated that the Earth has been visited for thousands of years by an ET race that has altered the human genome and helped to form human religious beliefs. Doty offered Howe the right to use thousands of feet of USAF film of UFOs and ET bodies, as well as footage of an alleged landing at Holloman AFB. Intrigued by the offer, Howe told HBO to make legal preparations for the receipt of the footage while she continued to speak with Doty and three other men via the telephone. After many months of stalling, the footage was denied and her contract with HBO expired. It was later disclosed that U.S. intelligence agents had participated in a disinformation scheme against her to sever her ties with HBO.

Marden witnessed the harassment of her aunt Betty Hill in the late 1960s. (See *Captured! The Betty and Barney Hill UFO Experience*.) Marden moved into Betty's home in Portsmouth, New Hampshire, soon after Barney's death in February 1969. Betty had felt threatened by odd occurrences in her home such as finding her kitchen chairs grouped in a circle in her living room and clothing from her closet heaped in a pile on her floor. A neighbor had observed unusual activity when Betty was not at home, and visitors were confirming that her phone lines appeared to be tapped. On one occasion Marden was at home during an illegal entry. Initially, she thought that Betty had returned home for lunch, so she ascended the stairs to Betty's apartment, intent upon greeting her. Although she had distinctly heard a door and footsteps Betty was not at home. Assuming that she had heard noises coming from outside Betty's home, Marden returned to her own apartment. Immediately, she heard a loud crash, followed by hurried footsteps and the slamming of the front door. She rushed to Betty's apartment, threw open the door (that was now unlocked), and raced down the hall in time to see a short, stocky man dressed in a light brown suit fleeing the scene. Returning to the apartment, she found a closet door standing open and a baseball bat on the floor. Betty soon realized that the only solution was to install a security system linked to the police station. After this there was one foiled illegal entry. Then this type of harassment ceased. Betty's emotional strength and stability carried her through several attempts to push her over the edge soon after Barney's death.

Kathleen Marden and Betty Hill, 2003

Marden has received numerous reports of attacks upon individuals in the UFO field. Questioning the veracity of these claims, she conducted a survey of 18 prominent UFO researchers and experiencers who had received widespread media attention. All but one reported that their computers had been hacked and damaged by viruses despite having excellent, updated security software. Others reported that they had received direct threats of personal harm unless they ceased their public exploitation of their abductions. In one case, a conference organizer's Website was hacked and modified to state that the conference had been sold out, when in fact it was not. This led to low attendance and financial loss for the conference organizer. Several experiencers reported that black helicopters have hovered low over the homes the day after an abduction has occurred. All reported evidence that their telephone conversations were being monitored. One experiencer suspected that her phone was being monitored, because there was a clear pattern of interference during radio shows. Immediately following one failed interview, her phone and that of her coauthor went completely dead after her coauthor made a sarcastic remark to the alleged third party listening in on the line. Her coauthor's phone service immediately went dead for 10 minutes, but the woman's service was still dead the following day. Her utility company's technician discovered a perplexing extra bundle of wires leading into her home and was forced to call his supervisor. The supervisor identified the extra bundle of wires as being similar to a Department of Defense bundle. Two radio show hosts claim they received direct threats to their families if they continued to address the topics they were discussing. Both left their shows. Two abduction researchers reported that they received thinly veiled threats at conferences. The problem is more widespread than Marden had imagined and by far exceeds any of the Durant Report's recommendations. Some people claim that the government doesn't have the resources to harass UFO and alien contact witnesses. However, the witnesses swear that they are not delusional.

If the CIA had carried out the Durant Report's plan to ridicule prominent cases and credible observers in order to dissuade the public from reporting UFOs, it couldn't have hired a better person to do the job than Philip Klass. Using his credentials as a mainstream journalist and his connections with government scientists, Klass launched ad hominem attacks on many upstanding advocates for the scientific investigation of UFOs and witnesses alike. Edward Condon's letter of recommendation to Klass's boss at McGraw-Hill started his career as the go to guy for television and radio talk shows and documentaries. The evidence in his archival collection reveals that he was a conniving prevaricator who creatively constructed hypothetical scenarios around every case he sought to destroy. Honest, productive citizens were portrayed as delusional kooks. Law enforcement officers were transformed into hoaxers or as perceptual deficients. Experienced airline pilots were told that they were incapable of differentiating between a fiery UFO and a firefly stuck in the airspace between an airliner's windows. His papers reek of a narcissistic personality, so convinced of his investigative skills that he bragged of transcending experienced investigators for both the military and the FBI. No human was capable of making an accurate assessment unless they agreed with Klass and his cronies, and there was no UFO report, regardless of how credible, that he couldn't easily dismiss.

Major Hector Quintanilla revealed in his unpublished manuscript, "UFOs: An Air Force Dilemma," his high regard for Klass and Menzel and his disdain for Dr. Allen Hynek. He stressed that Hynek was not an Air Force scientific consultant, only a Project Blue Book consultant, and accused him of lying when he stated that he worked for the Air Force.

The public was demanding an open congressional hearing on UFOs in 1966, after a record number of 1,112 UFO sightings had been reported to Project Blue Book that year. A UFO flap in Michigan had carried like wildfire to the media and the American public when Dr. Allen Hynek had identified it as swamp gas. His explanation was totally inadequate and in the public's mind smacked of a cover-up. Quintanilla felt that Congressman Gerald Ford had "stacked the deck" against him or "didn't really complete his homework" when he pushed for an open hearing. In Quintanilla's book section titled "The Beginning of a Congressional Coup," he laments that General Cruikshank blew his stack over it, telling his secretary, "Get me that God damn Quintanilla."[11] It would be his and Hynek's job to make a brief statement at the hearing that followed, after Secretary Brown read an official statement that had been prepared by a team of air force lawyers, scientists, administrators, and information specialists. Quintanilla reflected on how the meeting began as a closed-door executive hearing that ended when the chairman of the House Armed Services Committee pulled "a coup from which NICAP and the UFO buffs have never recovered." He opened the doors and effectively "pulled the rug out from under the advocates of a public hearing."[12] Hynek angered General Corbin and Quintanilla when he produced an unplanned and unapproved five-page statement from his briefcase calling for a scientific investigation of UFOs. Quintanilla wrote, "The truth of the matter is that Hynek has never made a meaningful or profound statement with regard to UFOs since I have been on the program." He called Hynek "disloyal."[13]

Dr. James E. McDonald was also perceived as untrustworthy because he had previously taken the Air Force to task over its plan to place titan missiles in the Tucson area. Now he was back causing trouble again, only this time he had presented evidence to General Cruikshank that Project Blue Book was doing an inadequate job. Quintanilla wrote that he was now dealing with "a different set of bad guys."[14] Cruikshank appointed a Blue Ribbon Panel of three officers to investigate Project Blue Book, and in the end Quintanilla stated that the Air Force was satisfied. However, when General De Goes ordered Quintanilla to take care of McDonald in his absence, his temper flared. He unsuccessfully requested a transfer, stating that he had lost objectivity, did not believe that UFO sighting could be vehicles from space, and was tired of fighting off the press, professional agitators, and inquisitors. McDonald and his cohorts had become Quintanilla's enemy and were causing major problems for him and the Air Force by gathering strength in the press as proponents of a serious scientific evaluation of UFOs. At his April 22, 1967, speech before the American Society of Newspaper editors, McDonald addressed this very issue. He also stated that the CIA had instructed the U.S. Air Force to adopt a policy of debunking flying saucers. Quintanilla called the statement "pure crap."[15] The record shows that McDonald was correct and Quintanilla was debunking UFOs with the assistance of both Klass and Menzel. He thanked Menzel for the assistance that he had given to the USAF on numerous occasions and was infuriated at McDonald for criticizing the Condon Committee for its failure to conduct a serious scientific evaluation of UFOs. The record shows that he adopted Klass's debasing terms for the scientists who advocated for the scientific study of UFOs, referring to them as "charlatans and phonies."[16]

In the end, the Air Force used the Condon Report's negative pronouncement and its endorsement by the National Academy of Sciences to hammer the lid shut on Project Blue Book. Quintanilla's wish was granted. A follow-up study by a sub-committee of the American Institute of Aeronautics and Astronautics revealed that of the 117 cases that the Condon Committee had studied in detail, 30 percent could not be identified after all possible explanations had been exhausted. Yet this significant data fell on deaf ears. No additional government funds would be allocated for the scientific study of UFOs, except for psychological studies of UFO reporters to determine why people continue to see things that officially do not exist.

In contrast to Quintanilla's treatment of Hynek and McDonald, he held Menzel and Klass in high regard. He stated:

> Numerous other individuals and organizations have helped the project office from time to time. Dr. Donald Menzel, who authored "The World of Flying Saucers" has helped me on some very ticklish cases. I consider Menzel to be a true scientist and not a publicity grabbing charlatan. Philip J. Klass, who wrote "UFO's-IDENFIFIED" offered the project office a number of UFO cases that turned out to be beauties. I consider Klass to be an excellent investigator. Neither one of these gentlemen has ever asked for one cent of payment and yet, these men have produced work of the highest caliber.[17]

What nonsense! Klass and Menzel's true motives have been demonstrated time and time again.

After the decision had been made to close Project Blue Book, on December 18, 1969, Menzel voiced his strong approval of the decision to Dr. Robert C. Seamans, department of the Air Force at the Pentagon, and offered his recommendation for a speedy closure. He advised Seamans that local members of NICAP had been urged to continue contact with their local Air Force bases to establish themselves as Project Blue Book's successors. He criticized the Air Force for failing to issue a directive for local bases to cease in giving information to "unauthorized amateur groups."[18] He also recommended that the Project Blue Book files be completely closed for a decade in order to prevent McDonald, Hynek and the amateur groups from accessing them. Fortunately, Menzel's plan to withhold access to the files was not carried out. They were maintained at Maxwell AFB, requiring approval by the Secretary of the Air Force for access to them. He also informed Seamans that NICAP was deeply in debt and "on its last legs" and thought that the actions he recommended would "help pull the carpet out from underneath them."[19] Copies of the letter were sent to Klass and Quintanilla, Menzel's two associates who were cooperating in a conspiracy to close Project Blue Book. NICAP closed its doors in 1980.

In the end, Robert Low and Edward Condon were appreciative of Klass's assistance to the Project. In a letter dated February 27, 1967, Robert Low wrote to Klass:

> I know that you're aware that Ed and I are very grateful to you for the help you gave during the course of the project. You were a constant source of assistance and encouragement. There never was a time that we didn't have lots of friends who told us we were virtuous and right, but few of them, it seemed, were in a position to do anything about it. You, on the other hand, by keeping us informed of late developments and by warning us of events about to take place, performed an invaluable service. I think you kept us from getting so very jumpy that we might have lost our cool. It is much better to know, even though knowing means bad news, than it is not to know at all.[20]

He was referring to Klass's intelligence gathering efforts against individuals such as Dr. James E. McDonald, Dr. David Saunders, NICAP leaders, and others. Low was pleased by the press's decision to forego coverage of UFO news. Three months later, he wrote, "the same old gang keeps cranking out the trash."[21]

Condon, in a campaign to end government funding for the study of UFOs advised Klass, "If you hear of serious efforts to get additional federal money for UFO study, such as McDonald advocates, I would appreciate being tipped off so I can oppose them."[22] Menzel, too, pushed for an end of funding for UFO studies, stating in a letter to Klass (copied to Markowitz, Condon, Quintanilla, and Boyd), "I want to do everything I can to scuttle the boat of Hynek and McDonald for money to be spent on UFO studies...I may well kick my hat out of the ring at the appropriate time. And when I do so, would gladly join you and Mark in letting our objections have the widest publicity."[23]

CHAPTER 7

KLASSICAL FICTION

What would motivate an aviation journalist, supposedly dedicated to the search for truth, to devote nearly all of his free time to speculative arguments and ad hominem attacks against credible UFO witnesses and investigators? Were his assaults politically motivated? Was he working for a federal agency? The Church congressional hearings demonstrated that there were hundreds of journalists who were on the payroll of the Central Intelligence Agency or working without pay out of a sense of loyalty to their government. Obfuscation for political reasons has often gotten in the way of progress. Our book *Science Was Wrong* discusses case after case of the concealment of scientific evidence in favor of political expediency. Was Philip Klass carrying out a political agenda designed to maintain the status quo out of fear of the public's reaction to an ET presence? Or was he an emotionally driven fanatic with a penchant to harm anyone who disagreed with him?

He entered the UFO debunking scene in August 1966, by speculating in *Aviation Week and Space Technology* that the September 1965 multiple-witness close encounter near Exeter, New Hampshire, was nothing more than plasma on telephone lines. His first substantial investigation took him to Socorro, New Mexico, on December 16, 1966, for a two-day investigation of police sergeant Lonnie Zamora's April 24, 1964, sighting of an unexplained object. It was 32 months after Zamora's sighting of a landed and airborne craft and two humanoid figures associated with it. Klass was convinced that he could accomplish what an extensive investigation by the Air Force, the FBI, and top UFO investigators had failed to do: find a conventional explanation for Zamora's sighting. He had written to New Mexico Senator Clinton P. Anderson asking him to request State Police sergeant Sam Chavez's cooperation in his investigation. Chavez had arrived at the scene moments after the mysterious craft had disappeared from sight and had written the first report based upon Zamora's statement. Klass's request for political intervention with regard to his investigation raises questions in this book's authors' minds. We know that months of media attention had worn thin on the witness and investigators. Had they refused Klass's request? Did this require an official request by a political leader from New Mexico? Or was Klass there in an official capacity? The following segment will examine Klass's investigation, his modus operandi, his interpretation of the evidence, and his case disposition.

Officials from the Air Force and the FBI had investigated Zamora's sighting immediately after it occurred. The official reports state that Lonnie Zamora was heading south in pursuit of a speeding black Chevrolet on the outskirts of Socorro at approximately 5:45 p.m. on April 24, 1964, when through an open window his attention was drawn to a loud roar and bluish-orange flames rising into the air in the vicinity of a dynamite shack. He made the decision to abandon his chase and hurried in the direction of the flames, fearing that the dynamite shack might have blown up. He turned onto the rough gravel road that led to the dynamite shack and attempted to negotiate a steep hill of loose gravel and rock with his '64 Pontiac police cruiser. Zamora finally crested the hill on his third attempt. He continued to drive westward looking for the dynamite shack, when to his left he spotted a shiny aluminum or white object, 12–15 feet long, resting on the ground approximately 150 to 200 yards in the distance.

He told officials that he had briefly observed two figures dressed in white coveralls standing next to the vehicle. From Zamora's vantage point in the driver's seat, they appeared to be about the size of small adults or large children. One of the figures spotted the patrol car and seemed startled, jumping quickly. Zamora hastened to drive closer in order to assist what he still thought were probably teenagers next to an overturned car standing on its trunk or radiator.

Zamora radioed the sheriff's office to report a possible 10-44 (auto accident) and to ask for assistance. He stopped approximately 100 feet from the scene of the "accident" and informed the radio operator that he was leaving the cruiser to investigate. As he was leaving his car, he fumbled and dropped the microphone, then put it back in place. He heard two loud metallic banging sounds, like doors closing, as he walked toward the arroyo for a closer look, and noticed that the two figures were no longer visible. This is when he realized that the vehicle was not an overturned automobile, but an oval-shaped object resting on legs slanted outward toward the ground. Suddenly he heard an intense roar that started at a low frequency and rose to a higher pitch. Dust began to swirl as the craft rose straight up—slowly. Zamora saw a light blue flame with an orange tinged bottom shooting out from the craft's underside.

He then noticed a strange red insignia on the side of the smooth, windowless craft about 1 1/2 to 2 feet in height and shaped like a crescent, with a vertical line in the center below it, and slanted lines to the top right and left of the vertical line, similar to an arrow head. There was a straight horizontal line beneath the vertical line.

Oil on canvas by artist Patrick Richard of retired Socorro police officer Lonnie Zamora. Painting donated in his memory to the City of Socorro

Fearful that the vehicle would blow up at any moment, Zamora fled for cover. As he dashed toward the back of his patrol car, the official reports state that he bumped the rear fender and fell down, losing his sunglasses and prescription glasses in the fall. Picking himself up, he ran in a northerly direction, glancing back at the object from time to time. When he was about 25 feet north of his patrol car, Zamora saw that the craft was now level with his car. He continued to flee and jumped over a hill, where he took cover, shielding his eyes with his lower arm. When the roar ceased he uncovered his eyes and watched the craft leave. It traveled over the top of the dynamite shack, clearing it by only about 3 feet. Returning to his car, and picking up his glasses on the way, Zamora called radio operator Nep Lopez and instructed him to look out the window for what looked like a balloon, but his window faced north so he was looking in the wrong direction. Zamora watched as the craft gained speed and traveled toward the southwest covering an estimated 6 miles in three minutes before disappearing from view. He sketched the insignia on the side of the craft while he was waiting for backup to arrive.

State Police Sergeant M. Sam Chavez arrived at the scene moments after he heard Zamora's call for backup. He described Zamora as "perfectly sober and thoroughly frightened"[1] and "badly shaken, pale and shaking."[2] Chavez stated that although Zamora was reluctant to enter the area where the craft had landed, the two walked to the site and observed smoldering vegetation and indentations in the soil. Chavez secured the area and took photographs of the evidence. He then notified the FBI, and in turn agent D. Arthur Byrnes, Jr. notified Army Captain Richard T. Holder, Up Range Commander at Stallion Range Center, White Sands.

The following day, Byrnes and Holder interviewed Chavez and Zamora and conducted a search of the area securing soil and plant samples before curiosity seekers had arrived. They found four irregularly shaped areas of smoldering vegetation and four 6x16-inch depressed areas in a rectangular pattern approximately 12 feet apart and 2 inches deep. Three smooth circular marks approximately 4 inches in diameter were noted. A check for ground radiation was made indicating, in the official documents, that no radioactivity was present. A sample of the vegetative material, soil samples, and Zamora's lengthy statement were sent to the Albuquerque FBI Office. Hours later, Project Blue Book director Major Hector

Quintanilla ordered his chief analyst, Sergeant David Moody, who was on temporary duty at Kirtland AFB, and Major Connor, a less-experienced UFO investigator at Kirtland, to conduct an immediate investigation at Socorro. They arrived at noon on April 26, to find that Chavez and Holder and taken numerous samples of the vegetation, soil, and rocks.

Thirty-two months after Zamora's harrowing experience and the painstaking investigation by the New Mexico State and local police, the Air Force, and the FBI, Klass set out to debunk the story and everyone who disagreed with his opinion of it. His first plan of action was to write off the entire sighting as a plasma ball or dust devil or something else, and his 1968 book, *UFOs—Identified*, does just that. It didn't matter to Klass that the object bore not even a remote resemblance to a dust devil, nor that government investigators had collected physical evidence samples on the ground. Nor did it matter that the atmospheric conditions precluded plasma as a viable explanation. Klass was hell-bent on destroying the case.

He had invited Dr. Charles B. Moore, an atmospheric physicist at New Mexico's Institute of Mining and Technology, to meet him at the landing site in December 1966. (Moore was later awarded the prestigious American Institute of Aeronautics and Astronautics Otto C. Winzen Lifetime Achievement Award). In *UFOs— Identified*, Klass misinformed the naïve public that Moore was an "ardent UFOlogist" who'd been investigating the Zamora case since he'd arrived in Socorro.[3] Moore countered Klass's claim by stating that he was an agnostic on the subject of UFOs and had made his first visit to the site in mid-1966 at the request of meteorological physicist Dr. James McDonald. Moore speculated that Zamora had observed an early version of the Lunar Excursion Module, not an alien spacecraft, as Klass would have us believe. Several modules had been built in 1962 and 1963, but a thorough search by Project Blue Book director Hector Quintanilla found that none were operational in 1964. Moore told McDonald in a private communiqué that, when he arrived at the site, he attempted to join into a conversation with Klass, Zamora, and Chavez, who were already there. But Klass was "aggressive," twisting his statements and answering his "questions before he was half way through his replies."[4] Moore stated that Klass argued with him about plasma physics and explained away the landing marks as gopher holes—speculations that Moore simply could not accept considering the evidence.

Klass claimed in *UFOs—Identified* that he found significant discrepancies and damaging evidence in Zamora's statements that cast serious doubt upon his story. Speaking of Zamora's harrowing experience as an adventure, Klass twisted the facts with regard to the sequence of events and criticized investigators for missing the so-called obvious inconsistency in Zamora's statements. For example, Klass insisted that Zamora saw the object's two legs from a distance of 800 feet, but the Project Blue Book and FBI reports consistently state that he noticed the legs from a distance of 103 feet. He also cast doubt upon Zamora's observation of figures next to the craft, emphasizing the idea they were in view for "two seconds or so."[5] The documented evidence reveals that although Zamora saw the figures only briefly he was able to describe their attire and behavior. Given Zamora's excellent character assessment and his skills as an experienced police officer, there is no reason to believe that he lied. In addition to this, Klass introduced fiction to the story by leading readers to believe that the major part of Zamora's sighting took place after he lost his glasses. If this were the case, Zamora's 20/200 vision would have precluded a clear description of the symbols he observed on the side of the craft. Again this is false. Klass had copies of the official Blue Book documents, so how could he have been so wrong? The obvious answer is that he was motivated by an overwhelming desire to discredit Zamora and destroy the case.

A tourist traveling north on U.S. 85 reported that he saw the craft just before it landed in the gully. Opal Grinder, manager at the Whiting Brothers Service Station, told Hynek that the witness had remarked on the funny-looking craft that passed low over his car and his observation of a police car heading up the hill. Hynek tracked down the man through a lead in the Dubuque, Iowa, *Telegraph-Herald*. Klass wasn't buying it. Convinced that Zamora had made the whole thing up, he accused Grinder and the witnesses of lying.

Several additional witnesses registered reports with Project Blue Book in the same general time frame. The record indicates that despite the credibility of the witnesses and medical testimony by an examining physician of facial burns and eye irritation in one witness, all reports of UFO sightings and landings were given conventional explanations. A close encounter with a landed craft that fit the description of the one Zamora reported that left identical ground markings was investigated by a police captain and military officers from Kirtland AFB. Yet, Project Blue Book "explained" away every report.

Thirty-two months after the event occurred, Klass argued that Zamora was lying because no charcoal was found in the trace evidence samples that had been analyzed by a scientific laboratory. It was another deceptive move by Philip Klass. He had copies of the Project Blue Book reports stating that the vegetation was smoldering, not flaming. He also knew that Dr. Donald Menzel had questioned Dr. J. Allen Hynek about the "burning bush." Hynek had written that at no time did anyone report smoke rising from the smoldering vegetation. The green snakeweed and green greasewood, which are difficult to ignite, showed evidence of being seared by a hot flame, not burned as Klass claimed.[6]

A rumor had been circulating that fused sand was removed from the landing site. But evidence of this could not be found in any of the official reports. Moore had reported to Klass that "bubbly rock" had been found at the center of the pad prints. When Klass inquired about this Zamora paused for seven seconds before replying. He interpreted this as an indication of Zamora's deception.

In 1968, Stanton Friedman was in Las Vegas to deliver a lecture to the local American Nuclear Society section when Mary Mayes, a member of the audience, spoke to him after the lecture. She told him that she had been asked to analyze plant material from the Socorro site in 1964, when she was a graduate student in radiation biology at the University of New Mexico. She stated that following her analysis, the Air Force had collected all of her notes and samples and instructed her and two other graduate students involved in the analysis not to discuss it. Friedman passed the tip to Dr. James McDonald.

McDonald interviewed Mayes extensively over the phone and in person. She revealed that she was a graduate student under Dr. Howard Dittmer in 1964, when she was asked to go to the landing site on the morning of April 25, 1964, to collect samples of scorched vegetation and melted, fused sand. She and two other graduate students, whose names she was never able to find, analyzed the samples. She discovered that the plants were scorched and completely dried out. Sap had burst out of and through the surface of the plants, but they were not charcoaled. She found two organic substances on the plant samples that were not identified. No propellant or radiation was found. She hadn't analyzed the fused sand, but she stated that it was a 25x30-inch patch .25-inch thick, like glass with holes on the edge. She wrote to Wright–Patterson AFB for additional information, but was not able to acquire it. The scientific analysis has never been released by the Air Force or the FBI.

Klass accused investigators of distorting the facts and embellishing the evidence, but most certainly Klass added his own fiction. The truth is that federal investigators left no bases unturned in their search to identify the vehicle Zamora observed. An unsigned official report in Project Blue Book's files states:

It is therefore essential to consider this one of the major UFO sightings in the history of the Air Force's consideration of the subject, and to spare no effort in establishing whether maneuvers of any sort were taking place in the locality either on the part of the Air Force, the Army, or even the Navy. However, I am quite certain that it will not be sufficient for the Air Force in this case to indicate that the sighting was 'probably a new type of craft being tested', or that a secret war maneuver was in progress, unless the log of such maneuvers is produced, and better yet, the entire "crime" reenacted, preferably in Zamora's presence. I recognize that this will be a very difficult task, but in view of the importance of this case, I think every attempt should be made to do this. It will require, very possibly, the attention of the Secretary of the Air Force himself.... The object which produced this, if it is a new device or under test or in maneuvers, [should] be brought to same location and movies be taken of it departing in the manner described by Zamora, and under the same lighting conditions. This then could be played at any future hearings on flying saucers. This, it seems to me, could go a very long way toward exploding the myth of flying saucers, and might do more good than all of the previous years of propaganda.[7]

Holloman's Balloon Control Center and all weather stations were queried, but all denied having balloons in the air at the time of Zamora's sighting. The possibility of an undocumented balloon was eliminated because winds were blowing strongly from the south–southwest, yet the object traveled west against the prevailing winds. Helicopter activity and government and private aircraft were checked. An inquiry was sent to the FAA for the identification of the symbol Zamora observed on the craft. The FAA had no knowledge of any country that used symbols as reference to their registration. A joint military operation known as "Cloud Gap" was taking place in New Mexico at the time of the incident, but the OSI in Albuquerque advised that the craft was not related to any military operation or Cloud Gap operations being conducted 100 miles north of Socorro. The reconnaissance division in the Pentagon was checked. Even the White House Command Post was queried, but did not have an operation in the area. The weather was clear, so the possibility of meteorological phenomena was ruled out. Quintanilla was so determined to find a solution to the problem that he obtained permission to travel to Holloman AFB. Four days later, he left feeling dejected. He began a letter-writing campaign to Lunar Landing vehicle manufacturers in search for a match, but to no avail.

Quintanilla stated, at the end of an exhaustive investigation, that no conventional explanation could be found. The case remained puzzling. He wrote:

> There is no doubt that Lonnie Zamora saw an object which left quite an impression on him. There is also no question about Zamora's reliability. He is a serious police officer, a pillar of his church, and a man well versed in recognizing airborne vehicles in his area. He is puzzled by what he saw, and frankly, so are we. This is the best documented case on record, and still we have been unable, in spite of thorough investigation, to find the vehicle or other stimulus that scared Zamora to the point of panic.[8]

Klass was convinced that a craft with a radically new type of propulsion system and aerodynamic shape could not have been developed in classified programs without journalists getting wind of it. He wrote in a letter to Jim Moseley, "In the US, rightly or wrongly, journalists enjoy the privilege of reading classified documents, and even publishing them, without any possible criminal action—thanks to the US Constitution."[9] He advised Moseley that he had read a report, classified "Secret," one week before it was delivered to the White House. He felt it was inconceivable that the government could cover up a new technological development for years, especially because Zamora's sighting had compromised its secrecy. He did not mention that he avoided prosecution for releasing classified information because it could not be declassified.

As if Klass felt his fiction wasn't convincing enough, he introduced character assassination to his ploy to demolish public interest in the Zamora case. He told the American public that Lonnie Zamora was a liar despite the fact that all military and civilian investigators had deemed him a man of unquestionable integrity. His final assessment of the experience was that it was a hoaxed event perpetrated by Zamora and Socorro mayor Holm Bursum, Jr. His devious mind linked newspaper articles in the *El Defensor Chieftain* and *The El Paso Times*, to stimulate tourist dollars to the New Mexico economy, as a motive for the alleged hoax.

Menzel had written a letter to Hynek in 1965, introducing the suggestion that a hoax had been perpetrated. He replied that he and Quintanilla had considered the possibility of a hoax, but had agreed that if it were a hoax, Zamora, Sergeant Chavez, Opal Grinder, and FBI Agent Byrnes were in on it. Project Blue Book investigators had considered the possibility that college students had perpetrated a hoax by launching a balloon. But the balloon conjecture was ruled out, because the craft that Zamora had sighted traveled west against a strong wind. The possibility that local teenagers wanted retribution against the police for harassing them was also ruled out. Hynek's report noted that UFOs had not received publicity in the Socorro area in 1964, and no evidence of a hoax was ever found. No propellant was discovered. No paraphernalia was found at the site. There were no human footprints at the site when Zamora and Chavez investigated it immediately after the sighting. And there were no fresh tire tracks leading to the site, except the ones left by Zamora and Chavez. Hynek left Socorro after planting the idea that student "neophyte intelligence officers" should continue with the investigation of a possible hoax.[10] But no hoaxers were identified. The hoax hypothesis has been resurrected periodically, but when all of the evidence is carefully weighed, it has not been supported by factual information. The origin of the craft that startled Zamora and confounded the Air Force in 1965 remains a mystery.

By 1975, Project Blue Book had been closed for five years and the Air Force had ostensibly turned its back on the UFO problem. Klass was in his stride developing highly imaginative speculative arguments to discredit credible reports. When the evidence was so compelling it couldn't be easily dismissed, Klass separated the evidence into tiny packets of information and used "science" to dismiss each packet independently. Virtually no level of evidence passed his test for acceptability. Ad hominem attacks kept potential witnesses at bay and credible people were threatened with legal action or told to shut up or be declared prevaricators.

This was the debunking climate Travis Walton faced five days after he disappeared from the forest near Heber, Arizona. His case has been shrouded by dubious investigative reports, strong personalities, and false claims promoted by disbelievers. It is considered one of two top abduction evidence cases in history. Walton's story is presented in his book *Fire in the Sky* and Jennifer Stein's compelling documentary *TRAVIS*. An inaccurate presentation of his case was dramatized in an earlier movie. The authors have investigated Walton's case both in Arizona and through an examination of the archival documents. We have discovered a paper trail that reeks of deception and obfuscation of the facts by certain investigators. We are convinced that the credible evidence speaks for itself.

Briefly, on November 5, 1975, Walton (22) was one of seven woodsmen working on the Turkey Springs tree thinning contract in the Apache-Sitgreaves National Forest. Around 6:00 p.m., he, John Goulette, Dwayne Smith, Kenneth Peterson, Mike Rogers, Jeff (Steve) Pierce, and Allen Dalis piled into crew boss Mike Rogers's 1965 International Crew Cab truck for the rough ride toward Heber. They noticed a bright, glowing light in the distance that took on form as they approached it. A golden, flattened disk hovered only 20 feet or so above the ground, less than 30 yards in the distance. Walton, who was in the front passenger seat, opened his door and impulsively walked toward the craft. As he drew closer he detected a barely audible high-pitched beeping and low rumbling sounds emanating from the craft. Suddenly the vibrating sound increased and the disk started to wobble on its axis. Just then a blue-green beam shot out from under the craft in Walton's direction. It threw him backward into the air and down to the forest floor 10 feet from where he had been standing.

Rogers's immediate reaction was to escape from the craft because he and his crew were in grave danger. He drove recklessly down the logging road toward the gravel access road, but upon reflection stopped to collect his thoughts. He glimpsed what he thought was the craft rising above the trees and streaking toward the northwest. A few minutes later, he turned around and headed back to the spot where Walton had been lying on the ground. With only the truck's headlights and a flashlight, the men scoured the area, calling Walton's name over and over again. He had apparently vanished.

The men headed back to Heber and phoned the sheriff's department. Moments later, Navajo County Deputy Sheriff Chuck Ellison took statements from the visibly shaken crew. Two of the young men were so upset that they wept during their testimony. An hour later, sheriff Marlin Gillespie and undersheriff Ken Coplan arrived. The younger crew members were transported to their homes, while Rogers joined the police in a thorough but futile search of the area.

At about 1:00 a.m., Coplan and Rogers carried the upsetting news to Walton's mother, Mary Kellett, at her summer cabin 10 miles east of the abduction site. Rogers later testified that that Kellett was too shaken to drive, so he transported her to her daughter's home outside Snowflake. She called her son Duane, in the Phoenix area, at 3:00 a.m., and he immediately headed for Snowflake.

Klass touted a different version of the story. He promoted the idea that that Walton's mother had not exhibited the strong emotional response one would anticipate from a mother whose son was missing and possibly dead. This led him and a skeptical police officer with whom he was collaborating to suspect that she was violating the law by concealing her son in order to perpetrate a hoax. Kellet and the Walton family vehemently denied the allegation and requested polygraph exams to prove their honesty.

Duane submitted to a polygraph exam on February 9, 1976, administered by George Pfeiffer, Jr. He asked if he was aware that Travis was missing before he received the telephone call from his mother; if he had participated in a hoax to pretend that Travis was missing; if he believed that Travis had participated in a hoax to pretend that he was missing; if he knew where Travis was located during the several days that he was missing; if he believed that Travis was sincere when he described his experience while he was missing; and if he (Duane) had told the truth. He passed the polygraph exam with no sign of deception.

Despite the efforts of search crews there was no trace of Travis. Suspecting that he had been the victim of foul play, the sheriff's department asked the crew to submit to polygraph exams. Polygraphs record blood pressure, pulse, respiration, and galvanic skin response, related to perspiration. Changes in the variables that differ from the baseline measures indicate an emotional response that can be interpreted as deception. On November 10, 1975, the suspects attempted to prove their honesty. C.E. Gilson, the polygraph examiner from the Department of Public Safety, asked three questions that pertained to whether or not a member of the crew had caused physical injury or death to Walton and had hidden or buried his body in the Turkey Springs area. The fourth question asked was "Did you tell the truth about actually seeing a UFO last Wednesday when Travis Walton disappeared?"[11] All but one crew member, Allen Dalis, passed the exam. Dalis, a troubled young man, stormed out of the examination room before it was completed. C.E. Gilson's final report concluded, "These polygraph examinations prove that these five men did see some object that they believe to be a UFO and that Travis Walton was not injured or murdered by any of these men, on that Wednesday (5 November 1975). If an actual UFO did not exist and the UFO is a manmade hoax, five of these men had no prior knowledge of the hoax."[12] In 1993, Allen Dalis passed a polygraph with no sign of deception.

Travis Walton, Kathleen Marden, and Stanton Friedman

Klass refused to accept the enormity of this evidence. Instead he stated that sometimes celestial bodies, such as Jupiter, which was particularly bright that night, are mistaken for UFOs. This argument is weak indeed. The men had all observed a low, hovering craft. The blue-green beam that struck Walton and threw him backward caused them to fear for their lives. Apparently Klass realized that his argument was weak when he added, "If they were all partners in a pre-arranged hoax, all might be able to answer 'yes' to this one UFO–related question without displaying overt signs of telling a significant falsehood."[13]

Walton has consistently stated that he awakened on the side of a winding, hilly stretch of highway just west of Heber, several miles from the site of his disappearance, five nights after his disappearance. The craft shot vertically into the air, and in an instant disappeared from sight. Dazed and in a state of shock, he ran down the hill toward Heber, stopping at a lighted building. His desperate knocks on the door did not rouse the occupants, so he ran farther to a row of phone booths at the Exxon station. He asked the operator to call his sister, who lived about 33 miles northeast of Heber near Snowflake. It was 12:05 a.m. when Walton's brother, Duane, and brother-in-law, Grant, found him collapsed in the phone booth.

Philip Klass used a fragment of incorrect information in the *National Enquirer* to support his claim that Walton was lying. The reporter had mistakenly written that Walton had phoned his mother when in fact she didn't have a phone. Klass used this small error to conclude that Walton had lied. The evidence in Klass's archival files indicates that Walton's sister told Klass that her brother was "slumped in the bottom of the phone booth...so shook up, he was so upset...he was very panicky...even talking to us was a real strain. He was very upset."[14] Klass believed she was lying.

Klass speculated that Duane's decision to whisk his brother to Phoenix was a ploy to prevent law enforcement officers from seeing him in a confused state of mind, possibly from injecting LSD. The fact is that blood tests did not find drugs in Walton's system, nor did the doctor who examined him find a puncture wound over a vein. Despite the evidence that Walton had not injected LSD or any other drug, Klass played the drug card, claiming that Dr. Steward told him that Walton might have been experiencing drug withdrawal symptoms from a combination of LSD and PCP. We know that Klass was highly manipulative and often put words into people's mouths. It is indeed difficult to understand why a psychologist who knew nothing about Walton would jump to the conclusion that he had been on a drug binge. The fact is LSD can be detected in urine for 12 to 24 hours and PCP for 24 to 48 hours. But why would Klass let the facts get in the way of a good debunking story?

The real reason behind Duane's decision to whisk his younger brother away from Snowflake was because the press had descended and was relentlessly pursuing Walton's mother. According to credible reports she was in no condition to do media interviews. Concern over Travis's physical and emotional well-being was a priority when Duane made the decision to transport him to Phoenix for a medical evaluation.

William Spaulding, of Ground Saucer Watch (GSW), a small UFO group in Phoenix, had advised Duane to take Travis to Dr. Lester Steward, a GSW member, for medical care. He had recorded magnetic and ozone readings at the abduction site and was concerned. They arrived at Dr. Steward's office at approximately 9:15–9:30 in the morning and left at approximately 10:15–10:30, upon discovering that he was not a medical doctor, but a psychologist and hypnotist. Spaulding and Klass later stated that Steward had interviewed the men for two hours, a statement that Duane disputed and later proved with phone records from his home. Duane, who had taken charge of Travis, was angry and disappointed that a licensed MD was not present as promised, so he refused to cooperate with Spaulding despite his repeated requests to become more involved in the investigation. The Aerial Phenomena Research Organization (APRO) convinced Duane that they would find funds and doctors for Travis's care.

Klass's transcript of his teleconference with Spaulding, on January 4, 1976, states that he declared the case a hoax when he learned that the Waltons had agreed to cooperate with APRO, not GSW. He allegedly told Klass that although physical trace evidence was found in the area, he shied away from occupant cases. Klass's correspondence with Spaulding suggests that the two joined forces to refute the Walton case. In a letter to Klass dated February 18, 1985, Spaulding referred to himself as a "near-skeptic" about UFOs.[15] However, in a letter dated November 5, 1976, Jim Lorenzen, director of APRO, informed Klass of Spaulding's decision to withdraw his acceptance to take a lie detector test with regard to the veracity of his statements. Lorenzen added, "During the show he also said that if he had known that the Walton case would develop as it has [meaning the dissention, I think] he would have said it was a good case from the beginning. He also said that G.S.W. had come out strongly against the case because the Waltons had 'chastised' him."[16]

APRO arranged for funding by the *National Enquirer* to carry out medical and polygraph exams for Travis. At the conclusion of his medical examination Dr. Kandell described him as both disturbed and depressed. Klass's failure to comprehend Walton's apparent traumatic reaction suggests that he lacked a basic understanding of human psychology and compassion toward others. He perceived every detail as evidence of deception and used minor inconsistencies that occur in human communication as proof of deception.

Travis was anxious to take a polygraph exam to prove his honesty. Dr. Rosenbaum, the psychiatrist involved, advised against it because he thought it would be meaningless. APRO's James Harder was concerned that Walton would fail the test due to his "extraordinarily nervous condition."[17] Harder likened him to a man who'd just been taken out of an electric chair after being administered a nearly fatal dose of electricity. Klass's files reveal that James Lorenzen described Walton's demeanor as "like a caged wildcat" when he first saw him. "It really freaked him out that five days had passed and he could only remember two hours. That was hard for him."[18] Lorenzen told Klass that the first thing Travis had viewed on TV were distortions of the facts and this upset him. It was too close to the date of the abduction and a false positive result was a distinct possibility. But despite the warnings, Walton was anxious to prove his truthfulness, so he took the polygraph exam, and failed it due to his highly charged emotional state. The examiner, who was later accused of bias, stated that Walton had shown signs of deception when he held his breath briefly after he was asked a question. He failed to mention that Walton's emotional state prevented any significant determination from being made. Lorenzen explained that two of the questions were so poorly constructed that Walton would have failed them whether he answered yes or no.

On February 9, 1976, polygraph examiner George Pfeiffer, Jr. asked Duane eight questions pertaining to the case. The polygraph examiner concluded, "It is the opinion of this examiner that Duane Walton has answered all questions truthfully according to what he believes to be the truth in this incident and has not attempted to be deceptive in this area."[19] Travis was administered a polygraph exam on the same day. Among other questions, he was asked if he was a UFO buff before November 5, 1975. *No.* Had he been completely truthful with James Lorenzen (APRO) in this area? *Yes.* Did he see a UFO on the evening of 11-5-75? *Yes.* The polygraph examiner stated that Travis had answered all questions in a manner that he himself "is firmly convinced to be truthful regarding the incident on 11-5-75."[20] Currently, he and his co-workers have passed several polygraph exams. Despite the overwhelming evidence that all witnesses have told the truth, it fell upon Klass's deaf ears.

Realizing that their decision for an early polygraph exam had not done Walton justice, APRO suppressed the initial results. But, a few months later, Klass uncovered and publicized the early polygraph results in his refutation of the case. He failed to place importance on the fact that Walton tested normal on the Minnesota Multiphasic Personality Inventory, administered by a licensed psychologist. The MMPI is a widely used test of personality and psychopathology. To this Klass wrote, "Apparently it is quite 'normal' to hope to be abducted by a UFO!!"[21] Travis's polygraph test indicates that Klass was prevaricating.

Fed up with Klass's constant attacks, Mike Rogers challenged him to a test of credibility. He and his crew, along with Duane Walton and Mary Kellet, requested another lie detector test under the condition that, if all parties passed the polygraph exam, Klass would accept the results as proof of the truth and retract his accusations of a hoax. The astute Rogers pointed out that Klass had played both sides of the coin with regard to the validity of polygraph exams, stating that if the results favored Klass's preconceived notion that UFOs are bunk, he promoted it. On the other hand, if the witnesses passed the polygraph exam, he stated that the results were invalid.

Klass had initially agreed to test all of the witnesses involved in the case except Mary Kellet, under the condition that if one of the witnesses failed to pass one or more of the relevant questions, the group would issue a public statement that the whole thing was a hoax. But there was one catch: Klass refused to honor the witness request for the questions to pertain only to the UFO incident. Rogers countered that this opened the door for emotional distress that might register a negative physiological response on the polygraph test. In addition to this, Klass insisted upon being present during the tests. Rogers declined, stating that the excessive agitation caused by Klass's publicly made "derogatory insinuations" and "erroneous accusations are not taken lightly by those wronged."[22]

The record shows that Klass had badgered the proposed polygraph examiner, accusing him of bias and dishonesty. Rogers swore that if a panel concluded the witness statements were false, he would publicly confess to being dishonest and pay all attorney's fees. He offered the qualifying statement: "I cannot accept your 'challenge' because it is in deliberate error concerning my actual statements of 7/25/76 and 10/5/76. Only a very devious and dishonest man would demand me to prove the truth of statements I never even made."[23] (Klass had misrepresented Rogers's statements with regard to a dispute over the conditions of their polygraph challenge.) Klass's lie detector testing was never carried out. But when subsequent polygraph exams were administered and passed, Klass inserted himself in the mix, attempting to pit examiner against examiner to discredit their work.

Klass's dogged pursuit of a prosaic explanation for the Walton abduction carried him down many avenues. He had spoken with the chief deputy clerk of the Navajo County Court, who had informed him that Walton had no criminal record. However, Klass was somehow able to extract information on an earlier conviction that had been expunged from the record due to Travis's good behavior. He made a big deal out of a stupid decision Travis had made as a teenager that resulted in both boys being charged with taking checks from the Western Molding Company in Snowflake. Klass spoke with Robert Gonsalves, president of the company, who informed him that Travis hadn't taken the checks and was not in the company's office when a young employee had torn two checks out of the back of the company's checkbook during a coffee break. However, both teens had used the money to purchase a new boots and were caught when the bank statement came in. Gonsalves stated that Walton, during his high school years, had worked part-time for his company and sometimes spent the night at Gonsalves's home during the frigid winter months. He vouched for Travis's good character and stated that he and Golsalves's son were friends. When asked about the UFO abduction Gonsalves stated, "I sure know that after this episode he sure was a changed individual, I'll tell you that.... As soon as he re-surfaced I met him right away and shortly thereafter. He had always been somewhat of a jokester, and always laughing and joking and he was sure quiet, spooky...as far as personality change...he was sure quiet and jumpy like he had been involved in something. He sure wasn't the same as he had been."[24] Despite this, Klass promoted the information in Walton's expunged record and failed to reveal the less-incriminating information he had received from Gonsalves. Walton was denied opportunities that might have been open to him were it not for Klass's unrelenting attempts to destroy his character.

Klass's telecons reveal a confrontational interrogation style with anyone that he considered unsympathetic to his cause. It would not be an overstatement to assert that he viewed them as the enemy. For example, on July 11, 1976, he grilled Mike Rogers, the owner of the company that employed Walton, in a long interview. Klass made it clear that he was attempting to catch Rogers in a lie, not through direct information, but as the result of his hostile and suspicious attitude. He had already acquired extensive information about

Rogers's business and forestry contracts. If his response wasn't consistent with what Klass wanted to hear, he was accused of fabricating information. Klass allegedly put words into his mouth in a confrontational style. For example, Rogers explained to Klass that the forest service would like contractors to take their deadlines seriously, but were always willing to give extensions when the work wasn't completed on time. Klass retorted, "So you didn't take your 200 working days seriously. Is that what you mean?"[25] Rogers explained that he was working on several contracts at once, as were several other contractors, and did take their jobs seriously. He had been given many extensions in the past and even defaulted in the past, so this was nothing new. He was not alone in this. It is not uncommon, even among large contractors. Klass repeatedly asked the same questions over several phone calls, making it clear that he was attempting to catch Rogers in a lie. Rogers was clearly fed up with Klass's allegations of dishonesty and unhappy that four men in his crew refused to return to the job or to go outside at night. Klass was out for bear.

He interviewed the forester in charge of the Timber Stand Improvement Office, who informed him that Rogers had done nothing wrong. He did not have to pay a penalty and was paid for most of his work. However, his last inspection had failed resulting in nonpayment for three weeks of work. The reason it failed is because Walton's brother had torn all of the slash piles apart searching for his brother's body. Klass coveted this information and twisted the facts to make it appear that Rogers was guilty of wrongdoing, when clearly he was not.

With the fervency of a fanatic, Klass doggedly pursued Rogers, claiming that he was part and parcel to a hoax, not only with regard to the Walton abduction, but also for setting up a situation that would relieve him of his forest service contract. Rogers was then audited by the IRS, which is not surprising considering Klass's habit of reporting suspected wrongdoing to government agencies.

Klass's book *UFO Abductions: A Dangerous Game* was aptly titled. As long as Klass was alive, it was dangerous to have endured an alien abduction. Not only would you suffer the trauma related to the experience, you would be traumatized by Phil Klass's relentless attacks.

CHAPTER 8

MORE FICTION

Klass's white paper exposé on the Walton case states that "hoaxes ought to be exposed and the failure to do so can only hurt the 'UFO movement'."[1] Marden and Friedman agree that hoaxes and credulous reports serve only to detract from serious research. The great difficulty we have with Klass's statement is that it is disingenuous. Klass had no interest in increasing the integrity of UFO research. His modus operandi clearly spells out a negative agenda focused upon ad hominem attacks, the distortion of factual information, malicious gossip, and the unethical manipulation of individuals and facts. He impugned nearly every prominent investigator's character and motives, and labeled every contact report a hoax or psychological case. An egregious example of his unethical behavior can be found in his attempts to discredit Betty Cash and Vickie Landrum, who observed an unconventional craft on December 29, 1980, at 9:00 p.m. and suffered serious, life-changing medical consequences.

Betty Cash (51) was in the driver's seat of her 1980 Oldsmobile Cutlass, traveling toward her home in Dayton, Texas, about 37 miles northeast of Houston, with Vickie Landrum (57) and Landrum's grandson Colby (7) after a night out in search of a bingo game. The two friends and young Colby had discovered that the regularly scheduled bingo games in nearby Cleveland and New Caney had been cancelled due to the holidays. But their trip was not a total waste. They made the decision to stop at a truck stop restaurant at U.S. Route 59 and Farm to Market Road 1485 with an all-day breakfast menu. They left the restaurant before 9:00 p.m. and headed on their 28-mile journey home on Farm to Market Road 1485. After they had driven approximately 12 miles, they spotted a bright light in the distance that sparked their curiosity because of its luminosity and unusual appearance. Little did they know that soon they would round a curve and encounter a fiery craft hovering over the road near the tops of the pine trees. The ominous craft, only 130 or so feet in the distance, was belching flames. Betty made the split-second decision to brake rather than risk driving under the craft. Suddenly, the motor went dead and Betty could not remember if it had simply died or if she had turned it off. She and her passengers could now see that it was as large as a water tower, and possibly 60 to 80 feet above the road. It was surrounded by a glow that made it difficult to discern its shape. Vickie remembered an oblong shape with a rounded top and pointed bottom, whereas Colby recalled its diamond shape. All agreed that although it was only 40 degrees Fahrenheit, the craft's heat warmed the area. When it ascended, a red-orange flame shot out from its underside and when it stopped it emitted a sound similar to air brakes. In addition to this the trio heard a shrill beeping noise.

Vickie stood beside the passenger door with her hand on the roof of the vehicle, looking toward the strange object. She held her terrified grandson close, shielding him from the intense light and heat. Neither of the women held a prior belief in extraterrestrial visitation, so they relied upon their religious beliefs for an explanation. Vickie, a fervent Christian, believed that Jesus would emerge from the glowing object and told her hysterical grandson to look toward the dark part for Jesus. Less than five minutes after they stopped, Vickie began to fear that Colby might run into the woods to hide, so she pushed him under the dashboard and shielded him while she steadied herself on its soft, padded surface. Despite her curiosity, after a few moments Vickie gave in to Colby's incessant pleas to join him inside car.

Betty walked to the front of the car for a better view of the craft, shielding her eyes from the intense light with her upper arm. She could feel the heat radiating from the craft, but remained outside for five to seven minutes longer than Vickie and Colby. Finally, she conceded to Vickie's pleas to return to the safety of the vehicle, but as she attempted to enter her Oldsmobile, she discovered that the door handle was too warm to touch. She protected her hand with her leather coat and opened the driver's side door to discover that, despite the 40-degree outside temperature, the car's interior was uncomfortably hot.

Finally, the craft emitted a huge burst of flames and rose into the air, departing southwest in the direction of Houston's Intercontinental Airport. From a distance the witnesses could see helicopters streaming toward it. For the witnesses, the ordeal was over, they had survived, and it was safe to drive to their homes in Dayton. Little did they know that moments later, when Betty made a right-hand turn onto connector road FM 2100 toward FM 1960, they would again encounter the ominous craft. This time it was surrounded by up to 23 helicopters, some with dual rotors and some with single rotors. Cash thought that she saw a U.S. Air Force

151

insignia on one of the helicopters, but Landrum did not notice a marking. This time the trio sped toward the safety of their homes.

The events on the night of December 29, 1980, changed the course of their lives forever. Suddenly and nearly immediately after the encounter the three witnesses suffered a constellation of significant physical effects that could only be attributed to their exposure to the fiery aerial object. They had been in good health prior to their encounter, with the exception of Betty's hysterectomy in 1958 and heart surgery in 1976. She was under the care of a cardiologist, but had been enjoying excellent health and had ambitious plans for the future. She had never undergone chemotherapy or radiation treatments, nor did she exhibit evidence that she had ever been the victim of an electrical shock. Vickie's health had been good except that she was overweight. She too had undergone surgery for a hysterectomy 22 or 23 years earlier, but had not suffered complications. She had been caring for her grandson and working nights as a waitress.

When Betty Cash pulled into her driveway at 9:50 p.m., she had blisters and swelling on her head, face, back, and neck, and felt as if she was burning from the inside out. The skin under her ring that had been exposed to the craft's heat as she shielded her eyes was burned. The next day, she was too ill to care for herself. A blinding headache, extreme weakness, nausea, vomiting, and diarrhea overtook her. On January 2, 1981, she was admitted to Parkway Hospital in Houston, where her cardiologist Dr. V.B. Shenoy worked, and remained there for 12 days. Initially, she felt too apprehensive to tell her attending physician about her experience with the craft and how it had led to her injuries, out of fear that he would believe that she was delusional. She later told investigators that she was unrecognizable to her own family because of the swelling and weeping sores on her face and head. Her release from the hospital was short-lived. Her condition degraded and she was forced to spend an additional 15 days in treatment. This time she confessed the cause of her injuries to her medical team and was seen by an ophthalmologist, a radiologist, a neurologist, a doctor who performed an EEG, and a doctor who checked for heavy metal poisoning.

Mysteriously, some of the information pertaining to her condition vanished from her medical records. The results of her early blood tests completely disappeared from the hospital and could not be located even by her physician. As her health declined, her radiologists noted that her symptoms were somewhat typical of a person who had been exposed to whole-body radiation on a high level. The perplexing part was that the whole-body radiation victims at Hiroshima and Nagasaki had perished, but Betty didn't die, as had been predicted in textbook cases.

After Betty was released from the hospital, she was too ill to care for herself, so she went to live with her brother in Houston and later was cared for by her mother and sister in Fairfield, Alabama. Her doctor in Birmingham, Dr. Brian McClelland, had treated military personnel with radiation damage caused by radar systems. He stated that pulsed non-ionizing radiation can have an ionizing component that clouds the textbook explanation of radiation damage. He had seen it manifested in a variety of victims and perhaps this was the cause of Betty's demise. Whatever the cause, Betty was never able to lead a normal life again. Her injuries were permanent and debilitating.

Betty's medical records indicate that she experienced ongoing severe headache and nausea, abnormal redness of the skin, scarring and loss of pigmentation, eye inflammation, vomiting and diarrhea, swelling of her neck, loss of her fingernails on one hand, excessive hair loss and regrowth of a different texture, weight loss, and extreme fatigue. Her medical bills amounted to $10,000. This information became part of the supporting evidence that was submitted by attorney Peter Gersten to the U.S. District Court for the Southern District of Texas in case # H-84-348, a lawsuit against the United States of America. He argued that Betty had been exposed to radiation as the result of negligence and reckless misconduct when the military allowed an experimental aerial device to fly over

153

a publicly used road and come in to contact with her. He asked for 10 million dollars in punitive damages.

Vickie Landrum, who had less exposure to the craft than Betty, suffered general weakness, burns to a lesser degree, ongoing stomach pain, nausea, and diarrhea, eye inflammation and partial loss of vision, and partial hair loss and regrowth of a different texture that started six weeks after her exposure to the craft. She also suffered fingernail loss on the hand that rested on top of the car, loss of skin pigmentation in the area of her burns, and 24 pounds in weight loss. As is often the case with low-income families, her financial status precluded immediate access to medical care, so she treated her grandson and herself at their home. She stated that she had spoken with her family physician, but he had advised her that he didn't know how to treat her and her grandson's illness. Later, she spoke with Cash's physician in Houston, but did not receive medical treatment from him. When her vision began to fail she was forced to seek medical treatment from an eye doctor in Liberty. For this she had incurred approximately $600 to $700 in medical bills. Peter Gersten represented her in the lawsuit against the USA asking for five million dollars in punitive damages.

Young Colby, who'd been terrified and hysterical, had less exposure to the craft than his grandmother or Betty. Even so, he suffered from ongoing stomach pains and diarrhea, weight loss, eye inflammation, a small amount of hair loss on top of his head, an increase in tooth decay, anxiety, and nightmares. Like Betty and his grandmother, he suffered photosensitivity, burning easily when he was exposed to the sun. But his symptoms were not long-lasting. It was the emotional impact of the event that caused problems for Colby. He experienced nightmares and was fearful of helicopters, and when the event played out in the press his classmates at school teased him and called him a liar. This was indeed disconcerting for an innocent little boy who had suffered greatly from both physical and emotional scars. For this Peter Gersten requested five million dollars in punitive damages.

John Schuessler, the civilian investigator on the case, stated that Betty's new 1980 Oldsmobile Cutless had multiple electrical system problems after the event. Schuessler is a retired manager of flight operations for McDonnell Douglas at NASA and in 1981 became assistant director of the Mutual UFO Network. Later he assumed the role as MUFON's executive director and is a top notch investigator. He reported that the plastic material on the steering wheel had irritated Betty's hands when she drove, and soon began to crumble and fall off in large chunks, leaving the metal exposed. Investigators, in an attempt to find a prosaic explanation for the damage, searched for but could not find other Oldsmobile steering wheels, new or old, that exhibited this type of damage. The steering wheel was not the only part of the car's interior that was damaged. Vickie's handprints left permanent indentations on the padded, hot dashboard when she exerted pressure upon it as she leaned over Colby and looked up at the craft, waiting to see Jesus emerge. Schuessler reported a very unusual event that occurred when a film crew was training lights from the front of Cash's Oldsmobile toward the windshield in order to reenact the event as the three witnesses were seated inside the car. Although the lights were not projecting excessive heat toward the window, it shattered like it had been hit with a baseball bat, much to the film crew's surprise. Schuessler spoke with representatives at GMC, but they could not explain why the windshield had shattered.

Schuessler was aware of the case not long after it occurred and on January 26, 1981, spoke with a Houston area doctor who had consulted with Betty's doctors for an overview of the case. He received informal updates from the doctor until Betty was released from the hospital on February 9.

On February 16, Betty phoned the NASA Public Affairs Office and the Johnson Space Center in Houston to inquire about their ownership of helicopters. Because she mentioned her encounter with a UFO, she was referred to John Schuessler. On February 17, Vickie phoned Robert Gribble of the National UFO Reporting

Center in Seattle, Washington, to report the incident. On February, 22, Schuessler visited Betty and her mother, at her brother's home in Houston, to record her testimony and take photographs of her injuries. Six days later, he interrogated Vickie and Colby Landrum at their home. Betty had given him a release to speak with her attending physician, Dr. V.B. Shenoy, and his investigation into her medical condition began.

He discovered that there were CH-47s at Ellington AFB in South Houston and at the Dallas Naval Air Station. The Air Force denied that it had twin rotor helicopters or any involvement in the incident even though a photograph of one was featured in the August 17, 1982, issue of *The Houston Chronicle*. Shuessler's extensive investigation via military officers found that there were no civilian Chinooks flying in 1980. However, he was informed by Commanding Officer Major Dennis Haire of the 136th Transport Unit, a reserve group stationed at Ellington AFB Major, that eight Chinook helicopters in his unit were operated by the Army National Guard and an additional 16 were in Dallas. Additionally, there were four Hueys and four 58s assigned to Houston. Major Haire told Schuessler that helicopter pilots are very light sensitive at night and would avoid approaching a bright object such as the one described by Cash and Landrum because it would ruin their night vision. He stated that he was 99-percent certain that the CH-47s were not part of an operation on December 29, 1980.

A report by Schuessler titled "Cash-Landrum Case Investigation by U.S. Army Inspector General" states that on February 24, 1982, he received a call from Captain Jenny Lampley from the U.S. Air Force's Liaison Office in Washington, DC, stating that she had been assigned to determine if USAF helicopters had been involved in the Cash-Landrum case. This had come as the result of a congressional inquiry.

Lieutenant Colonel George Sarran from the Department of Army Inspector General's Office phoned the inspector general to inform him that Fort Hood had a number of twin rotor helicopters, but carried out its testing and operations at the Ft. Hood reservation. Ft. Hood, located between Waco and Austin, Texas, was within close reach of the Cash-Landrum sighting. However, the military denied having helicopters in the area that night. A long investigation ensued and on May 25, 1982, Colonel Sarran flew to Houston to investigate the case. John Schuessler met him at the airport and the two spent the day in interviews with all available witnesses.

It should be noted that Colonel Sarran did not have a top secret security clearance and was not able to gain access to information about highly classified operations. However, he would not have been able to reveal the truth had he known, because it would have been classified top secret. An investigation by Colonel Sarran concluded that a military operation was doubtful because it was Christmas week and most military installations allow most of the troops to go home for the holiday.

The Vehicle Internal Systems Investigative Team, a scientific research organization comprised of NASA aerospace engineers, tested the veracity of the military's denial of operations during Christmas week by watching for helicopter operations in the Houston area on weeknights during the Christmas holiday. On Tuesday, December 28, 1982, CH-47 Chinook helicopters with Army markings were observed at 3:01 p.m. landing at Ellington AFB and at 6:19 p.m., 6:41 p.m., and 7:19 p/m/ flying out of Ellington AFB. Later flights were mixed with F-4 Phantom flights until after 9:30 p.m.

Senators Lloyd Bentson and John Tower had urged Betty and Vickie to file a claim with the Judge Advocates Claims Office. They met with personnel at Bergstom Air Force Base, where they were interrogated, to file their claim on August 17, 1981. Vickie Landrum told representatives that she had attended an "Aircraft Day" event and spoke to the military representative (Chief Warrant Officer Willie Culberson) by a landed Army National Guard CH-47 Chinook helicopter about helicopter activity on the night of her event. According to Landrum's statement, the officer informed her that the Montgomery County sheriff's department had called the

Army Air National Guard on the night of December 29, 1980. She added that others had denied that they had been notified. An interview with Warrant Officer Culberson by Colonel Sarran confirmed Landrum's statement, but Culberson stated that they were "just talking."[2] He had not taken part in a mission on the night in question and did not know of anyone else who took part in a helicopter operation that night. He stated that when he was pushed for additional details he refused to comply due to reasons of national security. Major Haire countered Culberson's statement by saying their unit could not legally respond to an emergency called by a sheriff, adding that this might not apply to an Army Reserve Unit such as the one located at Tomball, northwest of Houston. On the day that Schuessler and Colonel Sarran visited the Montgomery County sheriff's department they discovered that all personnel had been replaced on January 2, 1981, only three days after the Cash-Landrum event. They were not able to speak with any of the people working there on the night of the event, but were informed that it was not standard procedure for the sheriff's department to call the Army Air National Guard.

The investigation brought out other witnesses who observed helicopters flying on the night of the Cash-Landrum sighting. Police officer Lamar Walker and his wife had observed three groups of three Chinook helicopters flying in V-formation within 5 miles of the sighting on the night of the incident, and an additional group behind the others, approximately three hours after the Cash-Landrum sighting. They were flying lower than usual and the lead helicopter of each group was shining a spotlight on the ground as if it was searching for something. Law enforcement officers that he discussed his sighting with speculated that the helicopters were part of a Quick React Force that operated in both Louisiana and Texas. However, Colonel Sarran denied the presence of a Quick React Force in the Texas–Louisiana area, stating that only Ft. Bragg, North Carolina, Ft. Devens, Massachusetts, Panama, and Europe had Quick React Force units.

Bill English, the first investigator from the Aerial Phenomena Research Organization, stated that he found three additional witnesses to the unidentified object that night. But only one of the three was willing to take the risk of stepping forward with testimony. The other two feared the negative consequences that publicity might cause them. English sold his story to a tabloid and was expelled from APRO for violating confidentiality.

Nearly eight months after the Cash-Landrum event occurred, two men from the Texas Department of Health surveyed both sides of roads FM 1485 and FM 1960 in a 7.2-mile stretch of the area where the aerial vehicle was observed. Using a Ludum 14-C and an NA I probe they tested for radioactive material but found nothing above background levels. Three soil samples were collected but were negative for radioactivity. The Texas Department of Health's report states that the question of whether the trio had been exposed to a source of sealed radiation could only be determined from clinical findings. John R. Haygood, administrator for the Texas Department of Health, stated that gamma rays or x-rays from a source or machine would leave no indication of radiation, but loose contamination might be found in the soil.

Dr. Richard C. Niemtzow, an Air Force radiation oncologist and former medical consultant to APRO and MUFON, contacted Philip Klass on January 10, 1982, to inform him of a proposed panel of specialists to consider the Cash-Landrum radiation case. Although Klass had not visited the site of the event or interviewed any of the witnesses he stated that he and two of his cohorts, Robert Sheaffer, vice-chairman of CSICOP's UFO Subcommittee, and Dr. Gary Posner, a young internist from Florida and member of CSICOP's UFO Subcommittee, should comprise half the panel. He believed it would give balance to John Schuessler, who had actually done an outstanding investigation, and the two radiologists, Dr. Peter Rank, who had reviewed Betty Cash's medical records and had spoken to Betty's physician, and Dr. Niemtzow. The idea that biased naysayers would contribute anything productive to a panel of specialists seems ludicrous to this book's authors. Schuessler informed us that Klass had repeatedly attempted to obstruct the investigation, stating that Klass never did an investigation of the case except from his arm chair. However, he often threw out suggestions that created problems and contributed to the level of misinformation in the literature.

Klass contacted Dr. Peter Rank, director of the department of radiology at Methodist Hospital in Madison, Wisconsin, a consultant to MUFON on the case, to request copies of Betty Cash's confidential medical records. Dr. Rank informed Klass that he was bound ethically and legally with respect to a patient's right to privacy and could not release the medical reports to him without consent. He stressed that he was concerned over the amount of personal and sometimes-embarrassing information that reached the media in UFO cases and did not want to be a party to it. Klass then attempted to trick Rank into releasing Betty's medical information by requesting a probability ratio on the chance that her injury had a prosaic cause versus an extraterrestrial or nuclear device cause. But Dr. Rank did not fall for the ruse. He explained to Klass that he was bound both ethically and legally to respect a patient's right to privacy, without exceptions. He wrote, "I would not begin to comment on the pre-incident medical condition of either Betty Cash or Vickie Landrum, nor will I comment on their hospital care, nor will I comment on their post hospitalization condition."[3] In the next paragraph he added:

> Again, I must say it would be unethical for me to transmit any medical information to an interested third party, regardless of their journalistic or other credentials.... I do not agree with the philosophy currently among people who style themselves as Ufologists, of transmitting personal information about the informants or witnesses, and I have no sympathy for the journalistic model under which you are laboring. There is no doubt that we have caused many citizens a great deal of inconvenience, embarrassment,

and harassment by going public with names and private details of their lives as they relate to the entire UFO question. I will not be a party to this in any way.[4]

It appears that Klass was furious with Rank's comments and his refusal to submit probability ratios with regard to Betty's medical condition. He retorted that Betty Cash and Vickie Landrum had forfeited their right to privacy and anonymity when they allowed themselves to be interviewed by UFO investigators. Not so. MUFON respects the individual's right to anonymity and privacy unless the witness requests that their information be open to the public. Klass had no legal right to confidential medical information.

When it became clear to Klass that Dr. Rank would not violate medical ethics, he requested assistance from his associate at CSICOP, Dr. Gary Posner. Dr. Posner told Dr. Rank that Dr. Niemtzow had hoped that he would release enough medical data for a panel of scientists to evaluate the case. Dr. Posner stated, "Although the principals have not specifically authorized you to go public with details of the case, they certainly have done so in their own way."[5] He was referring to ABC's *That's Incredible* show that aired on April 1, 1982. Betty and Vickie had agreed to appear on the show in an attempt to elicit more interest from the government and scientists. Dr. Posner stated that it reinforced his skepticism with regard to the reality of the case.

He quoted several textbooks symptoms of radiation poisoning that did not seem to fit the text book expectations. As was stated earlier, Dr. Rank and others were aware of this and knew there were variables when one experiences radiation poisoning. Not everyone responds in precisely the same manner. Dr. Rank knew that the type of injury reported could have been caused by ultra-violet, infrared, low energy x-ray or particulate radiation and was not necessarily the type of whole-body ionizing radiation that had killed so many in Hiroshima and Nagasaki. But the young internist thought he had a more reasonable explanation. He stated that the photographs of Betty's skin lesions were suspicious because they should not have been "discrete, round, coin sized macules."[6] He could only imagine a burn having such an appearance if the limb had been covered with a template and burned with a UV light, thus setting up CSICOP's final conclusion that Betty had induced her own injuries in order to perpetrate a hoax.

Dr. Rank replied that dermal lesions following irradiation could persist for long periods of time after exposure, depending on many factors. In a follow-up letter he advised Dr. Posner that his assumption that Betty and Vickie had been exposed to a whole-body dose of radiation is based upon insufficient information. But it is clear that their symptoms and signs are consistent with exposure to ionizing radiation. Hair loss could occur anywhere from a few days to up to a year. Diarrhea can persist for days or weeks. Dermatologic symptoms can be acute, chronic or a mixture of both and radiation dermatitis can result in non-healing ulcerative lesions. He urged Posner to familiarize himself with the diversity of radiologic symptoms and recommended a medical book that would provide additional information on the topic.

Posner reported to Klass that Rank had given him a vague response to his questions and had obviously made up his mind in favor of radiation exposure. He simply could not understand how part of a body could be exposed to more radiation than another part. The reasons for the uneven exposure are stated in this chapter.

Philip Klass proclaimed the Cash-Landrum incident a hoax. He based his conclusion on the fact that the military had denied the presence of an experimental craft or an operation involving helicopters on the night of the event. He ignored all evidence that did not support his negative assessment of the case, and assailed the character of Betty Cash, Vickie Landrum, and Colby Landrum, assuming that they had lied about their experience and burned themselves. Posner and Sheaffer stated that the burns on Betty Cash's arms were not consistent with radiation burn patterns, but were consistent with burns that had been created by placing a template on her arms and intentionally burning them in order to impress her doctors. He does not mention how Vickie Landrum and her grandson sustained similar burns. Today, Sheaffer states on his blog "Bad UFOs" that it seems likely Betty Cash's medical records contained the words "Munchausen syndrome." Does he also believe that Vickie burned her own flesh and then inflicted wounds upon her grandson? This would have been a criminal act. A preposterous explanation such as this is not only slanderous, it is an affront to scientific investigation. CSICOP's well-known reputation for extreme bias and ad hominem attacks upon witnesses and investigators worked against them in this case. Physicians protected the victims from the abuse that would surely have been heaped upon them. It is unfortunate that Betty, who suffered greatly from her injuries, was accused of having a psychiatric illness that led to her debilitating condition.

In contrast to this, Lieutenant Colonel George Sarran conducted an investigation on site in Texas. He interviewed John Schuessler, Vickie Landrum, Betty Cash via the telephone, and doctors Rank and Niemtzow, who were in other locations. Of the victim's health he wrote, "The medical evidence of deterioration of health is almost irrefutable...."[7] Further, he assessed Cash, Landrum, and police officer Lamar Walker and his wife as credible witnesses.

In contrast to CSICOP's investigation, John Schuessler's MUFON investigation involved up to seven people, all of them experts in their fields. As the investigation progressed, they discovered that some of their early assumptions were erroneous, so they refined them as they went along and acquired more information and evidence. They held brainstorming sessions periodically to plan the next steps in their investigation, all in an effort to acquire all of the evidence possible through unbiased investigation. In all, Schuessler collected nearly 15,000 pages of records on the case, including hours of taped interviews and the victim's medical reports from various hospitals. He stated that his team ran down leads and suggestions given to them by "arm chair investigators", but most of leads were based upon "useless speculation." The team wasted a lot of time on these useless "leads," but in the end it became part of the record.[8]

Sarasota, Florida's *Herald Tribune* journalist Billy Cox wrote that he had faced a reality check when Klass informed him that Cash, Landrum, and others had perpetrated a hoax. He said Klass was a go-to journalist whenever he and his colleagues had to write about UFOs and referred to him as "Mr. Insider, the establishment's sensible 'reality check' authority you could always count on for balance. Klass never met a UFO he couldn't explain."[9] He knew that Klass's allegations of a hoax were false because he had traveled to Texas and investigated the case himself. His interviews with Cash, Landrum, and the other witnesses who had observed the helicopters that escorted the UFO on the night of December 29, 1980, and the medical records that Cash and Landrum had authorized MUFON's John Schuessler to release to him convinced him that a very real and tragic event had occurred. He wrote of Klass's discussion of the Cash-Landrum incident, "I got the first queasy feeling that the American press was routinely quoting a man who had a pathological disregard for the truth...one thing we'll never know is the full extent of the damage Phil Klass did to American Journalism's trepid inquiry into The Great Taboo. The first word that comes to mind: Irreparable."[10]

In January 1984, attorney and president of Citizens Against UFO Secrecy Peter Gersten represented Cash, Landrum, and Landrum in a civil suit against the United States of America in case number H-84-348. The case was dismissed on August 21, 1986, because the Colonel William E. Krebs, chief of the Tactical Aeronautical Systems Division at Air Force Systems Command, declared that no such craft as described by the plaintiffs was owned, operated, or in the inventory of the U.S. Air Force on December 29, 1980, nor was the U.S. Air Force in possession of a CH-47 Helicopter. The acting chief of Aviation Systems Division, Richard L. Ballard from the Office of the Deputy Chief of Staff for Research, Development and Acquisition for the U.S. Army, declared that no craft meeting the plaintiffs' description was owned, operated, or in the inventory of the U.S. Army on or about December 29, 1980. Federal Judge Ross Sterling dismissed the case on August 21, 1986, stating that the plaintiffs had failed to prove that the U.S. government was in possession of the CH-47 helicopters on December 29, 1980, or that the U.S. government was in possession of the diamond-shaped craft they described.

Betty Cash died on December 29, 1998, exactly 18 years after her exposure to an unknown craft that forever changed her life. Vickie Landrum passed on September 12, 2007. Colby Landrum has not suffered long-term physiological effects from his exposure to the craft. The origin of the craft that irreparably damaged Betty Cash and wreaked havoc with the lives of Vickie Landrum and her young grandson remains unknown.

CHAPTER 9

FRAUDULENT CLAIMS BY SCIENTISTS, WHISTLEBLOWERS, AND SELF-PROMOTING CONTACTEES

One of the major difficulties for anyone seriously attempting to get to the bottom of the UFO question is trying to determine the validity of the claims being made by both proponents and opponents. So much of what has been claimed seems to be by proclamation rather than as a result of investigations, epitomizing the notion of "Don't bother me with the facts; my mind is made up." Particularly galling is the fact that many of these claims are made by professional scientists. One would expect them to know better. A typical foolish and completely unsubstantiated claim was made by British astronomer Royal Lord Martin Rees, who in September 2012 loudly proclaimed that "Only kooks see UFOs."[1] No reference is given for this absurd statement.

In Blue Book Special Report 14, the better the quality of the sighting (as evaluated by four Battelle Memorial Institute scientists under U.S. Air Force Contract), the more likely to be unidentifiable. Of the highest quality cases, 35 percent were listed as UNKNOWNS. Of the poorest only 15 percent were UNKNOWNS. Dr. Peter Sturrock, a Stanford University astrophysicist, in his book *The UFO Enigma*, gives results of surveys of the American Astronomical Society membership as well as the San Francisco area–based section of the American Institute of Aeronautics and Astronautics. There were plenty of sightings by astronomers. We presume Dr. Rees doesn't think astronomers are kooks. Dr. J. Allen Hynek, then-chairman of the astronomy department of Northwestern University, noted sightings by astronomers in his book *The UFO Experience*.

There have been loads of sightings by military and airline pilots as reported not only to the old USAF Project Blue Book, but also to NARCAP (National Aviation Reporting Center for Anomalous Phenomena).We presume that Lord Rees doesn't consider professional pilots to be kooks. Gert Herb reported on a survey of 1,805 amateur astronomers who were members of the American Astronomers League. Twenty-three-point-nine percent claimed to have seen a UFO. It should be stressed that normally amateur astronomers spend a great deal of time outdoors looking at the sky and often using small telescopes. Most professionals are normally indoors and use sophisticated instruments looking at preselected targets and not a having a wide view of the sky. Friedman has checked hundreds of times after his lectures and found that 10 percent of the attendees believe they have seen a UFO, but 90 percent didn't report what they saw because of fear of ridicule. Rees, of course, provided no basis for his claim.

Often we have heard that there is only anecdotal data. The definition of anecdote is "a brief story of an interesting, amusing or biographical incident."[2] The famous RB-47 incident on July 17, 1957, involved six highly trained crewmembers of an USAF RB-47 Reconnaissance Bomber flying over the Gulf of Mexico and then

Texas and Oklahoma. They observed the UFO visually and with their radar. They received radio signals from it. It was also observed simultaneously by a ground-based military radar crew. The observations lasted for an hour and were described in detail by Dr. James E. McDonald, an atmospheric physicist at the University of Arizona.[3] He spoke with all six of the crew members. Friedman noted this case during a visit with Dr. Carl Sagan. Carl's first comment was that that it was probably "spoofing." This involves electronically creating a target on a radar screen even though no target is physically present. When informed that it was seen visually by all the crew, he said he would have to review it. There was no further contact about the case.

A major objection is that ET visitors would have to travel vast distances and it would take too long and too much energy. Some astrophysicists have also suggested visitors would, for reasons unknown, even have to come from stars in other galaxies. Andromeda is more than 2 million light years (LY) away. But the Milky Way is only 100,000 light years across and about 15,000 light years thick, a big spiral pancake having perhaps 200 billion stars. But it makes no sense to worry about aliens coming from "distant" stars. The nearest star to the sun, Alpha Centauri, is only about 4.3 LY away. Within 50 LY there are more than 1,000 stars. Or about 10,000 stars within 100 LY. The stars are *not* uniformly distributed in space. The general consensus these days based on the detailed measurements made by the remarkable Kepler satellite, is that on the average there is about one planet per star. Some stars like our sun have around nine planets (Pluto is still being argued about). Others have none. Also some stars have next-door neighbors. The base stars in the Betty Hill Star map are Zeta 1 and Zeta 2 Reticuli in the Southern sky constellation of Reticulum. They are only 39.3 LY from the sun and, much more interesting, they are only about an eighth of a light year apart from each other, or more than 35 times as close to each other as the sun is to Alpha Centauri. They do not form a double star orbiting closely around each other. This means that from a planet around one, the other star is visible all day long and that it would be far easier for one to travel to the other than for us to travel to Alpha Centauri. Also it would be much easier to determine the characteristics of the planet or planets around the other. In addition the likelihood of developing interstellar travel soon would be enhanced the closer one's neighbors are. Some have suggested using Kepler to find out more. Sorry, that cannot be done. Its orbit allows it only to observe a small portion of the Northern sky about the size of a fist at arm's length.

Some have already claimed they aimed their radio telescopes (in the Southern Hemisphere) at Reticulum and haven't received a signal, so there must be no one there! Of course SETI specialists have so far not found any signal indicating an intelligence sent it. On the other hand, it seems extremely unlikely that intelligent beings out there have no better technology than we do. Our first long-distance radio signal was only sent in 1901. The earth is 4+ billion years old. So it seems very unlikely that nobody got started sending or listening until we did. SETI personnel make stronger statements than that. Dr. Seth Shostak, in his book *Confessions of an Alien Hunter* says, "Consider that the closest extraterrestrial society to us is probably hundreds of light years distant."[4] What an incredible statement! We have no data yet on where there are any ET societies. One needs data of which we have none about ET civilizations, but we do know that there are probably more than 10,000 planets within 100 light years. What possible justification is there for saying there is only one within hundreds of light years? There certainly has been plenty of time for a civilization to have been colonizing and migrating for a mere million years, no less a billion. There are certainly cities thriving on earth now where there were none 500, no less 1,000, years ago. Think Las Vegas, Los Angeles, or Sydney, or San Francisco.

Shostak then says, "If alien rockets are no better than our own, than their time to arrive at Roswell or some similarly glamorous destination is millions of years."[5] It takes real chutzpah to suggest alien rockets are no better than ours, and to denigrate Roswell. It was, after all, at that time (1947) the only base on Earth to have nuclear weapons and was not far from White Sands Proving Ground,

Stanton Friedman and Seth Shostak

where powerful rockets were being tested. Presumably both would be of interest to ET visitors, if not to SETI specialists. Yuri Gagarin made man's first space flight in 1961. Less than 60 years later more than 500 Earthlings have orbited the planet. In short, once space travel gets going, it seems to blossom rapidly. The basic rule for technology is that progress comes from doing things differently in an unpredictable way. Look at traveling around the Earth. Magellan's sailing vessel took roughly three years to circumnavigate the earth, arriving home in 1522. The space station takes about 95 minutes in 2015. Submarines during World War II could stay underwater for only about a day because their diesel engines needed air. Nuclear submarines can travel around the planet underwater. The Triton nuclear-powered submarine was there first and went around the world entirely underwater in 60 days ending in April 1960.

171

Shostak compounds his ignorance of space flight by then saying correctly that "[c]hemical rockets are entirely inadequate for such velocities."[6] Of course. And most engineers don't use slide rules any more, and we don't build TV sets with vacuum tubes anymore, either. "Nuclear fission or fusion rockets seem marginal as well."[7] It is very dubious that Shostak knows anything at all about either fission or fusion rockets. He certainly doesn't mention the three powerful nuclear rocket engines ground tested at the nuclear test site outside Las Vegas in the 1960s. They were built by Aerojet General of Sacramento, by Westinghouse Astronuclear Lab of Pittsburgh, and by Los Alamos National Laboratory of Los Alamos, New Mexico. The power levels were 1000 Megawatts, 1100 MW, and 4400 MW, respectively. The exhaust temperatures for the hydrogen, which cooled the reactors, were all in excess of 4,000 degrees F., and all the cylindrical reactors were less than 8 feet in diameter. For comparison, the Hoover Dam produces only 2200 MW and is much larger. Friedman worked at Westinghouse on the NRX A-6. He also worked earlier at Aerojet General Nucleonics of San Ramon, California, in 1962 on a small, nine-million-dollar study for the USAF on fusion propulsion for deep space travel. Using the right isotopes, one can exhaust charged particles having 10 million times as much energy per particle as in a chemical rocket. Our first fusion weapon, the H-bomb (in 1952), produced as much energy as would be produced by exploding 10 million tons of TNT. The Soviets largest fusion device later released the energy of 57 million tons of TNT. Because nuclear fusion produces almost all the energy produced in the galaxy by the stars, every advanced civilization will get around to fusion. The AGN study was done under the direction of Dr. John Luce, who had directed the Oak Ridge National Laboratory fusion work in the 1950s.

One objection to fusion rockets is the simple fact that we haven't yet successfully operated a fusion power plant on Earth. There are several good reasons. One is that the fusion process requires a vacuum. Outer space provides one with no effort. A second is that in terms of producing electrical power so vital for our civilization, several different techniques have had major development. These obviously include burning coal, oil, and natural gas. We have been able to build and safely operate hundreds of nuclear fission power plants. We have solar and wind power plants as well as many hydroelectric plants. Most important, there is no question that developing a star-faring nuclear fusion rocket would be very expensive and at the moment would not seem to be a realistic goal for planet Earth with all its battles. Back in 1958 the U.S. Air Force and Atomic Energy Commission spent 100 million dollars on an early attempt at developing an Aircraft Nuclear Propulsion system. The General Electric Aircraft Nuclear Propulsion Department in 1958 employed 3,500 people, of whom 1,100 were engineers and scientists. Much research was done, but no nuclear powered airplane was built. The military budget in 2015 was roughly a trillion dollars. It will be sometime before a major fusion propulsion research and development program can be justified.

Anti-UFO groups frequently try to show that only kooks and quacks believe in the reality of flying saucers. Arch debunker and disinformant Philip Klass falsely claimed in his book *UFOs Identified* that the ratio of believers to nonbelievers in flying saucers was one to 11. Better numbers would be three to two, or four to one. There have been a host of opinion polls conducted over the years. All recent ones show that there are more believers than nonbelievers. But the debunkers continue to claim falsely that only a small percentage of people believe Earth is being visited. There is an entire chapter on the results of polls about UFOs in Friedman's *Flying Saucers and Science* (2008). Another aspect of the UFO problem that is often discussed is with regard to the ability of governments to keep secrets. Even Ted Koppel, when hosting *Nightline* on ABC TV (June 24, 1987) and talking to guests Stanton Friedman and Philip Klass, indicated that Washington was notoriously leaky when it came to keeping secrets. The facts are very different. The NSA before 1985 released 156 pages of TOP SECRET UMBRA UFO documents on which one can read one sentence per page. Everything else was whited out. The CIA released dozens of pages of TOP SECRET

UMBRA CIA UFO documents with almost everything blacked out. Unexpurgated pages have not been released. The media seems totally uninterested in trying to open these files. Friedman had copies of many of these highly redacted pages with him but was not allowed to bring them into the studio! Strange as it might sound, he and Klass were sitting two feet apart but were told to look only at their cameras, not at each other. Koppel, who was in another room, could only be heard through an earplug and could not be seen.

The expensive and extensive Corona spy satellite project, which obtained all kinds of data about Russian military installations (after 12 failures), was kept secret for 30 years. The breaking of the German and Japanese military codes at the beginning of World War II was fortunately kept secret for 25 years after the war ended, though 12,000 people had worked at Bletchley Park in England intercepting, decoding, translating, and very carefully distributing the TOP Secret German military communications. None of them spoke out. The Stealth aircraft program of Lockheed spent 10 billion dollars in secret over 10 years. The *Washington Post* admitted three years ago that the US Military Intelligence Budget was 52.6 billion dollars that year (NSA, CIA, NRO). Surely very little of that information was open to the public. Furthermore, the spy satellites and radar installations are owned and operated by the government. Their information is not available in the published scientific literature, nor to the media. Both communities seem to falsely believe that no secrets can be kept from them.

More fiction in the guise of scientific "fact" was presented by Dr. Don Lincoln in his book *Alien Universe: Extraterrestrial Life in Our Minds and in the Cosmos.* He is a senior scientist employed by the very prestigious Fermi Laboratory outside Chicago. He is also affiliated with the Large Hadron Collider in Switzerland and has published 500 scientific papers, some even dealing with the Higgs Boson. One might reasonably expect a scientific approach to the question of alien life. Unfortunately, although he seems very knowledgeable about the aliens of science fiction movies, TV shows, and various books of fiction, he has not done his homework on flying saucers in the real world. Ostensibly his purpose is to convince his readers that there is really nothing to flying saucers, but that the world has been influenced to think so by all the fiction. He has apparently not read any of the more than 10 PhD theses done about UFOs, nor studied the several large scale scientific studies that one might have hoped would be the basis for his conclusion about the unreality of alien visitations.

The UFO section of his "Suggested Reading List" offers only 13 titles, three by contactee George Adamski and one by ancient astronaut expert Eric von Daniken. We should probably be pleased that he included our book *Captured! The Betty and Barney Hill UFO Experience*. He also lists John Fullers's *The Interrupted Journey* and *The Roswell Incident* by Charles Berlitz and William Moore. Judging by the gross inaccuracy in his discussion of both the Hill case and the Roswell Incident, we seriously doubt that he really read either. He does mention *The UFO Experience* by astronomer and UFO researcher Dr. J. Allen Hynek. He doesn't mention that he was the scientific consultant on UFOs to the USAF Project Blue Book for more than 18 years and was chairman of the astronomy department at Northwestern University. He notes that Hynek defines Close Encounters of the First, Second, and Third kind, but says nothing about any of the 70 cases he covers in his book.

There is no mention of *The Scientific Report on Unidentified Flying Objects*. The study was done at the University of Colorado under noted physicist Dr. Edward U. Condon, at a cost to the taxpayers of $539,000. Of course there was no mention of the fact a special UFO subcommittee of the American Institute of Aeronautics and Astronautics found that 30 percent of the 117 cases studied in detail could not be identified. Lincoln makes no mention of the congressional hearings of July 29, 1968. The 247-page proceedings included the testimony of 12 scientists. All but Friedman had a PhD. We think the most important paper was the one presented by Dr. James E. McDonald, an atmospheric physicist and physics professor at the University of Arizona. He detailed his investigations of the top 41 cases of the more than 500 he had looked into. These included reports by pilots, radar operators, astronomers, and meteorologists. As one might expect from the above, Lincoln makes no mention of the largest scientific study of UFOs ever done for the USAF "Project Blue Book Special Report No. 14." It has more than 200 charts, tables, graphs, maps, and quality evaluations. One would think, wrongly, that the fact that 21.5 percent of the 3,201 sightings investigated by professional scientists at the Battelle Memorial Institute could not be explained, would be considered important especially because they were completely separate from the 9.3 percent listed as Insufficient Information. With the Hill case and the Roswell Incident he ignores the facts and really botches the discussion of them.

Here is how he summarizes Roswell:

A UFO crashed outside Roswell, New Mexico. Government agents generally known as "The Men in Black" swooped into town and confiscated the flying saucer and the saucer's occupants which included actual aliens. The saucer and the aliens were transported to Area 51. One or more of the aliens died and subsequently an autopsy was performed. A film of the autopsy was leaked in 1995 and shown on Fox TV. This most famous of alien reports has been the obsession of UFO enthusiasts for more than 60 years.[8]

As with so much of his verbiage, he provides no sources for his outrageous claims, and they are almost all nonsense. "Men in Black" certainly wasn't used at the time of Roswell (1947) or for years thereafter. The military personnel at Roswell did all the handling. They just happened to be the 509th Composite Bomb Group, the most elite military group in the world, having dropped the atomic Bombs on Hiroshima and Nagasaki in 1945, and two more during

Operation Crossroads in 1946. Area 51 wasn't built until years later. Friedman was in the Fox Network show about the alien autopsy and denigrated it after having talked twice in person to Ray Santilli, who sold the phony footage to Fox. There were no UFO enthusiasts back then and the word *UFO* was actually not in use until years later. There was brief interest in Roswell in early July 1947, until the USAF explained it away as a radar reflector-weather balloon combination within a day. Almost nothing more was said about Roswell until the Berlitz book in 1980, to which Friedman was a major contributor.

Then Lincoln changes his story and says: "Here is what really happened. An unnamed rancher [Mac Brazel's name was noted from the start and his picture was even in the *Roswell Daily Record*] notified the local sheriff that he had an instrument on his premises. A major from the local Roswell Army Air Field took a detail of soldiers to the ranch and recovered the disk."[9] Of course Lincoln doesn't give the name of Major Jesse Marcel, nor note that he was the Intelligence Officer for the 509th, nor that the commander was Colonel William Blanchard, who went on to become a four-star general and was vice chief of staff for the USAF when he died of a massive heart attack at the Pentagon in 1966. There was no detail of soldiers, just Major Marcel and Captain Sheridan Cavitt of the Counter Intelligence Corps at the 509th. All of this is spelled out in detail in several books, including Friedman's book with aviation writer Don Berliner, *Crash at Corona: The Definitive Study of the Roswell Incident*. Lincoln mentioned the book but apparently couldn't be bothered reading it, though he quotes one paragraph. Then he makes more absurd comments:

> Things got really interesting in 1989 when the TV show "Unsolved Mysteries" devoted an episode that "reconstructed" what was supposed to have happened. That prompted a mortician from Roswell to contact Stanton Friedman and tell his story. The outcome of the subsequent interview was published in the 1991 book *UFO Crash*

at Roswell in which the now well-known story came into existence, alien bodies recovered, aliens walking around, small coffins, an army colonel making death threats, the disappearance of a nurse who knew too much, a dramatic series of events that make for an excellent story.[10]

What balderdash!! Friedman was the scientist who had instigated the *Unsolved Mysteries* program seen by 27 million people the first time around. He had earlier obtained mortician Glenn Dennis's name from Lieutenant Walter Haut, an outstanding WWII bombardier and the base PR person who had issued the July 8, 1947, press release at the direct order of Colonel Blanchard.

Friedman had called Glenn Dennis, who had indicated there were some things he had not spoken of. Friedman sent him information about his professional background as an industrial nuclear physicist working on various classified advanced nuclear and space systems. When Friedman was flown to Roswell for the *Unsolved Mysteries* filming, he called Glenn who agreed to speak with him out in Lincoln, New Mexico, where Glenn was hosting at the hotel celebrating Billy the Kid Day. Another former 509th Officer, Robert Shirkey, drove Friedman to the hotel dining room, where he taped a long interview while a Mariachi band was playing in the background. Friedman met with Dennis on several occasions and even visited him at the Baird Funeral Home in Roswell where he had worked. There was no talk of aliens walking around or death threats. Glenn hadn't called Friedman.

Dr. Lincoln is equally cavalier in his treatment of the Betty and Barney Hill case. He refers to John Fuller's book *The Interrupted Journey* and to Marden and Friedman's book *Captured! The Betty and Barney Hill UFO Experience*. He calls Friedman "an avid ufologist." No mention of "nuclear physicist." He mentions the *UFO Incident* on TV, starring James Earl Jones as Barney. He doesn't mention that Kathleen Marden was Betty's niece and her first hearing of the case the day after it happened. He doesn't mention her comparative analysis of what Betty and Barney each said under hypnosis. Nor does he mention the fact that Marden conducted an extensive investigation in an attempt to debunk the alleged abduction. It is clear that significant details in their descriptions of the event matched, but did not match Betty's dreams. Again we get the clear impression that he didn't read the book. He grossly misrepresents Marjorie Fish's star map work, saying:

> In 1968 amateur astronomer Marjorie Fish read *The Interrupted Journey* and was interested in the star map. Over a period of 5 years she made a three dimensional model of stars near earth using beads and string. She even visited Betty Hill in the summer of 1969 (Barney having died earlier that year) to get as much information as possible. When the model was completed, she walked around the model with Betty's map in her hand. She finally found an angle that seemed to match. She concluded that the aliens had come from Zeta Reticuli 1 as it is a binary star system.[11]

Once again we have balderdash! Marjorie built 23 different 3D models, not just one, each involving tedious computation of star coordinates, which she had to copy from various star catalogs at the Ohio State University Library. Her largest model had 256 stars in it. Lincoln might have mentioned the 10-page chapter about the star map in *Captured*, or the testimony of how accurate her work was by Dr. Mitchell, chairman of the OSU astronomy department and noted in the DVD *UFOs ARE Real*, or by Dr. David Saunders, who was able to use a computerized star catalog and also verified her accuracy. Lincoln didn't mention that Ms. Fish was a member of Mensa and had become a technician at Oak Ridge National Laboratory, where she worked for many years.

Dr. Lincoln is clearly unaware of how easy it is for government agencies to keep secrets. He says, "This being the 21st century, secrets are impossible to hide and a Facebook or Blog Post is made, the press gets wind of the story and people are told."[12] Does he really believe that classified information is routinely put on Facebook or in blogs?! Perhaps he can tell us what is under all the whiteout on the 156 TOP SECRET UMBRA NSA UFO pages that were obtained via a Freedom of Information Act (FOIA) legal action on which one can read only one sentence per page, or what is on the dozens of pages of highly redacted CIA UFO documents on which only a few words per page can be read? It is easy to understand how government agencies can so easily cover up so much when top scientists and journalists are so ignorant about how security works. He also just can't imagine aliens being humanoid, or visiting, or governments keeping secrets—surely a splendid example of naiveté.

Another questionable claim about aliens was very recently put forward by one of the best-known astrophysicists, Dr. Michio Kaku. He is a professor at City University of New York. He is a co-founder of string theory and has had the courage to get involved in public discussion of UFOs. He interviewed Friedman on his radio talk show and was with him in Riyadh, Saudi Arabia, in January 2011, at the fifth annual Global Competiveness Forum talking about UFOs where each participant spoke as did Dr. Jacques Vallee, Nick Pope, and an Arab scholar. He was also one of the few bright spots in the Peter Jennings ABC mockumentary of February 24, 2005. There was an interesting post from him on the Internet on November 4, 2015, on "Why Aliens May Exist, but Aren't Landing on the White House Lawn." He was talking of some measurements with the Allen Radio Telescope Array in California suggesting there might be a large artifact around Star number K1C8462852.

His comment (from *The Observer*) was:

> Some people say if there are intelligent life forms out there, and I think there are, how come they don't visit us? Why don't they land on the White House Lawn, announce their presence and give us their technology? Well, if you

are walking down a country road and you see an anthill, do you go down to the ants and say I bring you gifts, I bring you trinkets, beads. I bring you nuclear energy, take me to your ant queen? Or do we have this strange urge to step on a few of them? If aliens are so advanced that they can land on the White House Lawn, then we are like ants to them, we have nothing to offer them so the reason that they don't announce their existence to us is that we are boring, they have seen it all. We have nothing to offer a civilization that advanced and that's why I think they don't visit us. We are arrogant to think that we are so interesting, extraterrestrial beings would travel thousands of light years just to visit us. So that's why they don't visit us, we're just not that interesting.[13]

We beg to differ on several levels. In the first place, the White House is in a "no fly" zone guarded by radar monitoring the sky and linked to interceptors and anti-aircraft rockets, ready to shoot down any intruders. Remember that there were a large number of UFO sightings including radar visual cases over Washington in the summer of 1952. In the second place, we are convinced that a major concern of all governments (national or galactic) is to protect their inhabitants from being attacked by hostile beings. Pearl Harbor comes to mind. Defense is not a trivial activity on Planet Earth with a total of one trillion dollars being spent this year on defense activities on Earth—half by the United States of America. Every major country has an Air Defense Command with radar early-detection systems, spy satellites, and attack planes and rockets ready to shoot down intruders. Any civilization in our local galactic neighborhood would certainly have Earth on its watch list. Not only did we Earthlings kill 50 million other Earthlings during World War II and destroy 1,700 cities, but we have exploded more than 2,000 nuclear weapons afterward. The largest, a Soviet fusion device, released the energy of 57 million tons of TNT! We have large nuclear-powered aircraft carriers and icebreakers and submarines. Large nuclear fission rockets have been successfully operated. The stars are now within reach. We can go, if we want to spend the dough. We are clearly a threat to take our brand of friendship (hostility) out to the neighborhood. The basic rule here is to shoot first, ask questions later. Think of all the reasons people poured across the Atlantic after Columbus. Some came to steal gold, others to convert the heathens, others to steal the land, and others to escape persecution or to establish businesses.

We also should pay attention to the fact that the Earth is the densest planet in our solar system and has more exotic heavy metals such as rhenium and iridium than the other planets in the solar system. It is easy to forget that uranium, also very dense, was once used primarily as a yellow coloring agent for dinnerware. No longer is that permitted. It is easy to forget that periodically on the Earth there have been rapid huge migrations of people searching for gold or oil or other valuables despite the rigors of the journey (for example, during the California and Alaskan gold rushes). Their purpose was certainly not to have tea with the natives or to give them advanced technology. We should also point out that there has been a clear indication of interest on the part of aliens in our nuclear power and nuclear weapon activities. Check out Robert Hasting's book *Nukes and UFOs* and Robert Salas's book *Unidentified*. Salas was an Air Force officer at the Malmstrom Air Force Base Minuteman Missile Launch Facility when aliens caused 10 missiles to go offline one after the other even though that is supposedly impossible. Perhaps we should also note that it would be rare for an advanced civilization to share its advanced weapons with primitive societies whose major activity is tribal warfare.

There is another serious problem with Dr. Kaku's comments talking about aliens having to travel thousands of light years just to visit us. It would appear that the notion among astronomers these days, thanks to the splendid Kepler satellite's findings, is that, on the average, each star has one planet.

UFO debunkers like Dr. Lincoln or, as discussed earlier, Philip J. Klass or Dr. Donald Menzel, are, of course, not the only ones who make false claims about UFOs. Early on there were the contactees such as George Adamski, "Dr." Dan Fry, and "Dr." Frank Stranges. Venus was described by these intrepid travelers as a nice place to visit. It was only later that it was discovered that the temperature at the surface of Venus was 864 degrees Fahrenheit, hot enough to melt lead, and was toxic. Defenders claim that Venusians reside in a different dimension and are therefore not subject to the effects of the heat. Adamski claimed he worked at Mt. Palomar at the Observatory. Instead he actually worked at a nearby hamburger stand. Fry's and Stranges's PhDs were phony as a three-dollar bill. Friedman actually spoke with Stranges's parole officer back in the late 1970s. (He served time for smuggling a big batch of drugs.) He was holding a huge conference in Los Angeles and said that two astronauts would be speaking there. Friedman spoke with both and found that neither would be there.

There is no question that many people were favorably impressed by the book *The Day After Roswell* by Retired U.S. Army Colonel Philip J. Corso (1915–1998) and Dr. William Birnes. Corso made a number of impressive claims, such as being chief of the Foreign Technology Division of the U.S. Army Research Group under General Arthur Trudeau at the Pentagon (1960–1962). Supposedly Corso had been a member of President Eisenhower's National Security Council during Ike's first term (1953–1957), and later was given a filing cabinet of hardware from the Roswell crashed saucer by General Trudeau and ordered to find all the new technology generated from back-engineering the wreckage. This was to be quietly inserted into U.S. industry without anybody knowing that the source of the information was recovered alien technology. He took credit for the transistor, the microcircuit, fiber optics, and Kevlar. The introduction to the book was written by Corso's close associate, long-serving Senator Strom Thurmond. The book was released at the 50th anniversary celebration of the Roswell event in Roswell, New Mexico, in July 1997.

Friedman tried without any success to verify Corso's claims. This was made difficult because there are no references in the book and no copies of any evidence. There was no question that Corso served in the army from 1942 to 1963. He didn't actually become a full colonel until retirement, which was sort of a reward for long service. There was no indication of his having any scientific background. Friedman employed a researcher in Carlisle, Pennsylvania, to review Trudeau's 95 boxes of papers at the Military History Institute Archives. Fifteen boxes covered 1958–1964.

Boose Educational Services (in Carlisle, Pennsylvania) provided copies of relevant material, including the 1962 roster of those working for General Arthur Trudeau. It listed 114 names, including two in the Foreign Technology Division (FTD). The director was Colonel J.T. Spengler. The other member was Lieutenant Colonel Corso. Friedman managed to locate Spengler, who was in the hospital but died before he could be interviewed. Friedman has a letter from Eisenhower Library Archivist, Herbert Pankratz, indicating that, though Corso was connected to various NSC subgroups, he was not a member of the NSC and never attended an NSC meeting. There has been considerable unsuccessful effort expended to try to validate the technology claims. Probably the best effort was a 30-page paper, "The Development of the Transistor and the Integrated Circuit; Exploring Col. Corso's Claims of Extraterrestrial Reverse Engineering," by Marcel Kuijsten. He has more than 100 references and also deals in detail with claims similar to Corso's by Jack Shulman. "Unless the information and dates provided in his book are incorrect, Col. Corso most likely was in no way directly involved."[14] It should be noted that a Nobel Prize was received by Drs. Shockley, Brattain, and Bardeen for the transistor, with almost all their work done at Bell Labs long before Corso could have had anything to do with it. Jack Kilby received a Nobel Prize for the integrated circuit years before Corso worked at FTD. Many others have been unable to find any link between Corso and the advanced technology seeding claims which he put forth.

In addition Corso claimed that while at Ft. Riley, Kansas, on July 6, 1947, his bowling buddy helped open a large container enclosing a blue fluid containing the body of an alien supposedly shipped by truck from Roswell to Ft. Riley on its way to WPAFB. If there was one thing they had at Roswell it was large airplanes, such as B-29s. The July 6 date doesn't jibe with events at Roswell, such as the trip from Roswell to the Foster ranch by Major Marcel and Captain Cavitt.

Another problem is that Friedman has found that many people have confused Corso's Army FTD with the USAF FTD at Wright-Patterson Air Force Base which is where Project Blue Book was located. Friedman had professional dealings with the USAF FTD in the early 1960s and was very impressed with the technical people whom he encountered there. There is every indication that wreckage from Roswell was sent to the USAF FTD at Wright-Patterson AFB in 1947. It would seem strange indeed if nothing was done by anybody with the Roswell wreckage until 13 years later. Also the roster includes such highly technical groups as Air Defense Division, Atomic Division, Chemical Biological Division, and Missiles and Space Division, all of them larger than FTD.

Marden weighs in slightly differently than Friedman, although she accepts Friedman's meticulous research findings. Her concern is that Corso's advancing age or other factors might have created the inaccuracies in the book. This is partly due to U.S. Senator J. Strom Thurmond's (1902–2003) strong character assessment of Corso, whom he knew well. His foreword in *The Day After Roswell* states:

> Colonel Corso was brought to my attention by two of my former staff members. The colonel had a great deal of credibility and expertise not only as a military officer but also in the fields of intelligence and national security. A veteran of World War II and Korea, Corso had also spent four years working at the National Security Council.

In short, he was very familiar with issues that concerned me and my colleagues on the Senate Armed Services Committee, and he very quickly became a valued source of bountiful information that was insightful and, most important, accurate.[15]

Given Strom Thurmond's strong endorsement of Corso, it is difficult to reconcile the belief that Corso's story was completely and intentionally fraudulent. It is clear, however, that the book contains several major historical inaccuracies, and this casts doubt on Corso's claims. It is entirely reasonable to acknowledge that memories morph over time and that an elderly man might have been mistaken in his factual details. Corso died a year after the book was published. He might have exaggerated his own importance and his relationship with men like J. Edgar Hoover, with whom he claimed to communicate with approximately once every six months after Corso left government service. Yet it is possible to verify some of his claims. His military record shows that he was in Ft. Riley, Kansas, from March 1947 until April 1950. He was transferred to Washington, DC, in May 1950, and attended the Strategic Intelligence School. He then became a strategic intelligence officer and in 1953 was appointed chief of special projects. In 1956 he was transferred to Ft. Bliss, Texas. He was awarded the Legion of Merit award for his Far East tour. He was appointed staff officer in the Foreign Technology Division in Washington, DC, in July 1961, in the Research and Development Division, and chief of the Foreign Technology Division on April 18, 1962.[16] It is difficult to reconcile an intentional fantastic deception from a man who spent his entire life in honorable service to his country, had an excellent character reference, and achieved a high military rank.

Perhaps the best known of those who claimed inside knowledge of flying saucers was Robert Scott Lazar. In the late 1980s he claimed to be a nuclear physicist with a master's degree in physics from MIT and a master's in electronics from the California Institute of Technology. He claimed to have worked at Los Alamos National Laboratory and then at S4 Area 51 outside Las Vegas, where he worked on back-engineering several flying saucers that were being kept there. He supposedly determined that they used element 115 to create Gravity Wave Amplifiers. His story was touted as true by John Lear, son of the founder of the Lear Jet company and himself a pilot working for the CIA. Element 115, which now has the official name of ununpentium, was presumed to exist and, contrary to what many people believed, was not discovered by Bob. Four atoms of it were discovered in 2003 by operating the huge accelerator at the Joint Institute for Nuclear Research in Russia for weeks. The half-life was as expected very short, less than one fourth of a second. Bob's claim that Los Alamos had 500 pounds of element 115 was absurd. With such a short half-life there is no way one can accumulate 1 pound, no less 500. Essentially all trans-uranium elements (atomic number greater than that of uranium, which is 92) have short half-lives—at least those with an atomic number greater than 100.

Because many people knew that Friedman had worked as a nuclear physicist, they were asking about Bob and he decided he had better check. The obvious thing to do was check his credentials. He wasn't a member of the American Nuclear Society, the American Physical Society, or the American Institute of Aeronautics and Astronautics. Friedman belongs to all three. He contacted five different officials at MIT after a colleague could find no trace of him in yearbooks. Nobody had ever heard of him—not the registrar's office, nor the physics department, nor the office that kept track of diplomas. Nor the people who kept track of theses. At MIT one needs a thesis to obtain a master's degree. The legal counsel said there was no way for anybody, including the government, to effectively erase one from all records. Thanks to George Knapp, prize-winning newsman at KLAS TV in Las Vegas, who had talked to Bob and told his story, Friedman was given the name of Bob's high school. They were very helpful. Bob had graduated in August, not with his class. He had taken only one science course (chemistry) and was in the bottom third of his graduating class. The admissions office at MIT stated that normally one had to be in the top 15 percent of a high school graduating class to be admitted. Bob was listed in the phone book at Los Alamos as working at the world class Meson Accelerator for a subcontractor (Kirk Meier). Nobody has turned up any written statement of his job title. He certainly is highly intelligent and has technician skills. Bob had claimed at a public forum in Rachel, Nevada, when asked to name some of his college professors, that William Duxler was his physics professor at Cal Tech. Friedman found that Duxler was listed as a member of the American Physical Society and contacted him. He had never taught at Cal Tech, but always at Pierce Junior College in the San Fernando Valley, where he had actually had Bob in one of his night classes the same year when he was supposedly across the country at MIT. Bob did build a jet-powered car and put on fireworks displays and took over United Nuclear Corp selling many types of technical items. Ironically Friedman, when working at General Motors Allison Division in Indianapolis, had worked with a White Plains, New York, division of United Nuclear on the eventually canceled Military Compact Reactor Program in the early 1960s.

A recent development on the Lazar front was the production of a new short film, *Lazar: Cosmic Whistleblower*, from filmmaker Jeremy Kenyon Lockyer Corbell. The film was the winner of the best short film at the 2016 International UFO Congress Film Festival in Phoenix in February 2016. It purports to claim that Dr. Robert Krangle, who has often consulted (with a PhD from MIT) at Los Alamos Scientific Lab (LASL) verified that Bob was indeed a scientist at the lab. Friedman had had a long, friendly conversation with Krangle, noting that Bob had been listed in the LASL phone book for a short time years ago. He had been employed at the unique Clinton Anderson Meson Accelerator working for a subcontractor, Kirk Meyer. Krangle had noted Bob at the lab and said he looked like a typical physicist complete with a pocket protector full of pens. Friedman asked him if he happened to check on Bob's credentials with MIT or Cal Tech, as Bob had claimed degrees from both, or the lab. The answer was that he had no reason to. He had seen Bob at a security lecture so was sure he was employed there. Corbell has yet to provide any real evidence that Bob was actually a scientist as opposed to a technician—pocket protector or not.

There seems no doubt that Bob spent some time working at Los Alamos, possibly in a technical capacity. However, considering the absence of any degree from any college, any membership in a professional organization for physicists, and lack of any professional papers published, that he would have been chosen to work on such an important task as determining how an alien flying saucer works, seems highly unlikely.

CHAPTER 10

A HARD LOOK AT THE MEDIA, THE UFO COMMUNITY, AND THE TREND TOWARD SENSATIONALISM

History has demonstrated that the treatment of UFO news is cyclical. Televised programs present compelling evidence cases that increase the public's interest. When this occurs, public opinion polls register a rise in the public's belief that UFOs are real. However, when the public's interest is sufficiently high scoffers and disinformants are brought out to cast doubt upon credible cases and researcher integrity. In this turn of events, the facts are distorted and the naïve public is misled. This serves two purposes: to reduce public interest in the topic and to build a false mythology on the topic of UFOs.

One of the major problems in the 1960s and 1970s was the attitude of some arrogant talk show hosts. A typical example was the

David Susskind Show (1920–1987). His producer called Friedman while he was living in California to come to New York to request that he supply an alien abductee, a skeptic, and written materials for the show. Between segments Susskind told Friedman that he read the *New York Times* regularly and had certainly had not seen anything indicating flying saucers were real, so saw no point wasting his time on saucers. Friedman has often talked about the Susskind Syndrome: "I am so well informed that if this was true, I would already know about it. I don't, so it must not be true. Talk about arrogance coupled with ignorance!"

Another arrogant talk show host that Friedman had the displeasure of meeting was Mort Shulman, MD, in Toronto, along with Paul Kurtz, director of the Committee for the Scientific Investigation of Claims of the Paranormal. Shulman was smirking during his entire interview with Friedman although he clearly knew nothing about the subject and insisted that classified information could not be kept secret. Friedman spoke conservatively, and informed the audience of his credentials as a nuclear physicist and member of many professional organizations. He explained his position that disclosure of a neutral ET presence would impact the stock market and that mental hospital admissions would increase. But more importantly he stated that young people would adopt a new view of themselves, not as Canadians, American, or Russians, but as Earthlings. To this Shulman replied, "This is nonsense you're spouting!"[1] Schulman immediately changed the subject, asking Friedman "What are these funny little.... Do they look green?"[2] He asked ludicrous, insulting questions in rapid-fire succession such as "Are you crazy? Have you ever been in a mental institution? Have you ever had psychiatric care?"[3] To his credit, Friedman kept his cool, stating that he had never been under psychiatric care and was, in fact, a nuclear physicist with bachelor's and master's degrees in physics from the University of Chicago. He spoke of the professional organizations of which he was a member and the papers he had published in scientific journals. The fact is that, while employed in private industry, Friedman had a Q security clearance for his work on as nuclear aircraft, fission and fusion rockets, and compact nuclear power-plants for space applications. He was unmistakably not de-lusional as Shulman inferred. Shulman clearly had never had access to classified material, nor was he the least bit respectful to guests with whom he disagreed as a result of his ignorance of the subject matter.

Immediately prior to the commercial break, the narrator asked, "How does the bonafide field of science react to this?"[4], implying that scientists with an interest in the scientific evaluation of UFOs are not authentic scientists. Dr. Paul Kurtz was treated with respect and dignity by Shulman. He was introduced as a professor of phi-losophy and founder of CSICOP, who, like other members of the intellectual community, is extremely disturbed by the readiness of the public to accept total nonsense. Kurtz did not quote statis-tics that were remarkably different from Friedman's. In fact, he re-stated Friedman's assertion that most UFOs can be identified. But this time Shulman's formerly negative attitude had become posi-tive. Kurtz misspoke when he stated that people have examined the CIA and FBI files and have found no evidence of a cover-up. Friedman countered his claim by showing blacked-out documents that he had acquired through FOIA requests. But the camera did not focus upon them. Kurtz alleged that people believe UFOs are real because, for personal gain, Friedman has been concocting theories. This is complete nonsense! He then correctly stated that we have no hard physical evidence that proves UFOs are extrater-restrial, for which Friedman concurs. But Friedman argues that we do have large-scale scientific studies and the testimony of credible military officers and scientists, some of whom were witnesses and some of whom took part in the cover-up.

Fortunately there were some sensible hosts, such as Merv Griffin and Tom Snyder of the *Tomorrow* show. They asked reason-able questions, were courteous, and seemed to be really paying at-tention. Griffin was rational and respectful in front of a live audi-ence. Betty Hill, a social worker from New Hampshire, was first on Snyder's *Tomorrow* show. Hill and her husband, Barney, had a close encounter with a silent, hovering unconventional craft in New Hampshire's White Mountains in 1961, followed by a two-hour period of missing time. Later, hypnosis sessions with Dr. Benjamin Simon, a prominent Boston psychiatrist, revealed that the Hills had undergone a harrowing abduction by non-humans. There was physical and circumstantial evidence that was investigated by several technical and scientific people who supported the possibility that it might have been real. Betty had passed a polygraph exam after Barney's death in 1969, and both were deemed not to be suffering from a major mental illness. Friedman watched from the green room, and was then brought out live. Friedman mentioned off camera that the viewing audience probably didn't know that Betty was a social worker and well educated. The first question Tom asked Betty in that segment was about her background. He clearly treated his guests with respect and consideration.

In 2006, Discovery Canada pulled a demeaning deception upon Marden and Friedman. It was on *The World's Strangest UFO Stories* and featured the authors on location in New Hampshire's White Mountain region. Marden was prepared for the interview with evidence of the Hill's original investigation reports, scientific evidence reports, forensic drawings, and Betty's damaged dress. She and Friedman were surprised when the film crew showed little or no interested in the evidence. Nor did they seem particularly interested in conducting a serious interview. Marden was shocked when she read the release form requesting permission to slander her. Of course, she declined. But she and Friedman consented to an interview within reasonable limits. Months later, Friedman received a notice that the show, "I Had Sex With an Alien," would air soon. Prominently displayed on the advertisement was Friedman's image next to the show's title. The segment began: "Imagine for a moment that aliens really exist. What would they be like?... Perhaps there is only one thing aliens can't get anywhere else in the whole Universe. Have extraterrestrials travelled half way across the limitless expanse of space because they've got the hots for humans?

Maybe they just want to have sex with us."[5] Shortly thereafter, the viewer is informed that Betty and Barney were the first to experience a close encounter of a sexual kind. This is complete nonsense! We are then informed that their story captured the public's imagination and led to an overabundance of alien encounters of a sexual kind, perhaps because aliens find humans sexually irresistible. More nonsense! We are falsely informed that the male aliens wrestled Barney aboard the UFO and took an unnatural interest in his genitals. The truth is that Barney recalled undergoing a harrowing experience where he was floated aboard a landed UFO. Only the toes of his shoes were bumping over the rocks and this resulted in the real toes of his shoes being so deeply scraped that he was forced to purchase new ones. He was taken to an examining room, where the ETs showed an interest in his skeletal structure, his nervous system, his skin, and his mouth. Immediately prior to his release he felt a cuplike device applied over his genitals. There were no sexual advances made toward him. Nor did he experience pleasure or pain. We are then informed by the narrator that the other aliens turned their attention to Betty and stripped her naked before giving her a thorough internal probing. This is another line of baloney! Only Betty's dress and shoes had been removed. There was no sexual encounter, only a needle inserted into her naval. The show then offered a variety of slanderous explanations for the Hill's so called deception. The fact is the Hills had attempted to keep their revelations of alien abduction from the mainstream media. Both were honest, high-functioning members of society. All unbiased investigators have reached this conclusion. Neither was psychotic, as was suggested by the show's narrator. The show's content went downhill from this point, introducing several individuals who the narrator stated had positively orgasmic sex orgies with aliens. This loathsome piece of negative propaganda is typical of the distortion and slander that the Hills and other abductees have been subjected to.

More recently, Fox News offered up a perfect example of the media's treatment of the UFO topic in a segment on the 2016 International UFO Congress Conference, Fountain Hills, Arizona, on *Watters' World: UFO Edition*. Old video clips from television sitcoms were injected into the mix to encourage viewers to poke fun at experiencers. Two women described their alien contacts to the commentator while he grinned in disbelief. One told of being taken to the moon, where she was strapped down and straddled while a Mantis stared into her eyes. The emphasis was on another woman's purple hair. The experiencers were asked who they were going to vote for, to which they replied Trump! The public then watched a clip from Donald Trump proclaiming, "I love the poorly educated!"[6] Marden had been interviewed, but her segment was not included in the final cut, probably because she emphasized credibility and evidence. Thankfully it was not kooky enough to satisfy Fox News' requirements.

Deception by the media that causes harm to experiencers has led Marden to wage an advocacy campaign for their right to be treated with common decency. Whether the experience is physical, psychological, or spiritual, the individual does not deserve to be tormented or marginalized by naysayers. The history of humankind offers example after example of intolerance by the dominant culture against minority groups. Those whose experiences, appearance, or values place them outside acceptable political, religious, or social norms, find themselves on the receiving end of ridicule and harassment by outspoken members of the dominant cultural group. Much of this is emotionally driven through fear and the desire to maintain the status quo. However, some of it is generated by a loathsome desire to control target groups through intimidation, harassment, and persecution. This discrimination has been politically sanctioned by the powers that be and the dominant culture to the detriment of the target group. It occurs in our society both subtly and pervasively to experiencers and those who have expressed an interest in UFOs.

In recent years, the Hill case has been treated fairly on the Travel, History, and Destination America channels. Marden's statements have been supported by the documented evidence. Several scientists have given testimony pertaining to their analysis of the damage to Betty's dress and the pink powdery substance that mysteriously appeared on it. Evidence has been presented that confirms the Hills' backgrounds as stable, reliable people. Most people do not know that Barney was appointed to the U.S. Civil Rights Commission's State Advisory Committee and had received an award from Sargent Shriver for the volunteer work he performed with funds from the Office of Economic Opportunity. Betty was active in community affairs and a respected adoption worker for the state. Yet negative propagandists have been busy in their attempts to demolish the case, painting the Hills with a new brush and transforming Betty into a credulous, longtime flying saucer enthusiast and Barney into a weak man who believed the ravings of his kooky wife. It is clear that these disinformants have active imaginations and an overwhelming desire to misinform the public.

One historical example pertains to a false claim made in 1979 by Philip Klass, on WBZ radio's *Larry Glick Show*. He spoke of an incident that allegedly occurred when Betty accompanied a group to a spot in rural NH to look for UFOs. As the story was relayed to the audience, Betty was the only one who saw a UFO. This allegedly confirmed that her perceptual ability was extremely poor or she was delusional and was a theme that Klass promoted. The story was false, but has been repeated many times. The truth can be found in correspondence between Klass and John Quinn, a New Hampshire, newspaper reporter, at Klass's archival collection in Philadelphia. Quinn described Betty as an "articulate and sincere woman...and doubtless had a strange and enigmatic experience," adding, "I also have no real doubts as to the credibility of Betty Hill, despite the fact that I feel that some, at least, of the objects she reports with impressive regularity are the result of mistaken identity or perhaps wishful thinking."[7] Marden can attest to this. Hill had a habit of telling observers to look at a light in the sky that she thought might be a UFO. Over the next few minutes all focused upon the distant light. Sometimes it moved closer and could be identified as a plane or helicopter. Sometimes it took on an unconventional appearance.

Marden explained this in detail in *Captured! The Betty and Barney Hill UFO Experience.* Betty had been harshly criticized for publicizing her sky-watching activities, especially when she published photos of alleged UFOs. But several witnesses saw what they described as perplexing unconventional objects. Her archival collection contains several interesting photos that have a highly unusual appearance.

Over the next several months, Klass used his magic to assuage Quinn's thoughts about Betty and earned his trust by mailing him secret, damaging information about Dr. Allen Hynek that he had received from one of his younger associates. He used humor and satire in his chain of propaganda. As time passed, Quinn informed Klass, "You have succeeded in making a card carrying skeptic out of me!"[8]

Returning to the real story behind Klass's false remarks on Larry Glick, Quinn and a professor from Plymouth State College had accompanied Betty to a spot in southern New Hampshire for a night of sky-watching. They left the car, leaving Betty to adjust her malfunctioning camera. Suddenly, according to Quinn, a gold white light appeared on the tracks approximately 300 yards in the distance. He was stunned thinking that he was observing his first UFO. As it drew closer, he could feel a rumbling vibration and then watched as a 50-car freight train thundered past. The truth is that Betty was not there and had not made the statement that Klass attributed to her! Listeners had reported the misstatement to Betty and she was angry with Quinn. He explained to Klass, in private correspondence, that he did not want to be portrayed as an inaccurate reporter with regard to this event. Klass ignored Quinn's desire for credibility and simply reassured him that he had personally apologized to Betty for his mistake. The problem lies in the fact that Klass failed to retract his error. His false statement has been repeated time and time again.

A major problem for anyone trying to get to the truth about UFOs is the persistent failure of the major media groups to take the subject seriously. There is no question that they could dig in as solidly as the *Washington Post* did to try to determine the truth about Watergate and President Nixon's involvement in that scandal or as the *New York Times* did about the Pentagon Papers. The general rule has been that newspapers such as the *Washington Post* and the New York Times refuse to do their own UFO investigations. For example, the *New York Times* carried the crash test dummies explanation for the Roswell Incident on their front page. They apparently blindly accepted this explanation as divulged in the Air Force's 231 page "The Roswell Report: Case Closed," which was a sequel to the huge Roswell Volume One report "Fact Versus Fiction in the New Mexico Desert." Strangely, the author, USAF Colonel Richard Weaver, had stated in the first report that they would be saying no more about Roswell. They obviously were not telling the truth. Colonel Weaver had claimed, without providing any evidence, that the Eisenhower Briefing document was BOGUS. Friedman filed a Freedom of Information request for any and all evidence to justify that conclusion. Weaver said he had nothing to provide.

The Air Force had previously promulgated three other explanations for Roswell:

1. It was a flying saucer. (Nothing was said about an alien explanation.) July 8, 1947.

2. Sorry, it was just a radar reflector–weather balloon combination. July 9, 1947.

3. It was a super-secret Mogul balloon. 1997.

As it happens, #1 was correct. Much effort has been unsuccessfully made by researchers such as Dr. David Rudiak to verify the Mogul explanation. There was certainly such a project with the objective of using standard neoprene weather balloon trains connected with string at 20-foot intervals. Twenty to 25 balloons were tied together and carried appropriate pressure sensors, and other equipment. The idea of using appropriate ballast was to maintain a very constant altitude as they listened for sounds that would be expected to be produced by a Soviet nuclear explosion thousands of miles away. The records from the project show that it was the purpose that was highly classified and *not* the technology. No chase planes tracked the balloons to assure that the "secret" equipment would not be recovered by non-government people. Standard weather balloons were released all over New Mexico every day. Some press coverage even foolishly showed huge balloons having nothing to do with MOGUL. No balloons released during any of their launches could have possibly been found by rancher Mac Brazel in early July 1947. The newspaper headlines of July 8, 1947, spoke of a saucer "found last week." However, the big USAF report spoke of June 14—hardly a week before July 8. There are many other problems, such as that Roswell Army Air Force Base Intelligence officer Major Jesse Marcel had taken a course about radar and weather balloons, and the ranchers in the area were all familiar with them. They certainly did not match the descriptions of the wreckage given by the rancher or the military people. The crash test dummies explanation was even sillier. The army used a picture of lieutenants Eugene M. Schwartz and Raymond Madson and one of the dummies. Friedman located Madson in New Mexico and met with him. There are just a few problems.

The dummies were made of wood, were 6 feet tall and weighed 175 pounds, and were in Army Air Force flight gear because the clothing affected the drag as the dummy fell through the atmosphere as well as the temperature. The major difficulty, of course, is that none were dropped until 1953, a full six years after Roswell. How could they possibly account for stories of small alien bodies found in 1947? Another problem was that often limbs of the dummies fell off when the dummies impacted on the ground. Surely nobody would mistake a wooden dummy with a detached limb for an alien body.

Unfortunately the *New York Times* had a front page story touting the dumb dummy explanation! Surely the *New York Times* could have talked to Colonel Madson, who was named and pictured in the Report. Friedman had no trouble locating him. He spoke freely.

Another example of poor press coverage involves the many articles repeating the false claim by CIA historian Gerald K. Haines, that most sightings were actually reports of such spy planes as the U-2 and SR-71. The hope was that the Russians and others would believe that people were seeing UFOs rather than the new intelligence devices. There are several problems with this notion. Dr. Bruce Maccabee, an optical physicist, was the first to obtain more than 1,000 pages of UFO info from the FBI using the new Freedom of Information path to document release. Bruce carefully collected data on the number of sightings reports made to Project Blue Book before and after these craft started flying. There was no increase. Surely they don't think that the public is so stupid as to presume that these high-speed, high-altitude planes with wings, tails, and noisy engines could hover, make right angle turns, land, and take off from very small areas of ground in the middle of nowhere while flying silently. They were barely visible when at high altitude. Bruce goes into considerable detail in his book *The FBI, CIA and UFOs*.

An almost-ludicrous example of unverified press coverage involved reporting of the claim by outstanding pilot and parachutist Joseph Kittinger, that he was responsible for the story that a red-haired officer was involved at Roswell. It is a fact that Kittinger had once appeared at the base hospital. He was indeed red haired. However, he was actually there in 1959, not 1947! It would appear that the same time travel device was used to transfer Kittinger as was used for the crash test dummies.

The active debunkers of UFOs such as the Committee for Skeptical Inquiry (formerly Committee for Scientific Investigation of Claims of the Paranormal) have often had their debunking claims blindly accepted by the media. Chairman Dr. Joseph Nickell has a PhD in English. Two examples, of many, indicate his failure to use the methods of science and investigation rather than proclamation. About Roswell, he claimed in an interview, also involving Friedman, that an anonymous public relations man at Roswell had made up and issued an unauthorized press release stating that a flying saucer had been recovered near Roswell. All the serious books had named Lieutenant Walter Haut. Friedman had known him for 20 years. He happened to have flown more than 20 bombing missions over Japan as a bombardier during WWII and was selected to drop the instrumentation package over one of the nuclear weapons tested in Operation Crossroads in the Pacific in 1946. One chooses one's best people because, without instrumentation, the test is almost worthless. He was directed by Base Commander Colonel Blanchard to issue the release. The military group at Roswell (the 509th Bomb Wing) just happened to have been the most elite military group in the world, having dropped the only atom bombs. Blanchard went on to be a four-star general and was vice chief of staff of the USAF when he died of a heart attack at the Pentagon. Nickel repeated this same false explanation in a cover story in a skeptical publication eight years later!

Nickell also released a statement claiming that what was observed in Flatwoods, West Virginia, in 1952 by a number of people was a 6-foot-tall owl! Nickell had gone to Flatwoods, but had talked to none of the witnesses and had not visited the field and woods where the "Flatwoods Monster" was observed. The story was carefully investigated by Frank Feschino, who visited the town many times, introduced Friedman to a number of the witnesses, and has written a detailed book (*The Flatwoods Monster*) about the case. Friedman only received laughter when he asked people in the area about 6-foot-tall owls. Frank was also the only one who spoke with National Guard colonel, Dale Levitt, who had quietly and officially been ordered to investigate the case with a number of troops.

A good example of the failure of major press groups such as the *New York Times* and *Washington Post* to take saucers seriously was demonstrated when neither of these two gave any space to a rather shocking story that appeared in many other newspapers on July 29, 1952, after many saucer sightings over Washington, D.C. The headline of the front-page story in the *Seattle Post Intelligencer* was "Air Force Orders Jet Pilots to Shoot Down Flying Saucers if They

Refuse to Land." The Fall River, Massachusetts, *Herald News* head-lined "Jets Told to Shoot Down Flying Discs." General Roger Ramey of Roswell fame even commented that more than 300 planes had been scrambled—just routine. These were based upon official press releases from the USAF.

It has been suggested by critics that the UFO community is its own worst enemy. Scientific UFO researchers, including Friedman and Marden, who painstakingly examine the evidence, are extremely concerned about this trend. Some less-rigorous propagandists have blurred the lines of credulity and accept eyewitness testimony based upon emotional content, not painstaking investigation. There is ample evidence of false claims being embraced by the UFO community and defended by some promoters despite evidence to the contrary. There is a new trend in the media toward reality television. This is a departure from the intelligent talk show discussions with respected researchers of years past. One television researcher who was soliciting experiencers for his upcoming reality series stated that he was seeking eccentric personalities because they were the most entertaining to the public. On some shows actors replace authorities in the field. Sometimes so-called experts have strong personalities but are not at the top of their field.

Sensationalism has been the driving force behind the dissemination of recent UFO conspiracy reports by some media outlets. Simultaneously, there has been a nearly complete lockdown on UFO reports in the mainstream media. The current trend is moving us away from science and meticulous research toward fantastic reports by individuals who lack evidence in support of their claims. False information feeds the imaginations of a viewing public that feeds off sensational, emotionally driven stories. We are advised that Reptilians have walked into the bodies of world leaders and are now controlling governments. U.S. military forces are working in collusion with evil Grey aliens on mind control and reproductive experiments. Carnivorous ETs are dining on the corpses of missing children. And aliens have developed a plan to replace humans with a hybrid race. Fear sells and drives people further away from the truth. But where is the evidence?

Occasionally, a well-known member of the UFO community brings disgrace to the field through a criminal act. For example, Stanton Friedman witnessed the presence of a suspiciously young girl in the home of retired Air Force lieutenant colonel and UFO investigator, the late Wendelle C. Stevens, shortly before he was arrested on child molestation charges. Stevens entered a guilty plea and was sentenced to seven years in prison, of which he served five, for furnishing obscene material to a minor, and possessing films and pictures of minors engaging in sex acts. Initially, he claimed that he'd been framed in retribution for his UFO research, but later entered a guilty plea.

Stevens had published a book promoting the ET contact claims of Swiss farmer Eduard "Billy" Meier. Meier alleges to have been in contact with Plejarian, later termed Pleiadian, visitors starting at age 5, as the result of an agreement he'd entered into prior to his birth. Much of his communication is said to have been telepathic and with an interdimensional race. Throughout his lifetime "Billy" has made claims of alien intervention and messages that foretell the future. But an investigation of the real Billy Meier casts doubt upon his claims. At age 14, he was incarcerated in a youth prison for assault, and again served time two years later. He escaped from prison and joined the French Foreign Legion, but defected and made his way back to Switzerland, where he turned himself in to authorities. He was again incarcerated. After his release, he worked as a day laborer in the Middle East, where he engaged in grave robbing. In 1964, he took his first photos of an alleged UFO in India, prior to being deported to Switzerland on charges of vagrancy. Finally, in 1976 his photos were published in an Italian magazine. This was the beginning of his fame as a Contactee. Over the years, he submitted evidence of UFOs in dozens of photos that he claimed to have taken as they hovered nearby. An early analysis of his photos did not find evidence of a hoax. However, some of his photos were exposed as hoaxes following more sophisticated scientific analysis. Meier defended himself by claiming that intelligence agencies had planted hoaxed photos in his collection. But in 1997, his former wife stated that his photos and ET contacts were nothing more than fabrications. The debate continues to rage on.

Metallurgic and spectrographic analysis of a metal sample he claimed to have received from a Plejarian was analyzed with mixed scientific findings. Two scientific groups observed highly unusual properties including rare earth materials, whereas another disagreed, stating that Meier could have tooled the metallic samples himself. In addition to this, a sound recording of an alleged UFO being pursued by military jets was analyzed with negative results. Despite the fact that most of Meier's claims have been debunked by unbiased scientific investigators, he continues to enjoy his cult leadership among thousands of followers.

Meier's history of criminal activities, hoaxed photos, and dubious character cause one to wonder why Wendelle Stevens endorsed him. Stevens had spent a considerable amount of time with Meier and seemed convinced that something real was occurring. Today, some researchers continue to endorse Stevens, primarily because he had dedicated 54 years of his life to UFO investigation and had a huge collection of UFO photos and books. Yet more discriminating researchers eye him with suspicion as a result to his conviction on a serious felony charge. These revelations are a bitter pill to swallow for those who admire both men and are not aware of their criminal records. Some will attack the findings of unbiased researchers, whereas others will take a closer look at the evidence.

There have also been cases when supposed investigators have misrepresented their credentials. One shocking example was that a well-known author, Philip J. Imbrogno, was found to have falsely claimed to have university degrees including a PhD from MIT and to have served in the U.S. Army Special Forces. A background check revealed that his credentials were bogus. No evidence was found that he had any degrees or had served. When this was discovered and publicized, he dropped out of the field. He was probably best known as a coauthor of a book by the late astronomer Dr. J. Allen Hynek (1910–1976) about the Hudson Valley, New York, UFOs.

It seems clear that ufology needs to be more careful about its own practitioners. Media personalities who engage in fantastic speculation need to be disconnected from careful credentialed researchers in the public's mind. Credibility is at stake. Of course the anti-ufology community needs to own up to many misrepresentations, including those made by Klass, Menzel, and Condon.

CHAPTER 11

THE PUSH FOR DISCLOSURE AND ITS POSSIBLE RAMIFICATIONS

There has been a great deal of noise about the question of government disclosure of the "real facts" known by the U.S. government and all aspects of the flying saucer topic. Two of the major exponents of full disclosure are Dr. Steven Greer, head of The Disclosure Project, and Steven Bassett of the Paradigm Research Group. Both seem to believe that the U.S. government knows all about flying saucers and should release all that it knows. Greer has also claimed that free energy has been developed and should be released for the benefit of humankind and even used to recommend investing in a company he claimed had solved the problem. Bassett's Extraterrestrial Phenomena Political Action Group, with the help of a large donation, even held a Citizen's Hearing on Disclosure, a mock

Congressional Hearing in Washington, D.C., from April 29 through May 3, 2013, to get attention for his claims. Six former members of Congress were paid $20,000 each to listen to a weeklong parade of ufologists. Friedman was one of them. None were paid. DVDs of the highlights were eventually distributed to serving members of the U.S. Congress. Both are pushing for real congressional hearings, though very little was accomplished by *real* hearings held on July 29, 1968, by the House Committee on Science and Astronautics. Friedman provided written testimony to those hearings. The testimony of 12 scientists was included in the proceedings. Interestingly, the former congressmen recommended that the place to see action now should be the United Nations, *not* the U.S. Congress.

So far as is known neither Bassett nor Greer ever held a security clearance. Neither seems to believe that there might be good reasons for *not* releasing everything. The world is spending a trillion dollars this year on military activities, including the development of advanced military hardware. Why would any nation, whether the United States or Russia or China, want to release technical data it may have obtained from the wreckage of a recovered crashed saucer or from measurements made by instrumented aircraft chasing UFOs or observed by satellites, if the other nations did not release what they have learned? A basic rule for security is that one can't tell one's friends without telling one's enemies. They read the newspapers and listen to the media.

There have also been strange claims that there is no government cover-up of UFO evidence. This claim is easily refuted by, among other things, the simple fact that the NSA has refused to release 99 percent of the text of 156 TOP SECRET UMBRA NSA UFO documents and that dozens of old, almost completely redacted TOP SECRET CIA UFO documents were "released." In addition there is the October 1969 memo from Brigadier General Carroll Bolender stating that "Reports of UFOs which could affect National Security are made in accordance with JANAP 146 or Air Force Memo 55-11 and are not part of the Blue Book system."[1] He also stated that even though closure of Blue Book would mean that the public had no government office to which to report UFO sightings, the "reports which could affect national security would continue to be handled using the procedures established for that purpose."[2] Friedman had a telephone conversation with retired General Bolender, who confirmed that indeed there were two separate communication channels for UFO reportage. It would appear that the reports that could affect national security and that didn't go to Project Blue Book went to Operation Majestic 12, about which the U.S. government has officially released nothing.

A discussion of disclosure of an alien presence must begin with speculation regarding the reasons why an unknown intelligence would be interested in our planet and its people. It would appear that aliens have been observed on Earth for thousands of years, judging by such excellent books as *Flying Saucers and the Bible* by Dr. Barry Downing. Obviously there may be many different reasons for checking out Earth, just as visitors to the New World in the 16th century had different motivations. Perhaps records are being kept of how advanced civilizations are changing. Obviously aliens could be interested in what grows here, what elements might be mined here, and whether we are friendly or war-like. Equally, what progress has been made in the development of advanced technology, and is there any reason to believe we might be a threat to others in our local galactic neighborhood? Perhaps they are interested in protecting themselves from our predatory behavior as we develop the technology that might cause problems for them, or perhaps they are motivated by a desire to monitor our development and offer minimal assistance in our growth. There are some large structures readily visible from overhead such as the Great Wall of China, the pyramids, brightly lighted skyscrapers, and numerous huge dams. Another concern might well be: Are there any signs that we will be able to visit and attack nearby civilizations?

One reason is that nuclear weapons could threaten the very survival of this planet and/or be carried elsewhere to threaten nearby civilizations. Prior to World War II, human warfare did not pose the threat to our existence that nuclear weapons cause. A large conventional bomb (10-ton Block Buster) used in 1944 in World War II released the energy of 10 tons of dynamite. It required a large B-29 aircraft to carry and deliver it. Many were used to attack cities and battle targets. We destroyed 1,700 cities during World War II. However the two atomic (fission) bombs exploded at Hiroshima and Nagasaki to end the war in August 1945 each released as much energy as exploding more than 15,000 tons of dynamite. The first hydrogen bomb, "Mike," a fusion device, as opposed to the early atomic devices, was detonated in 1952 in the Pacific and released the energy of 10 million tons of TNT. Several years later a huge Russian fusion weapon released the energy of 57 million tons of TNT. The fireball at the Mike detonation was an impressive 3 miles wide. Over the 70 years we Earthlings have exploded more than 2,000 nuclear bombs of varying destructive capacity. Any visiting civilization would quickly recognize two important facets of the new demonstration of nuclear technology. Earthlings killed 50 million of their own kind in World War II before they had nuclear weapons. Nuclear technology can be used for space travel both locally and to the stars. Nuclear navies have submarines that can circle around the globe under water without surfacing. Nuclear-powered aircraft carriers can operate for 18 years without refueling. A study done at Aerojet General Nucleonics for the Air Force in 1962 indicated that fusion propulsion systems could eject particles having 10 million times as much energy per particle as can be produced by a chemical rocket and send us to the stars. Fusion devices use isotopes of hydrogen and helium, the two lightest and most abundant elements in the universe, which is very handy if one is traveling.

One way is to determine our potential for interstellar travel. Obviously the largest source of energy in our solar system is the energy produced by the sun. It is of some interest that we did not realize that the sun (and all the other stars in the neighborhood) produce its energy by nuclear fusion, rather than by burning gas, until 1938. That same year we learned that when uranium-235 captures

Hiroshima after the bomb

a neutron (not discovered until 1932) it releases a huge amount of energy because of Einstein's E= mc^2 and also releases more neutrons. This made it possible to think in terms of chain reactions. The first operating nuclear pile was constructed at the University of Chicago under the direction of Dr. Enrico Fermi in 1942. The first nuclear bomb, exploded at Trinity site on July 16, 1945, in New Mexico, released the energy of more than 17,000 tons of exploding dynamite. We have exploded many fission devices since, including at Hiroshima and Nagasaki less than a month later. All nuclear weapons release a lot of neutrons and gamma rays and leave behind a substantial quantity of radioactive materials. It only took seven years more for us to explode the first hydrogen bomb, releasing the energy of 10 million tons of dynamite and producing a mushroom cloud 3 miles across. One might certainly expect that aliens would be interested in such displays of huge—physically small, but energetically enormous—amounts of energy. In 1956 the United States demonstrated a nuclear-powered submarine and then a nuclear-powered aircraft carrier. One might expect that smart aliens would recognize that we soon could be expected to use nuclear energy, especially fusion, for star travel. Fission nuclear rockets were ground-tested in the late 1960s at the nuclear test site in Nevada. Remnants of nuclear activities are detectable from a distance and from above. We have exploded 2,000 nuclear weapons at many locations.

There are two other very important applications of nuclear energy sure to be of interest to alien visitors. One is obviously the production of electricity in nuclear power plants. As of mid-2015 there were 438 operating nuclear power plants in 30 countries, with 67 new ones under construction in 15 countries. The other application is the nuclear warheads placed upon many intercontinental ballistic missiles and smaller nuclear weapons for use with artillery. Anybody checking out our deep space probes would also take note of the dozens of radioisotope thermoelectric generators that have been used. The Horizon space probe to Pluto, which took almost 10 years to get there, was powered by an RTG.

Many have suggested that the reason there were UFOs at Rendlesham Base in England back in 1980 is that there were nuclear weapons stored there, though that was not generally known among the people living in the area at the time. Books have been written by researchers Nick Pope and Peter Robbins.

We have also been informed of UFOs seen near operating nuclear power plants supposedly including the Chernobyl plant in Russia after it exploded on April 26, 1986. The Aetherius Society claims that UFOs came along and were able to minimize the damage. We could find no real evidence to substantiate that claim. There have also been claims that UFOs showed up over Fukishima, Japan, after the nuclear incident there in 2011. Also of interest are the many reports of UFOs seen over such national labs as Oak Ridge NL in Tennessee; Los Alamos Scientific Lab, Kirtland, Sandia, all in New

Mexico, as well as Hanford in Washington State. On the Internet we find Larry Hatch's NCP-03 "UFO Sightings and Nuclear Sites," which notes 193 UFO sightings near or around nuclear sites. Also, as noted earlier, Roswell was the home of the 509th Bomber Wing, which in 1947, when the Roswell Incident took place, was the only military group in the world that had (and had detonated) nuclear weapons. Given our behavioral characteristics, extraterrestrial visitors have reason to be concerned about human behavior and the ultimate survival of Planet Earth.

A benevolent advanced extraterrestrial civilization might be motivated to intercede in the case of widespread nuclear warfare to prevent a holocaust, as long as they believe that the world is worth saving. As mentioned earlier in this book, it appears that they have been monitoring our development for at least 75 years, having appeared in large numbers when the first nuclear weapons were tested. The Air Force and scientists speculated that flying saucers might have been byproducts of emissions from nuclear sites. However, it seems more likely that they were advanced extraterrestrials concerned about our behavior and the dangers that nuclear weapons pose to life on earth. Perhaps they experienced similar growing pains earlier in their own development. Or perhaps they have witnessed the destruction of other primitive societies elsewhere. Their presence makes it clear that they possess the technology to monitor life on earth. What have they learned from us?

Earth is comprised of 196 nations that are dominated primarily by groups whose primary goal has been to obtain, protect, and control natural resources and its population. A few despotic leaders have imposed tyrannical oppression upon millions, and this has led to great suffering, social strife, and war. The socio-cultural impact of European settlement caused widespread disruption of traditional lifestyles and values when technologically advanced societies from Western Europe imposed their dominance upon indigenous people around the world. It was tantamount to the enslavement of an entire population. They were given protection from warring tribes, and taught the dominant culture's Christian religion and how to communicate in the language of the dominant culture. In exchange, they were expected to work for their oppressors in exchange for these services.

Little respect was given to the sacred sites that the indigenous people valued. Burial grounds and seasonal habitation grounds were desecrated as European settlers ignored property lines and moved onto indigenous land in violation of contracts. Disease, slavery, maltreatment and starvation caused the extermination of perhaps millions of native peoples. Survivors were forced to wear Western clothing and attend Christian churches. Communities and family units were divided and displaced. Native children were removed from their families and taught European history and cultural values. Assimilation became a policy, where natives were forced to live in the Western way and hold western beliefs and cultural values, thereby wiping out their own beliefs and values. Sometimes native children were taken from their families and forced to live under foster care or in group homes. Diseases such as smallpox, measles, and plagues wiped out thousands—perhaps millions—of indigenous people who did not have immunity. Our own history cautions us of the potential grave consequences that a technologically superior civilization might bestow upon us. Visitors whose values are similar to our own might subjugate humanity in exchange for technology and the answers to the secrets of the universe.

Can disclosure be advanced without widespread disturbance, as occurred over and over again when technologically advanced human populations disrupted less technologically advanced indigenous people? What are the possible ramifications from a security standpoint? One must consider the level of information, to be disclosed, before we can speculate about the impact it might have upon the human population. Will the government concede that thousands of people have observed what appears to be unexplainable phenomena in our airspace, but inform us that it doesn't seem to pose a threat to national security, as Major General John A.

Samford did in 1952? Limited disclosure is likely to cause less disruption than full disclosure. Yet, it will raise many questions in the media, among religious groups, and in the general population, who have been lied to for 70 years.

British astrophysicist Stephen Hawking speculated in a 2011 documentary, *Into the Universe With Stephen Hawking*, that intelligent alien life forms almost certainly exist, but would pose a threat to humankind, especially if they are predatory. He speculated that having expended all of their planet's natural resources, they might exist in massive ships searching for planets they could conquer and colonize. An alien presence on Earth could pose the same dangers that the Columbian invasion carried to the Americas.

Michael A.J. Michaud, a space policy analyst and former diplomat, cautions us that if intelligence on Earth has been channeled to predators and if this is true throughout the universe, predatory species might play a dominant role throughout the cosmos. They might be technologically advanced but ethically compromised by our standards, which would be bad news for humanity. However, an ethical, technologically advanced alien civilization might avoid direct contact with humanity in order to ensure that the less technologically advanced society will develop at its own pace. The authors suspect that a destructive or aggressive predatory civilization might have destroyed itself before it could reach other planets with advancing intelligent life forms through interstellar travel. Or, perhaps a more advanced species has intervened before the predatory civilization self-destructed by assisting it along in its moral, ethical, and spiritual development. Recently, many experiencers have reported this type of monitoring and possible intervention.

Futurist Allen Tough's (University of Toronto) research points to the belief that a civilization 10,000 years more advanced than ours has survived its growing pains and is more altruistic than Earthlings. He speculates that advanced alien visitors might be inclined to help humans through intervention in order to avert a catastrophe, such as in the case of a nuclear war, an environmental disaster, or an asteroid impact. Advanced aliens might require humanity to reduce major risks in order to promote its ultimate survival. Yet he thinks they will be very different from us. He imagines aliens who have developed advanced psychic abilities that can influence behavior, and send and receive information across vast distances at the speed of light. Consciousness might be projected from one place or another, or there might be a collective consciousness that has eliminated violent or destructive behavior. Sound familiar? Many experiencers have informed us that the aliens possess many of these characteristics, especially telepathic communication and psychic awareness. In fact, the majority of experiencers have reported that they have developed increased psychic abilities after their initial contact. Tough reassures us that a predatory species had the opportunity to invade our planet and destroy intelligent life on earth a long time ago, but chose not to. There is reason to believe that a highly evolved civilization might be ethically, morally, and spiritually advanced. Tough speculates that perhaps they are only observing our development without causing unnecessary harm and interference, and will only intervene if we are in imminent danger of destruction.

SETI's Dr. Jill Tarter suspects that aliens might use their superior technologies to take control of Earth. In an article for the online website "Tech Crunch", she informs us, "If they show up on our doorstep that means they have technologies that are considerably advanced with respect to ours. And because of that, they're going to be the ones to set the rules."[3] Referring to research by Harvard psychology professor Steven Pinker, she adds that, in order for a civilization to reach a state of technological advancement, they may have learned to behave in a non-aggressive manner. Pinker's research indicates that humankind is becoming kinder and gentler as we evolve. Citing 20th-century statistics, he states that only about 3 percent of the world's population died as the result of manmade catastrophes compared to 13 percent of the Native American hunter-gatherer societies and one-third of Germany's population during the 17th century. He also notes the acceleration of moral progress such as women's rights, civil rights, gay rights, animal rights, and the rights of children.[4]

He doesn't mention that we exterminated nearly 200 million of our own kind in major and minor wars during the 20th century or that our primary occupation appears to be tribal warfare. Nor does he speak of the oppression of human rights elsewhere on our planet. Worldwide reports of sightings of unconventional flying objects and non-human entities in association with these craft and widespread reports of alien abduction seem to point to monitoring by one or more advanced alien species around the globe. This monitoring of our civilization could indicate that technologically advanced societies have outgrown their primitive, brutal behavior and developed a policy of respect and consideration for other cultures. If this holds true, we have less to fear from extraterrestrial contact as we move toward the possibility of official disclosure.

Of serious concern is the impact of an extraterrestrial presence that is entirely different from humankind in its social structure, cultural values, ethics, communication style, and species. Many experiencers have reported aliens who appear to possess a collective consciousness guided by empathic behavior. They seem to function as a unit with well-defined goals and a limited ability to make independent decisions. Communication is telepathic and is projected toward the human with little room for two-way communication. Some describe this intelligent presence as possessing a hive-like mentality, perceiving human behavior from the same perspective with which we perceive apes. Some are described as having a human appearance, whereas others are hairless, large-eyed Greys with spindly appendages and perhaps non-mammalian. Some experiencers have reported giant insectoid creatures, commonly referred to as Mantis types, with an intense demeanor capable of inflicting harm if they wished to. They are sometimes observed working in concert with the Greys. Still others report Reptilian types. If the presence of a non-human highly advanced species that is very dissimilar to humankind is true, we could suffer massive disruption as the result of disclosure regardless of how benevolent their behavior is toward humans. We must consider the traumatic effect that alien abduction has inflicted upon otherwise–emotionally stable, high-functioning individuals. What if it is true that highly advanced non-humans are conducting reproductive, genetic, and emotional experiments upon humans without consideration for human ethical and legal values? These purported intrusions have been highly disruptive in the lives of experiencers until they have reached the revelation that, before they were born, they volunteered to advance human development and spiritual growth through contact.

If these reports are true, and not the result of a massive space age delusion, disclosure could have dire consequences upon humanity. Social, economic, political, and religious institutions could be shaken to the core. This type of disclosure would have the greatest impact upon fundamentalist religious groups who believe that God could not possibly have created life elsewhere in the universe. Christians comprise about one-third of the world's population, and about 13 percent are Evangelicals who adhere to biblical text. Extraterrestrial contact is in direct defiance to biblical scripture, which states only one God created man and it was in His own image. All other creation and intervention are believed to be demonic. Experiencers who claim to have been abducted or to have consensual contact with aliens, who believe they have a dual soul connection with an alien consciousness, or who believe they have been genetically manipulated by aliens could be targeted for extermination by Christians who believe they have demonic roots.

Dr. David Jacobs has studied the UFO and alien abduction phenomenon for nearly 50 years. His research suggests that advanced aliens have begun a process of integration on Earth that is the outcome of ongoing reproductive and gynecological experiments. If he and other researchers are correct, a genetically modified human form that is indistinguishable from other humans is being integrated into human society.

From a Christian standpoint advanced aliens represent fallen angels who carry non-human DNA. Therefore they are no longer human, but modern-day Nephilim, the offspring of the sons of God and the daughters of man, such as those who inhabited the earth in biblical times before the Great Flood.

Other religions take a less-dire view of an alien presence on Earth. Surveys conducted by various religious leaders reveal that the majority of adherents believe their faith would not be fundamentally altered by an extraterrestrial presence. However, they are concerned that it would precipitate a religious crisis especially among adherents to traditional religious doctrine.

Gabriel Funes, chief astronomer at the Vatican Observatory and scientific advisor to the Pope, has stated that the Catholic Church would welcome extraterrestrial visitors as part of God's creation. The late Monsignor Corrado Balducci, a demonologist close to Pope John Paul II, conducted an in-depth analysis of UFO sightings and the non-human entities sighted in association with unconventional craft. He concluded that we must view extraterrestrials as God's creatures—not angels or demons—adding that an advanced race of aliens is probably more spiritually advanced than humans.

Islam, the second-largest religious group on Earth, comprises nearly one-quarter of the world's population, followed by secular groups at 16 percent and Hinduism at 15 percent. Seven percent are Buddhists and 2 percent are Jewish.[5] In an interview on the website "Educating Humanity," Dr. Shabir Ally, president of the Islamic Information and Dawah Center in Toronto, states that the Quran tells of the Lord of the worlds, not one world, indicating that life might exist on other worlds. He speaks of a world of human beings, a world of the Jinn (beings that are concealed from our senses but can manifest in physical form), a world of angels, and so forth. The 29th verse in the Quran's 42nd chapter states, "And of His signs is the creation of the heavens and the earth and what He has dispersed throughout them as creatures."[6] Thus, it appears that Islam does not limit its belief system to life on Earth, or the deceptive Jinn or angels.

Jewish theology offers various conflicting opinions. Ezekiel 48:35 speaks of 18,000 worlds over which God presides for the service of humankind. The purpose is said to be for repopulation when the earth becomes overcrowded.

Buddhist and Hindu populations, it seems, would have the least difficulty accepting an alien presence. Their religious beliefs embrace the idea that intelligent life resides elsewhere. Buddhists believe that thousands of worlds are inhabited, whereas Hindus speculate that humans and aliens reincarnate to one another's worlds.

To date, more than 20 countries have initiated partial disclosure through the release of government documents, UFO studies, and statements by military and political leaders. The Argentinean Air Force's UFO Commission has pledged to document, analyze, and study aerial phenomena in an orderly, systematic, and truthful manner. Brazil's Air Force meets openly with top UFO researchers to discuss UFO sightings and examine classified UFO documents. Rodrigo Bravo, a Chilean military aviator and correspondent for Brazil's *Revista UFO*, disclosed the following statement by the Chilean Army: "There is no longer any need to deny or ignore the UFO situation. They represent a real and very serious threat. Today we are challenged by a complex phenomenon whose characteristics cannot be explained within natural terrestrial confines."[7]

Hundreds of USAF files have been released through the Freedom of Information Act and the CIA has recently released some of its UFO files and published a history of its involvement in the study of UFOs from 1947 to 1990. Yet, despite the release of evidence by numerous government sources, there has been no official disclosure by the UN, the United States, or any of the heads of state worldwide.

Historically, a number of prominent figures have disclosed the UFO presence. In 1961, Roscoe Hillenkoeter (1897–1982), the first director of the Central Intelligence Agency, in a letter to Congress and reported in the *New York Times* stated, "Behind the scenes, high-ranking Air Force officers are soberly concerned about UFOs.

But through official secrecy and ridicule, many citizens are led to believe the unknown flying saucers are nonsense."[8]

Canada's former defense minister and deputy prime minister under Pierre Trudeau from 1963 to 1967, Paul Hellyer has voiced the unofficial statement, "UFOs are as real as the airplanes flying over our heads."[9] He stated that in 1961 war nearly broke out when 50 UFOs were tracked flying in formation across Europe. The Supreme Allied Commander was prepared to press the panic button. But the UFOs changed direction and headed over the North Pole. He told of a three-year investigation that concluded "4 different species, at least, have been visiting this planet for thousands of years," and is very concerned about our development of atomic weapons.[10] It is indeed unfortunate that he did not disclose the source of his information. It is clear that a government agency, such as the Canadian Air Force, carries more credibility than an unknown media source.

Mercury and Gemini astronaut Gordon Cooper (1927–2004), who in the mid to late 1950s was stationed at Edwards AFB at the Flight Test Engineering Division, disclosed that on May 3, 1957, his crew was setting up a precision landing system on the dry lake bed when a silent, saucer-shaped craft hovered over the men, put down three landing gear, and landed 50 yards away. When cameramen approached it, it lifted off and flew away at a high rate of speed. Cooper held the film up to the window and viewed clear close-up shots of a saucer that he believed was not manufactured on earth. On November 9, 1978, he wrote to Granada's Ambassador Griffith at the United Nations:

> For many years I have lived with a secret, in a secrecy imposed on all specialists in astronautics. I can now reveal that every day, in the USA, our radar instruments capture objects of a form and composition unknown to us. And there are thousands of witness reports and a quantity of documents to prove this, but nobody wants to make them public. Why? Because authority is afraid that people may

think of God knows what kind of horrible invaders. So the password still is: We have to avoid panic by all means.[11]

Apollo 14 astronaut Edgar Mitchell (1930–2016), who founded the Institute of Noetic Sciences in 1972, after experiencing a profound sense of universal connectedness during a journey into space, disclosed that he had acquired information about the UFO crash in Roswell, New Mexico, from people who were knowledgeable and under severe threat to maintain confidentiality or pay the price of disclosure. He carried the story to the Intelligence Committee of the Joint Chiefs of Staff at the Pentagon, asking for confirmation. An unnamed admiral confirmed that the story was true, but Mitchell was denied additional information. Retired Colonel George Filer met with Mitchell at the National Press Club during the Disclosure Project. When asked about evidence of an alien presence on the moon, Mitchell replied, "I signed a NASA strict security contract that I had seen no evidence of aliens; therefore I didn't see any evidence of aliens on the moon, but all my astronaut friends had," and added, "I have met with credible professionals within two governments who have testified to their own firsthand experiences with close encounters. They include members of military, intelligence, and government whose official duties involved the extraterrestrial presence. As is expected, they were all bound by strict security oath agreements which prevented them from disclosing any of this."[12]

Despite the exposé of the UFO presence by a number of prominent figures, there has been no disclosure from official sources of intelligent life elsewhere in the Universe or on planet Earth. Yet, public opinion polls indicate that increasing numbers of the U.S. population believe that UFOs could be a sign of extraterrestrial visitation. In 1996, a Gallup poll indicated that 71 percent believed the U.S. government was covering up the UFO presence. In 2002, a Sci Fi Channel Roper Poll revealed nearly the same results.[13]

The revelation that a UFO crashed in Roswell in 1947 and served as an impetus for some of our modern technological development would raise many questions. Was the craft intelligently controlled by sentient beings? Why was this covered up for nearly 70 years? Have we back-engineered their technology? Were there survivors? If so, how similar are they to humans? Are they benevolent? Where do they come from? What do they want from Planet Earth? Are we safe? Safety and stability are two of our greatest concerns. Without full assurance from military and political leaders that an ET presence does not pose a threat to the safety and security of the world's people, there could be widespread panic.

Certainly, safety and security are major concerns to military defense forces. Knowledge of a benevolent presence that does not wish to interfere with human development would cause less disruption than ignorance about the visitors' nature and motives. An innocuous presence that has been monitoring our behavior for centuries, without interference, would cause less disruption than visitors who are perceived as a potential threat. The public would be curious about their appearance, their behavior, their social values, their religious beliefs, or if they believe in a higher power. If they are perceived as possessing knowledge that is contrary to our understanding of human history, with regard to our scientific and religious beliefs, it could shake the foundations of our collective beliefs.

How would we treat the visitors with respect to the ownership of property and the right to reside in a particular country? Would non-human entities be considered illegal aliens? Would we allow them to become citizens? Would we attempt to deport them to their own planet or dimension? Their technological superiority would establish their dominance over Earthlings. How would the Earth's military power structure react to the knowledge that they are powerless to protect the planet against the alien presence should it decide to take over? Will world leaders apologize to abductees for failing to protect them? For the cover-up? For employing harmful tactics to destroy their credibility?

The fact is that, despite nearly 70 years of research and investigation, we know very little about the extraterrestrial intelligence that appears to be visiting planet Earth. Who are they? Where are they from? Are they from a distant planet? Are they interdimensional? Have they always resided on Earth, only in a hidden capacity? What if they have been surveying Earth periodically throughout human history, and have established bases under our waters and in our solar system? How do they differ from humans physically and emotionally? What is their social structure? Do they have cultural values? Do they subscribe to ethical values? Are they spiritual? Do they have an appreciation for art and music? What if they adhere to power structure values similar to our own?

Or, what if they are a highly advanced spiritual presence that is merely watching over our development, to ensure that we don't destroy ourselves? Perhaps the detonation of nuclear weapons sent shockwaves to the watchers of the Earth. If this occurred, they might be concerned that our technological development has exceeded the evolution of our emotional consciousness. Perhaps we are on the brink of survival or extinction depending upon humankind's ability to rein in our aggressive behavior. One might speculate that the alien visitors' reproductive and emotional experiments will end in positive evolutionary change to advance human development through the manipulation of our gene pool. Will this lead to ascension, as many experiencers believe? Or is it a smokescreen for a more nefarious plan?

The disclosure of an alien presence by world leaders could lead to disruption of our institutions and hysteria among those whose belief systems would be shaken to the bone. For all of the reasons mentioned, it seems unlikely that our leadership will disclose an alien presence anytime soon.

CHAPTER 12

FACT, *NOT* FICTION

The scientific investigation of unidentified aerial phenomena has been termed the "Great Taboo" by academic and industrial scientists who have been refused funding for its study. Historically, government scientists such as Dr. Edward Condon and Dr. Donald Menzel have lobbied in opposition to this forbidden science. Their influence has carried to the mainstream, and those perceived as heretics have been sanctioned. Efforts were made to damage the careers of Dr. James McDonald, Dr. Allen Hynek, and Stanton Friedman in the name of political expediency. In 1969, the National Academy of Sciences declared that no funding should be made available to study the physical evidence after Edward Condon proclaimed his personal opinion that UFOs are not real, an opinion that was not supported by the evidence studied by his committee of scientists. Although the AIAA UFO Subcommittee's follow-up study discovered that 30 percent of the cases studied by the Condon Committee could not be identified, as conventional vehicles or phenomena, the scientific establishment ignored the evidence. Edward Condon, Donald Menzel, Hector Quintanilla, and Philip Klass successfully lobbied against the allocation of federal funding for the scientific study of UFOs. Skeptics contend that the subject is not worthy of serious scientific investigation, stating that most reports are anecdotal at best and have no scientific merit. This has resulted in nearly 50 years of scientific denial by mainstream science despite the fact that many scientists who had studied the UFO evidence were forced to conclude that they were real.

One of the greatest obstacles to the objective analysis of the evidence has been the propensity of the scientific community to separate out parcels of evidence for analysis without considering all of the evidence in a particular case in its entirety. We believe that it is important to separate out physical evidence for scientific investigation. However, it should not be evaluated in a vacuum as if it were entirely separate from the case at hand. For example, when there has been a credible observation of a landed craft and physical trace evidence on the ground where the landing occurred, and the witness has experienced dermal burns in association with the craft, it is not appropriate for the scientific community to ignore the proximity of the witness to the heat-radiating craft. It is unscientific for scientists to ignore the witness's testimony and state that the burns could have been caused by thunderstorm activity in the area, especially when it is based upon speculation about the weather conditions. Likewise, if a UFO has been tracked on radar by a highly experienced operator and there is ground-visual and air-visual contact by military pilots, the radar report should not be dismissed as a ghost on the radar screen and the eyewitness observers dismissed as having misperceived information.

Radar anomalies were analyzed without regard for the radar operator's years of experience and expertise. Each parcel of information was dismissed when it was not analyzed in reference to the body of evidence concerning the case. In the past, radar-visual sightings have been evaluated separate from the pilot sightings and eye witness testimony despite the credibility of the observers. The experienced flight crew's visual observations of perplexing craft have been dismissed as weak, anecdotal evidence caused by human misperception. In one case, the speculation that a firefly had been caught between the windows of a jetliner was employed to dismiss a credible UFO sighting report by an experienced flight crew. This methodology has been the greatest challenge to overcome in the evaluation of evidence, partly due to the resistance by physical scientists to accept social science. This limited approach is evident in the scientific analysis of many of the compelling historical cases that have been discussed in this book. It is a fact that most sightings are not very exciting and that most can be explained in relatively conventional terms. However, it is simply irrational and illogical to assume that, because most sightings turn out to be conventional phenomena seen under unconventional circumstances, then all must be.

The primary body of UFO evidence consists of UFO sighting reports, multiple witness close encounters, radar-visual reports, photographic evidence (still and video), physical trace evidence (environmental changes in soil, vegetation, trees, etc.) produced by UFOs, eyewitness testimony pertaining to crashed vehicles, government documents, and major scientific studies, (Project Blue Book Special Report #14). Obviously, witness credibility is of utmost importance, and a single witness sighting carries less weight than a multiple witness sighting by law enforcement officers or military pilots.

An important multiple-witness close encounter occurred on April 17, 1966, and involved several law enforcement officers across two states. At about 4:45 a.m. Ravenna, Ohio, Deputy Sheriff Dale Spaur and Deputy Wilbur "Barney" Neff heard a transmission over their police radio that a woman in nearby Summit County had observed a lighted object as large as a house over her neighborhood. The officers did not take the report seriously until they stopped to investigate an abandoned vehicle and observed a craft rising up from a wooded area at near ground level. It emitted a humming sound similar to an overloaded transformer as it moved overhead. The wobbling big as a house craft flew over them at approximately 100 feet in the distance bathing the officers in intense light. They radioed headquarters and were instructed to follow the craft by Sergeant Schoenfelt, while he tried to dispatch a photo unit to the scene. In a game of cat and mouse, the officers chased the perplexing craft at speeds up to 105 mph for 85 miles. It maintained an altitude of approximately 300–500 feet and illuminated the ground below it. When they made a wrong turn, the craft stopped and waited for them.

As dawn streaked the sky the officers were able to see that the structured metallic craft was 50 feet across and 15–20 feet high. Additional officers who were rushing to the scene remained in radio contact with Spaur and Neff. Police officer Wayne Huston joined the chase 40 miles east of the starting point near the Pennsylvania state line. The Portage police cruiser was running low on gas so the officers stopped to enlist the assistance of Pennsylvania police officer Frank Panzenella, who called his dispatcher. The four officers stopped and the craft hovered above them until an aircraft from the Pittsburgh Airport passed under it. It then ascended vertically at a rapid rate of speed, stopped in mid-air, and continued to ascend until it disappeared from sight. Police Chief Gerald Buchert, from Mantua, photographed the object, but was instructed by Air Force officials not to release the photo. The NICAP investigator described the object as having the appearance of two saucers inverted upon one another. The upper half was lighter in color than the lower half. The photo has never been released for evaluation.

Project Blue Book's director, Hector Quintanilla, "identified" the UFO as a communications satellite and the planet Venus despite the credibility of the officers involved. He interviewed Officer Spaur for less than 5 minutes and used the word "mirage" in his questioning.[1] Spaur and Neff's superior officer Ross Dustman rejected Project Blue Book's explanation, stating, "It was not a satellite and it was not Venus. I've seen Venus many times, but I never saw Venus 50 feet above the road and moving from side to side like this was."[2] Finally, under Congressional pressure, Quintanilla traveled to Ohio and interviewed officers Spaur and Neff along with radio operator Sheriff Robert Wilson, who had been in radio contact with the two officers during their pursuit, and Sheriff Ross Dustman, who vouched for the good character of his officers. The officers' testimony made it clear that the craft exhibited none of the characteristics of a satellite, nor the planet Venus. They clearly recalled observing the moon and the planet Venus that night as well as the moving object. Despite the detailed information in their testimony, it was written off by Project Blue Book and the Condon Committee, and is continuing to be dismissed by debunkers who refuse to consider all of the evidence.

Ted Phillips is recognized as the world's leading expert on physical traces found at UFO landing sites. He has collected more than 5,000 samples of physical trace evidence in more than 80 countries. One of his most compelling cases occurred at 7:00 p.m. on November 2, 1971, in Delphos, Kansas. Sixteen-year-old Ronald Johnson was tending to his sheep in their pen only 250 feet from the back door of his family's farmhouse. His mother yelled that his dinner was nearly ready and he shouted that he'd be in soon. Moments later, he heard a rumbling sound and noticed an object that was glowing like a welder's torch only 75 feet in the distance. He told Phillips that the multicolored object, which was domed at the top and at the base with a slight bulge at the center, was hovering only 2 feet or so above the ground. It appeared to be about 9 feet in diameter and 10 feet high. The brightly glowing object seemed to be releasing a shimmering substance from its underside that was visible within its intense glow. The terrified young man remained frozen in place for several minutes behind a stand of small trees as he and his dog stood mystified. Finally, the object lifted into the air, emitting a high-pitched sound, and cleared a nearby shed by only 4 feet. As the sound changed in frequency and the glow of the object increased in intensity, Ronald became completely blinded. This persisted for several seconds, and led to headaches and sore eyes for several days thereafter. Finally, having regained his sight, the agitated young man ran to his house, screaming for his parents to watch the object leave. Now, half the size of the full moon, it departed toward the south.

Upon inspection of the landing site, they saw a gray-white glowing ring in the soil and luminosity on the nearby tree. When they touched it they felt a cool, slick, crust-like texture, as if the soil had crystallized. Their fingers felt numb, as if local anesthesia had been applied, and when Mrs. Johnson wiped her fingers on her slacks, her leg numbed under the substance. Their numbness persisted for days to several weeks. Mrs. Johnson photographed the luminous deposit that was glowing so brightly, she didn't need a flash. The family then drove to Delphos and reported the event to their local newspaper. The next morning the reporter and the local sheriff photographed the site and the sheriff collected soil samples. A month later, Dr. Allen Hynek was notified and Phillips began his investigation.

Phillips collected soil samples adhering to standard protocols and sent the samples to several scientific laboratories for analysis. The most thorough analysis was completed by Dr. Erol Faruk, an organic chemist who did post-doctoral research at Oxford and Nottingham before working as a development chemist at GlaxoSmithKline Pharmaceuticals. His papers have been published in peer-reviewed scientific journals. His analysis concluded that the ring soil was extremely water-repellent, comparing it to pouring water onto a glass plate. He mixed the soil with water in a centrifuge and exposed it to UV light. It fluoresced. He stated that the sample contained an organic compound that could emit light when exposed to air and postulated that a chemiluminescent spray had created the elongated section of the ring corresponding to the wind direction on the night of the near landing. Fairy rings, a natural fungus infection, was considered, but it did not conform to the properties of the ring. They start from the center and enlarge slowly over time. This did not occur in the Delphos ring. There was fungal matter in the ring, but it was insignificant in comparison to the soluble organic substance in the ring. His results concurred with those of Dr. Hubert Lechevalier, an expert on fungal diseases and Phyllis Budinger, MS, an analytical chemist with 35 years' experience at BP Amoco, formerly Standard Oil. Dr. Faruk submitted his paper to the scientific journals *Nature* and the *Journal of the British Interplanetary Society*. Both declined without reading his work. The latter stated that it did not intend to publish scientific papers on UFOs. He then contacted Seth Shostak, who had stated that he would welcome one very good physical evidence case for UFOs, but, according to Faruk, Shostak dismissed it as unworthy of scientific investigation because he needed to point to "one thing that was a clincher."[3] Faruk replied that an isotopic analysis of the isolated soil compound would identify anomalies and that all of the evidence should be considered, including chemical analyses which corroborated the witness' testimony. Shostak summarily dismissed eyewitness testimony, stating that it is unreliable, but recommended that Faruk submit his paper to a refereed scientific journal. Faruk found it remarkable that Shostak showed little natural scientific curiosity toward the evidence he submitted, but made another attempt to have his paper published. Again, he was informed that, regardless of the quality of his paper, the journal's policy was not to publish UFO papers. Despite his efforts, his paper was not deemed publishable in any mainstream peer-reviewed scientific journal.

It seems clear that most UFO evidence is more amenable to forensic analysis than the scientific investigation of a single artifact. However, single samples of physical evidence, such as metallic sample with highly unusual properties, have been analyzed. For this reason, the authors are advocating a multidisciplinary team of scientists and investigators to examine the evidence. It should include unbiased physicists, chemists, medical doctors, police detectives, psychologists, sociologists, parapsychologists, document experts, and highly experienced UFO investigators, who have examined and evaluated the many types of evidence in the most compelling cases. This should not be limited to recent cases, as it is important to evaluate the best evidence cases of all time. The preponderance of evidence is of vital importance.

There is no question that there have been many UFO sightings reported in conjunction with nuclear facilities, including research laboratories such as Los Alamos National Laboratory (Los Alamos, New Mexico), Oak Ridge National Laboratory (Oak Ridge, Tennessee), and the Hanford works in eastern Washington State. An outstanding source for information on this topic is the 602-page *UFOs and Nukes: Extraordinary Encounters at Nuclear Weapons Sites* by Robert Hastings (Author House, 2008). Sightings have occurred near nuclear power reactors, and nuclear weapons tests, and nuclear tipped InterContinental Ballistic Missile (ICBM) facilities. Hastings has been collecting such information for more than three decades. Certainly one would expect that alien visitors to our warlike planet might be expected to be interested in our nuclear activities.

There have been observations of UFOs near Minuteman missile launch facilities. In several instances they have apparently shut down ICBMs. The most detailed discussion of such an event was provided by retired Air Force Captain Robert Salas in his book, *Unidentified: The UFO Phenomenon: How World Governments Have Conspired to Conceal Humanity's Biggest Secret* (2014). We know of no one more qualified to tell of what happened at Malmstrom Air Force Base in 1967. Salas was a 1964 graduate of the Air Force Academy and a launch officer at the Minuteman Missile facility. The event makes fascinating reading. When a UFO showed up at the gate, suddenly the impossible happened: All 10 missiles went offline, one after the other. This supposedly was impossible, but it happened. As a humorous sidelight Bill Nye (often called the "Science Guy" for his TV work) said on Larry King that it was just a short circuit! It was triply protected from such events. There have been a number of other instances of such interference with nuclear-tipped missiles, including one in the Soviet Union when a UFO apparently caused several missiles to go online until the missile officer shut things down.

Soviet missiles have also been affected. Considering that we didn't discover the neutron until 1932 and that both fission and fusion weren't considered until 1938, we might reasonably expect that most other civilizations in our local neighborhood are aware of nuclear energy. There are about 10,000 planets within 100 light years. And we know that most stars are a few billion years old. There is no question that the Air Force was worried about sightings near nuclear installations. Were they operated by alien or Earth-based spies? Anyone wanting some historic data can check out on the internet "Nuclear Connection Project NCP Report no. NCP-03: UFO Sightings and Nuclear Sites" by researcher Larry Hatch. The article, compiled on September 13, 1998, has a list of 193 sightings in or about nuclear sites beginning in 1944. Security personnel at Oak Ridge, Los Alamos, White Sands, and so forth were certainly concerned.

It should be no surprise that there have been myriad UFO sightings by private, commercial, and military pilots. The first sighting to attract a great deal of media interest was that by private pilot Kenneth Arnold near Mt. Rainier on June 24, 1947. He had more than 4,000 flying hours. It was broad daylight and he was sensible enough to time the flight of the group of nine crescent-shaped craft that he observed. The speed came out in excess of 1,500 miles per hour. The speed record for aircraft was only about 700 miles per hour at that time. Thousands of pilot sightings have followed. There have been many fascinating compilations. Of most significance have been those of Dr. Richard H. Haines, a retired NASA scientist. He was also the founder of NARCAP (the National Aviation Reporting Center on Anomalous Phenomena). It is primarily a research organization with the very important virtue of providing anonymity for pilots wanting to make reports of their sightings of UFOs without any publicity. It is a fully accredited 501c3 nonprofit organization. He and executive director Ted Roe have collected more than 3,000 sighting experiences and released several reports. A primary focus has been to call attention to the possible dangers of close encounters between aircraft and UFOs. It is open to membership and can be found at NARCAP.org. A typical paper by Dr. Haines is "Fifty-Six Aircraft Pilot Sightings Involving Electromagnetic effects" (25 pages; copyright 1992). They have added many more such incidents to their files.

Ufology is certainly not the only area of science that the scientific community (primarily those in academia) has attacked. Our book *Science Was Wrong* has 14 chapters, each dealing with false claims by prominent, well-educated scientists who did most of their "research" by proclamation. Most stem from the assumption that we really know most of what can be known. Man will never fly in a vehicle; space travel is utter bilge; radio waves can only travel in straight lines; and so forth. No room was allowed for what we don't yet know or will be discovered. The neutron wasn't discovered until 1932. Nuclear fission and nuclear fusion were both "discovered" in 1938. The stars have of course been producing their energy by fusion for many billion years—despite our ignorance.

It is easier to understand the attacks from Harvard professor of astronomy Dr. Donald Menzel once we learned of his long-term connection with the National Security Agency and other intelligence agencies. But even without that specific connection, we know that there are many misconceptions about what drives academic scientists in their attacks on unusual phenomena. One thing is fear of ridicule. We have both heard "Please don't tell anybody about my interest in this or that unusual area of research whether it is telepathy, remote viewing, or ufology," even though opinion polls have shown that there are more believers in UFO reality than nonbelievers, and that the greater the education the more likely to accept this "oddball" area. One endemic problem is that academic scientists tend to believe that if information isn't published in peer-reviewed scientific journals, it is of no value.

This, of course, ignores classified research. Two different academics told Friedman that if Roswell had really happened there would have been a need to pull many physicists from their academic positions to investigate. This totally ignores all the scientists working in industry and at the national laboratories such as Oak Ridge, Los Alamos, Livermore, Sandia, Hanford, and so forth, all of whom require security clearances. A recent check showed that the total budget that year of the three nuclear weapons labs (Los Alamos, Livermore, and Sandia) was greater than the total expenditure of the National Science Foundation on all its research grants. Los Alamos alone employs more than 6,000 people and has an annual budget of more than two billion dollars. Though these scientists occasionally publish in a scientific journal, most of the work winds up in classified documents. If one looks at books by astronomers and SETI specialists, one rarely finds reference to such large-scale scientific UFO studies as "Project Blue Book Special Report Number 14" (data on 3,201 sightings, with more than 200 charts, tables, and graphs) or the "Symposium on Unidentified Flying Objects" (247 pages), which has papers by 12 scientists presented to the House Committee on Science and Astronautics.

Both the press and the academics seem blissfully unaware of the national security implications of alien visitations. It is clear that the national defense forces of every country would like to be able to duplicate the technological capabilities of alien saucers. The ability to both fly rapidly and silently with hyper-maneuverability, make right angle turns, hover, and land and take off from a small area would obviously be of great interest to all air and space programs. There are serious concerns with possible alien partnerships with national defense forces of one's enemies. For some in power, the religious implications of alien visitations could be quite threatening. Religion is still an important factor in the politics especially of the Middle East and elsewhere. Some people seem blissfully unaware of the simple fact that the total military budget on Earth this year is about a trillion dollars.

Many professors and journalists have expressed strong views that in today's world, with the Internet, no secrets can be kept. For example, Dr. William Markowitz, at the time a professor of physics at Marquette University in Milwaukee, made the following claim in the prestigious journal *Science*: "In regard to secrecy, the charge that the US Air Force is withholding information that UFOs are extraterrestrial is absurd. The prestige of announcing the existence of extraterrestrial beings would be so great that no scientist, journalist, politician or government whether of the United States, England, France, the USSR or China would hesitate for a moment to release the news. It could not be kept a secret."[4] Apparently he believes that the search for prestige (as opposed to power and profit) is the driving factor in academia. Next, I suppose he would have suggested that we would have shared the development of the atomic bomb because it would have added to the scientist or journalist's prestige. Ted Koppel, an ABC newsman, when hosting Friedman and Philip Klass on *Nightline,* said that Washington is notoriously leaky about secrecy. It is hard to believe that he ever had a clearance. The fact is that many billions of dollars' worth of labor on classified programs has been kept Secret or TOP SECRET or even TOP SECRET CODEWORD. Markowitz joined with Condon and Menzel in trying to keep the American Association for the Advancement of Science from holding their UFO symposium. I think we can guarantee that Markowitz did not know about Menzel working for the NSA and other agencies for 30 years. It was kept secret.

There is no question that Condon was an eminent, highly qualified theoretical physicist. Very few people have been president of the American Physical Society and of the American Association for the Advancement of Science, as he was. He had been elected to the National Academy of Sciences in 1944. This makes it all the more difficult to understand why the Condon Report and the study showed so many signs of being unscientific. Condon was apparently not involved in the investigation of any of the more than 100 UFO cases they looked at. Perhaps he relied too heavily on the advice of his old buddy Donald Menzel of Harvard, who wrote three very negative books about UFOs. A particularly strange aspect is the total failure to mention anywhere in the report the largest scientific study of UFOs ever conducted—namely, Project Blue Book Special Report No. 14. The study was done for the United States Air Force Project Blue Book by the large and very well-respected Battelle Memorial Institute in Columbus, Ohio. They looked at 3,201 UFO cases, and provided more than 200 charts, graphs, tables, and maps. They categorized all the reports as follows: Aircraft, Balloon, Astronomical, Psychological Aberration, Insufficient Information, or UNKNOWN. No sighting could be listed as an UNKNOWN unless all four of the scientists evaluating the cases agreed it was an UN-KNOWN. Any two could list it as a known. Obviously the UNKNOWNS should have been the focus of the study. UNKNOWN was defined as "Those reports of sightings wherein the description of the object and its maneuvers could not be fitted to a pattern by any known object or phenomenon."[5]

A very significant 21.5 percent of the cases studied in detail were listed as UNKNOWNS. The results consistently showed that the probability that the UNKNOWNS were just missed KNOWNS was less than 1 percent. This point cannot be stressed too strongly. The UNKNOWNS were not poorly reported sightings or those for which there was insufficient data. More than 60 percent of the UNKNOWNS were observed for longer than one minute and more than 35 percent were observed for longer than five minutes. Ten percent were observed for longer than 30 minutes. The great majority of the UNKNOWNS were found to be different in shape than conventional aircraft. Typically, they were described as metallic symmetrical discs or large, cigar-shaped objects into or out of which the disks would fly. In general, the UNKNOWNS lacked wings, external engines, tails, propellers, rotors, jets, and conventional lighting. They had very little if any exhaust, and were silent or made very little noise in comparison to conventional aircraft. The flight pattern was different from that of conventional aircraft. The UNKNOWNS were often described as accelerating or decelerating abruptly rather than over longer periods, as was required by conventional aircraft in the early 1950s. The UNKNOWNS were observed hovering motionless and without sound. They moved straight up and down or back and forth in a zigzag motion very rapidly, without turning as conventional aircraft did. They appeared capable of making abrupt turns at high speed.

One might think that perhaps Condon and his cohorts were unaware of the report. However, Friedman had sent Condon a letter calling attention to it and received a response from Condon. Marden had found, many years later, that Condon had actually sent a copy of that letter to Menzel. In addition, Friedman had found in Menzel's Harvard papers that he had a copy of the report as well, and he also never mentioned it in his UFO books or papers. There is no doubt that Condon was not shy about expressing strong views about such controversial areas as civilian control of atomic energy research. Condon was apparently very sensitive about his involvement in the study, and had told Friedman and others that the files of the University of Colorado study had not been preserved. But they were indeed preserved at the American Philosophical Society Library. Both authors have reviewed many of those papers at the APS. One has to ask: Why the omissions?

It is easy to prove that many government agencies have been involved with the enigma of flying saucers. But very difficult to determine just what they have learned. Most people are aware that for many years in the 1950s and 1960s, there was a group called project Blue Book located at Wright-Patterson Air Force Base in Dayton, Ohio, whose primary mission was to receive reports of UFO sightings mostly from civilians. They did a number of field investigations and issued brief annual progress reports. Supposedly it was *not* classified. It had been preceded by two other official projects: Project Sign and Project Grudge. Dr. J. Allen Hynek, an astronomer, was the official scientific consultant to Blue Book. Initially he had been at Ohio State University in nearby Columbus, Ohio. He then became chairman of the astronomy department at Northwestern University in the Chicago suburb of Evanston, Illinois. The Blue Book files contain more than 12,000 reports and eventually were sent to the National Archives in College Park, Maryland, after Blue Book was closed in October 1969. It was a full 10 years later in 1979 that a copy of the memo from USAF General Carroll Bolender was obtained and distributed by researcher Robert Todd of the Philadelphia area with a number of documents obtained as a result of a Freedom of Information request.

Bolender had no connection with Blue Book, but was an engineer on the Lunar Excursion Module (deputy director of development, DCS/Research and Development), which successfully landed and took off from the moon in July 1969. He had been asked to make a recommendation about the future of Blue Book. Officially Dr. Edward Condon, head of the University of Colorado study of UFOs, published in early 1969, had recommended that Blue Book be closed, as it seemed to be making little contribution to National Defense or Science. There were two very surprising comments in Bolender's October 20, 1969, memo:

1. Moreover, reports of unidentified flying objects which could affect national security are reported in accordance with JANAP 146 and Air Force Manual 55-11 and are not part of the Blue Book System.

2. Termination of Project Blue Book would leave no official federal office to receive reports of UFOs. However, as already stated, reports of UFOs which could affect national security would continue to be handled through the standard Air Force procedures designed for this purpose.[6]

These are both shocking statements, especially coming from an Air Force General. Surely from a military viewpoint, the reports that can affect national security should have been the most important. UNKNOWNS. UFOs crossing national boundaries could start wars, couldn't they, if not quickly identified? Friedman actually spoke with Bolender, and the general agreed that there were two separate channels of communications, one for those reports that could impact on national security, such as a case that Friedman mentioned of a saucer going down the runway at a strategic Air Command Base. Furthermore, ever since Project Blue Book was closed, the Air Force had said it was doing nothing about UFOs because there was no security concern. Along with these surprises is the simple fact that the Office of Naval Intelligence has constantly maintained that it has no information about UFO sightings. Most investigators have heard of reports of saucers seen by naval personnel and entering and leaving the ocean. So, obviously, one has to ask where those reports go.

There is a simple and straightforward answer: They went to a super-secret government agency established for that purpose. Operation Majestic 12 was a highly controversial briefing for President-Elect General Dwight Eisenhower in November 1952 after he had been elected but before he took office in January 1953.

Friedman has dealt at length with all the objections raised to the reality of Operation Majestic 12 in his book *TOP SECRET/MAJIC*. He made a particular effort to examine the facts in two areas:

1. How a hoaxer could have known a number of almost-trivial details not previously known before the documents were received, such as that Robert Cutler was out of the United States on the date the Cutler-Twining memo was written and hence could not have signed it, and it isn't signed.

2. The false claims by debunkers such as that of Philip Klass that the Cutler-Twining memo must have been phony because it was done in PICA type, not the elite type supposedly always used by the National Security Council. Klass had never been to the Eisenhower library and wound up paying Friedman $1,000 for providing more than 10 such documents. The library had 250,000 pages of NSC

materials. Obviously judging the type face of them based on a mere 10 documents (obtained by mail) is irrational.

An important aspect of the discussion is that careful research has shown that there is a great deal of UFO-related information that is actually classified as TOP SECRET CODEWORD and could not be found in documents classified only at the SECRET level, such as 156 pages of TOP SECRET UMBRA NSA UFO documents, which are completely redacted except for one sentence per page. The CIA also eventually released dozens of pages of almost completely blacked-out TOP SECRET UMBRA CIA UFO documents. In both cases the released documents all predated 1985. It should be stressed that the brief (one-week-long) CIA effort to review the UFO problem, referred to as the Robertson Panel, had been classified only secret and declassified for inclusion in the Condon Report, completed in 1968. It should be obvious that the reports that could affect national security, one would hope, would be of primary interest. One obvious answer as to where they went is the very highly classified Operation Majestic 12, which didn't come to light until late 1984. It took years to deal with objections to MJ 12 touted so strenuously by the UFO debunking community. The famous Twining memo of September 23, 1947, was also classified at only the SECRET level and could not have mentioned any TOP SECRET or TOP SECRET CODEWORD data, such as recovery of alien craft near Roswell and the Plains of San Agustin in July 1947, and another near Aztec in 1948. On the other hand, it is very important to look at the makeup of the original 12 members, and number 13, Walter B. Smith, who replaced the deceased James Forrestal the first secretary of defense. Note that there were two each from the Navy, the Army, and the Air Force. Further note that Souers, Hillenkoetter, Smith, and Vandenberg had all been directors of Central Intelligence. President Eisenhower had the highest possible clearance during WWII and as head of the European Military Organization prior to becoming president. One of his first presidential actions was to establish a group known as Operation Solarium to devise a new Cold War strategy with three separate committees each looking at a different means for responding to the Soviets. Their very existence wasn't released until 25 years later.

It is perfectly clear that there were a number of very important intelligence agencies thriving with new technology after the space race and the Cold War became so important. The NSA was created in 1952 and the NRO (National Reconnaissance Office) in 1960. The Defense Intelligence Agency began in 1962. In 2012 the *Washington Post* claimed that the total military intelligence budget that year was 52.6 billion dollars. (the NSA had 10.4 billion, the CIA had 14.3 billion, and the NRO had 10.2 billion.) There are, of course, no line items for Operation Majestic 12. It seems clear that there should be a centralized, unified approach to learning as much as possible about the capabilities of the extraterrestrial visitors, as opposed to separate efforts by Army, Navy, and Air Force groups. These special capabilities would include analysis of wreckage of crashed vehicles to learn what they are made of, and analysis of instrument data obtained by aircraft and satellites to learn more about operational capabilities.

An early failure of the U.S. intelligence community was the failure to predict how soon the Soviet Union would explode their first atomic bomb. General Leslie Groves, who headed the Manhattan Project to develop and explode the first atomic bomb in July 1945, was asked in 1948 how soon the Russians would explode one. He thought it might take about eight years. In fact they exploded their first one on August 29, 1949. They also built a number of aircraft in secret to deliver them. So spying became of great importance, leading to the U-2 spy plane and then the Corona spy satellites. The first 12 were failures. The 13th provided more data about Soviet capabilities than all the earlier U-2 spy plane flights. The CIA specialized in human capabilities within and over the Soviet Union, as opposed to spying from space.

The advantage of the agencies is that they operate in secret. Their data is all born classified and is not distributed outside highly classified communications channels. Whether looking for alien capability or Soviet capability, the task is the same: collect, review, evaluate, and distribute. Undoubtedly Operation Majestic 12 changed its name when the first public accounts were given by William Moore, Jaime Shandera, and Friedman. It should be obvious that the United States and USSR would also each want to determine what information was obtained by their enemies about visiting aliens.

CONCLUSION

Now that we have revealed to you what is fact and fiction in the historical record and in today's ufology and summarized by stating what we know to be absolutely true about flying saucers and about the military-intelligence community's knowledge of this fact, we'll leave you with these closing thoughts. Many authors apparently feel there is no need to visit document archives and collections of researchers' papers to provide facts that correct many of the false claims that have been made. Marden and Friedman have spent years visiting archives to research the new information presented in this book. We have provided chapter and verse about the pseudo-scientific debunking claims loudly made by Dr. Donald Menzel, a well-known Harvard University astronomer who, unknown to the public and scientific community, secretly worked for the National Security Agency for 30 years. We probed deeper than ever before into the vicious and false debunking claims by Washington-based aviation writer Philip Klass, his motives, and his modus operandi. And we have exposed government documents released through the Freedom of Information Act that clearly document the reasons for the government cover-up. Further, we have revealed new information that exposes, once and for all, the Air Force's directive to the project chiefs concerning the expensive University of Colorado official UFO study that would end Project Blue Book and its collusion with debunkers for the purpose of promoting an anti-science agenda. Additionally, we have quoted the biased and false anti-UFO claims by its director, well-known scientist Dr. Edward U. Condon, and his personal letters that shaped public opinion.

Many members of the general public and the media do not realize how scoffers have entered the public arena and disseminated patently false information with regard to the UFO presence. In this book, we have examined the work of many debunkers and the scientists who have disseminated false and misleading information, and the debunking treatises that falsely report interstellar travel is impossible because the distances are too great and that the travel time would be too long. We have disclosed key information in the historical records that we discovered in archival collections and documents released through the Freedom of Information Act, and their significance. We have connected the historical dots with regard to the raison d'être for the cover-up and introduced the major players, both military and civilian.

It has been stated by some researchers that the UFO community is its own worst enemy because of its failure to police those who make extraordinary claims without evidence. We have demonstrated that some UFO researchers promote false information for a variety of reasons ranging from a desire for publicity to faulty reasoning. We have also offered ample evidence that some government agencies, scientists, and journalists have failed to examine the evidence in an impartial manner. Inadequate investigation, bias, and false propaganda have distorted the public's perception of

our knowledge pertaining to UFOs. Finally, we have stated what we know to be absolutely true about flying saucers and about the military-intelligence community's knowledge of this fact. We hope that this book has provided food for thought that will facilitate our readers in separating fact from fiction with regard to flying saucers.

APPENDIX

Air Force letter on Big Blast Exeter

DEPARTMENT OF THE AIR FORCE
HEADQUARTERS EIGHTH AIR FORCE (SAC)
WESTOVER AIR FORCE BASE, MASSACHUSETTS 01022

REPLY TO
ATTN OF: DOOTO

2 4 NOV 1965

SUBJECT: UFO Sighting

TO: AFSC (TDEW/UFO)

1. In reply to your letter, same subject, 16 Nov 65, and telephone conversation between SMSgt Heffley, 8AF, and Sgt Moody, Hq AFSC, on 19 Nov 65, the following information is furnished.

2. Big Blast "Coco", a SAC/NORAD training mission, was flown on 2 - 3 September, 1965. By 03/0430Z, the operational portion of the mission was complete and participating aircraft were enroute to their home stations.

3. Ten B-47 aircraft from Pease AFB were involved in Big Blast "Coco" and were estimated to arrive at their initial approach fix (Pease TACAN 320° Radial, 10 DME fix), between 03/0444Z and 03/0535Z. The town of Exeter is within the traffic pattern utilized by Air Traffic Control in the recovery of these aircraft at Pease AFB, N.H. During their approach the recovering aircraft would have been displaying standard position lights, anti-collision lights and possibly over wing and landing lights.

FOR THE COMMANDER

WILLIAM A. McGILPIN Jr
Lt Colonel, USAF
Directorate of Operations

U.S. Air Force Denial of Refueling Mission

3 Sep 65, Exeter, N Hampshire   7 Sep 65, Leon, N York

TSgt David Moody called Griffis AFB, N York and talked with Sgt Hunt, 416 SW of the 4028 Operations Squadron. Informed that Farmer Boy refueling route had been changed to Fur Trapper. Records were checked and revealed that no refueling operations were conducted on the nights of 2-3 Sep and 6 Sep. The route Fur Trapper was closed from 03/0500 to 03/0600Z for an 8th Air Force Operation "Big Blast". Sgt Hunt informed Sgt Moody that a refueling area "Down Date" controlled at Loring AFB, parelleled "Fur-Trapper" adjacent to the old Farmer Boy area. Sgt Moody called Col Smith at Loring AFB. No flights were conducted on the morning of 3 Sep and one operation of a B-47, KC-135 from Loring entered the Speedway refueling area near Indianapdis at 07/0110Z. There were no refueling operations in the New England area during the time in question. Any information on "Big Blast" should be obtained from the 8th Air Force. Sgt Moody called Major Benanders at Westover AFB at the 99th Bomb Wing, DCOI, and requested him to obtain information pertaining to the lighting and type of aircraft used in operation "Big Blast" and their positions during the time period of 03/0500-0600Z.

The above was accomplished by telephone on 28 September 1965.

....

Hunt and Bertrand Big Blast Denial

December 28, 1965

Hector Quntanilla, Jr., Major, USAF
Chief, Project Blue Book
Wright Patterson AFB
Dayton, Ohio

Dear Sir:

Since we have not heard from you since our letter to you
of December 2, we are writing this to request some
kind of answer, since we are still upset about what
happened after the Pentagon released its news saying that
we have just seen stars or planets, or high altitude
air exercises.

As we mentioned in our letter to you, it could not have
been the operation "Big Blast" you mention, since the
time of our sighting was nearly an hour after that
exercise, and it may not even have been the same date,
since you refer to our sighting as September 2. Our
sighting was on September 3. In addition, as we mentioned,
we are both familiar with all the B-47's and B-52's and
helecopter and jet fighters which are going over this
place all the time. On top of that Ptl. Bertrand had
four years of refueling experience in the Air Force,
and knows regular aircraft of all kinds. It is important
to remember that this craft we saw was not more than
100 feet in the air, and it was absolutely silent, with
no rush of air from jets or chopper blades whatever. And
it did not have any wings or tail. It lit up the entire
field, and two nearby houses turned completely red. It
stopped, hovered, and turned on a dime.

What bothers us the most is that many people are thinking
that wew were either lying or not intelligent enough to
tell the difference between what we saw and something ordinary.
Three other people saw this same thing on September 3, and
two of them appeared to be in shock from it. This was
absolutely not a case of mistaken edentity.

We both feel that it's very important for our jobs and our
reputations to get some kind of letter from you to say that
the story which the Pentagon put out was not true; it could
not possibly be, because we were the people who saw this; not
the Pentagon.

Can you please let us hear from you as soon as possible.

Sincerely,

Patrolman Eugene Bertrand   Patrolman David Hunt

Exeter Police
Exeter, New Hampshire

SECRET
COPY

TSDIN/HMM/ig/6-4100

23 September 1947

TSDIN

SUBJECT: AMC Opinion Concerning "Flying Discs"

TO: Commanding General
        Army Air Forces
        Washington 25, D. C.
        ATTENTION: Brig. General George Schulgen
                   AC/AS-2

1. As requested by AC/AS-2 there is presented below the considered opinion of this Command concerning the so-called "Flying Discs". This opinion is based on interrogation report data furnished by AC/AS-2 and preliminary studies by personnel of T-2 and Aircraft Laboratory, Engineering Division T-3. This opinion was arrived at in a conference between personnel from the Air Institute of Technology, Intelligence T-2, Office, Chief of Engineering Division, and the Aircraft, Power Plant and Propeller Laboratories of Engineering Division T-3.

2. It is the opinion that:

a. The phenomenon reported is something real and not visionary or fictitious.

b. There are objects probably approximating the shape of a disc, of such appreciable size as to appear to be as large as man-made aircraft.

c. There is a possibility that some of the incidents may be caused by natural phenomena, such as meteors.

d. The reported operating characteristics such as extreme rates of climb, maneuverability (particularly in roll), and action which must be considered evasive when sighted or contacted by friendly aircraft and radar, lend belief to the possibility that some of the objects are controlled either manually, automatically or remotely.

e. The apparent common description of the objects is as follows:

(1) Metallic or light reflecting surface.

SECRET
COPY

U-39552

SECRET

Basic Ltr fr CG, AMC, WP to CG, AAF, Wash. D.C. subj "AMC Opinion Concerning "Flying Discs".

      (2) Absence of trail, except in a few instances when the object apparently was operating under high performance conditions.

      (3) Circular or elliptical in shape, flat on bottom and domed on top.

      (4) Several reports of well kept formation flights varying from three to nine objects.

      (5) Normally no associated sound, except in three instances a substantial rumbling roar was noted.

      (6) Level flight speeds normally above 300 knots are estimated.

    f. It is possible within the present U. S. knowledge --- provided extensive detailed development is undertaken -- to construct a piloted aircraft which has the general description of the object in subparagraph (e) above which would be capable of an approximate range of 7000 miles at subsonic speeds.

    g. Any developments in this country along the lines indicated would be extremely expensive, time consuming and at the considerable expense of current projects and therefore, if directed, should be set up independently of existing projects.

    h. Due consideration must be given the following:-

      (1) The possibility that these objects are of domestic origin - the product of some high security project not known to AC/AS-2 or this Command.

      (2) The lack of physical evidence in the shape of crash recovered exhibits which would undeniably prove the existance of these objects.

      (3) The possibility that some foreign nation has a form of propulsion possibly nuclear, which is outside of our domestic knowledge.

3. It is recommended that:-

    a. Headquarters, Army Air Forces issue a directive assigning a priority, security classification and Code Name for a detailed study of this matter to include the preparation of complete sets of all available and pertinent data which will then be made available to the Army, Navy, Atomic Energy Commission, JRDB, the Air Force Scientific Advisory Group, NACA, and the RAND and NEPA projects for comments and recommendations, with a preliminary report to be forwarded within 15 days of receipt of the data and a detailed report thereafter every 30 days as the investi-

COPY   **SECRET**   U-39552

SECRET

Basic Ltr fr CG, AMC, WF to CG, AAF, Wash. D.C. Subj "AMC Opinion Concerning "Flying Discs"

gation develops. A complete interchange of data should be effected.

    4. Awaiting a specific directive AMC will continue the investigation within its current resources in order to more closely define the nature of the pehnomenon. Detailed Essential Elements of Information will be formulated immediately for transmittal thru channels.

        N. F. TWINING
        Lieutenant General, U.S.A.
        Commanding

SECRET
COPY   U-39552

Members of the MJ-12 Group

Name	Date of Birth	Date of Death	Age in July 1947	Field
Lloyd V. Berkner	2/1/05	6/4/67	42	Scientist, explorer; executive secretary of JRDB; leader of space program; on CIA Robertson Panel
Detlev Bronk	8/13/97	11/17/75	49	Aviation physiologist; chair, National Academy of Sciences; National Research Council; pres. Johns Hopkins, Rockefeller University
Vannevar Bush	3/11/90	6/28/74	57	Head of NACA, OSRD, JRDB; other high-security R&D positions; MIT; Carnegie Institute
James V. Forrestal	2/15/92	5/22/49	55	Secretary of the Navy; 1st Secretary of Defense
Gordon Gray	5/30/09	11/25/82	38	5412 Committee; National Security advisor; other intelligence posts; Secretary of the Army
Roscoe H. Hillenkoetter	5/8/97	6/18/82	50	Admiral; Navy Intelligence; 1st director CIA; 3rd DCI
Jerome Hunsaker	8/26/86	9/10/84	60	Aeronautical engineer at MIT; head of NACA
Donald H. Menzel	4/11/01	12/14/76	46	Astronomer at Harvard; high-security consultant to NSA, CIA
Robert M. Montague	8/7/99	2/20/58	47	General, Army; commander of Ft. Bliss; Head Armed Forces Special Weapons Center, Sandia Base
Walter B. Smith	10/5/95	8/9/61	51	General, Army; ambassador to USSR; 2nd director CIA; 4th DCI
Sidney W. Souers	3/30/92	1/14/73	55	Admiral; intelligence consultant; 1st director Central Intelligence Group; 1st DCI; 1st executive secretary, NSC
Nathan F. Twining	10/11/97	3/29/82	49	General, Air Force; Head, AMC; Air Force Chief of Staff; Head, Joint Chiefs of Staff
Hoyt S. Vandenberg	1/24/99	4/2/54	48	General, Air Force; 2nd director Central Intelligence Group; 2nd DCI; Air Force Chief of Staff

NOTES

Chapter 1

1. General Nathan F. Twining, September 23, 1947, *www.nicap.org/twining_letter_docs.htm*. (See FOIA document in the Appendix.)

2. "Bolender Memo," USAF General Carroll H. Bolender, October 20, 1969, Unidentified Flying Objects, *www.nicap.org/Bolender_Memo.htm*.

Chapter 2

1. See document at *http://upload.wikimedia.org/ wikipedia/commons/6/62/1948top_secret_USAF_UFO_ extraterrestrial_document.png.*

2. Michael Swords, "Project Sign: An Estimate of the Situation," *www.nicap.org/papers/swords_Sign_EOTS. htm,* FOIA document, 474-475 in Swords, Michael, Robert Powell, et al., "Appendix," *UFOs and Government: A Historical Inquiry* (San Antonio, Texas: Anomalist Books 2012).

3. Nathan Twining, "AMC Opinion Concerning Flying Discs," letter to Commanding General U.S. Army Air Force, September 23, 1947, originally classified SECRET, *www.nicap.org/twining_letter_docs.htm.*

4. Edward Ruppelt, *The Report on Unidentified Flying Objects* (Garden City, N.Y.: Doubleday & Company, Inc., 1956), p. 60.

5. Ibid., p. 211.

6. "Washington National Sightings," July 1952, 1661. htm#Zero, *www.cufon.org/cufon/wash_nat/bb.*

7. Project Blue Book Case 1661, 12W2, 18/5A, Bx 35, RG 341 Records of the USAF, Project Blue Book, "Washington National Sightings," July 1952.

8. General Samford's Press Conference, DOD, Minutes of Press Conference, July 29, 1952, *www.nicap.org/waves/ pressconf_1952.htm.*

9. Ibid., p. 2.

10. Ibid.

11. Ibid., p. 3.

12. Ibid., p. 5.

13. Ibid.

14. Ibid., p. 19.

15. Edward Tauss, August 1, 1952 letter, FOIA document.

16. Swords, Powell, et al., *UFOs and Government: A Historical Inquiry*, p. 503.

17. J. Allen Hynek, "Are Flying Saucers Real?" *Saturday Evening Post*, December 17, 1966, *www.ufoevidence.org/documents/doc364.htm*.

18. Ibid.

19. Durant Report of the Robertson Panel. See *www.cufon.org/cufon/robert.htm*.

20. Air Force Regulation 200-2, issued August 1954, *https://en.wikisource.org/wiki/Air_Force_Regulation_200-2_Unidentified_Flying_Objects_Reporting#/media/File:Afr200- 21_jpg.jpg*.

Chapter 3

1. Menzel letter, APS, October 17, 1963.

2. Prepared statement by Donald H. Menzel, "UFO: Fact of Fiction?" presented to the Committee on Science and Astronautics of the U.S. House of Representatives, July 29, 1968, pp. 198–205.

3. Prepared statement by Stanton T. Friedman presented to the Committee on Science and Astronautics of the U.S. House of Representatives, July 29, 1968, pp. 207, 213–222.

4. Menzel statement, p. 203.

5. Prepared Statement by James E. McDonald presented to the Committee on Science and Astronautics of the U.S. House of Representatives, July 29, 1968, pp. 19–27, 32–85.

6. Friedman notes from Menzel's collection.

7. Memo from Klass to Menzel, July 19, 1968.

8. Ibid.

9. Hector Quintanilla, *UFOs: An Air Force Dilemma* (1974), p. 22.

10. Menzel, "Committee on Science and Astronautics," p. 98.

11. Wilbert Smith, Canadian Memo, November 21, 1950.

12. Menzel letter to JFK, August 13, 1960. Menzel Archival Collection, Harvard University.

13. Eisenhower Briefing Document. 4.

Chapter 4

1. Philip Klass, *UFOs Identified* (New York: Random House, 1968), pp. 9–10.

2. Ibid.

3. William McGilpin, USAF Headquarters document, *www.nicap.org/reports/650903exeter_docs1.htm.*

4. Eugene Bertrand and David Hunt, letter to Hector Quintanilla, December 23, 1965, *www.bluebookarchive. org/page.aspx?PageCode=MISC-PBB2-280.*

5. David H. Griffin, "Project Blue Book Report," HQ817th Combat Support Group, Pease AFB, *www.bluebookarchive.org/page. aspx?PageCode=MISC-PBB2-303.*

6. *www.bluebookarchive.org/page. aspx?PageCode=MISC-PBB2-267.*

7. Correspondence between McDonald and Klass, Klass's McDonald files, Klass Collection at the APS.

8. Ibid.

9. Correspondence between Condon and Allen, Klass Collection, APS, May 24, 1968.

10. Interdepartmental memo from Low to Klass, August 29, 1968, Klass Collection, Klass's Low files, APS.

11. Correspondence from James E. McDonald to Robert A. Frosch, September 25, 1968, Klass Collection, Klass's McDonald file, APS.

12. Anne Druffel, *Firestorm: James McDonald's Fight for UFO Science* (Columbus, N.C.: Wildflower Press, 2003), appendix 9-C, p. 549.

13. Klass memo to Menzel, July 19, 2968, APS.

14. Correspondence in Klass's file from Condon letter to Klass, October 31, 1969, APS.

15. Correspondence in Klass's Condon file from Klass to Condon, June 7, 1971, APS.

16. Letter from Philip J.Klass to Clarence Kelly (FBI director), June 14, 1975, Klass's FBI File, *www.cufon.org/cufon/Klass_FBI.pdf.*

17. Interdepartmental memorandum from Mr. Moore to Mr. Heim, Klass's FBI file, February 21, 1975, *www.cufon.org/cufon/Klass_FBI.pdf.*

18. Ibid.

19. Letter published in full at *keyholepublishing.com/New%20Klass%20Letter%20 Found.htm*, visited May 18, 2011.

20. Letter in Stanton Friedman's private collection, December 18, 1987.

21. Friedman's personal files.

22. Letter to Master Mike Arbaugh, March 6, 1976, Klass's Correspondence files, APS.

23. Marcello Truzzi, UFO Skeptic.org, *Zetetic Scholar,* #12–13, 1987.

24. Ibid.

Chapter 5

1. David Saunders, and R. Roger Harkins, *UFOs? Yes!, Where the Condon Committee Went Wrong* (New York: Signet Books, 1968), p. 35.

2. Quintanilla, *UFOs: An Air Force Dilemma*, p. 47.

3. Ibid., p. 49.

4. Ibid.

5. Saunders, and Harkins, *UFOs? Yes*, p. 47.

6. Dick Olive, "Most UFOs Explainable Says Scientist," *Star Gazette* (Elmira, N.Y.: 1991), *www.nicap.org/docs/HipplerLetters.pdf*, 5.

7. Quintanilla, *UFOs: An Air Force Dilemma*, p. 78.

8. Saunders and Harkins, *UFOs? Yes!*, Appendix A, pp. 242–244.

9. Philip Klass to Robert Low, December 30, 1966, Klass's APS files.

10. Robert Hippler letter to Edward Condon, Condon File, University of Colorado, January 27, 1967.

11. V. Vaughn, editor, James McDonald, *UFOs and Science: The Collected Writings of Dr. James E. McDonald* (Washington, D.C.: One Reed Publications, Fund for UFO Research, 1995), p. 91.

12. Klass's personal notes on his meeting with Robert Low, August 3, 1967, Klass Collection, APS.

13. Ibid.

14. Edward Condon letter to Klass, May 24, 1968, Klass Collection, APS.

15. Edward Condon letter to Klass, February 27, 1968, Klass Collection, APS.

16. Edward Condon, "Conclusions and Recommendations," *The Scientific Study of Unidentified Flying Objects*, p. 28.

17. "Review of the University of Colorado Report on Unidentified Flying Objects by a Panel of the National Academy of Sciences," Attachment 2, Archival document, 1969.

Chapter 6

1. J. Allen Hynek, *The UFO Experience: A Scientific Inquiry* (Chicago, Ill.: Henry Regnery Co., 1972), p. 169.

2. Ibid.

3. Frederick C. Durant, "The Durant Report of the Robertson Panel Proceedings," *www.bibliotecapleyades. net/sociopolitica/esp_sociopol_mj12_3a6.htm.*

4. Quintanilla, *UFOs: An Air Force Dilemma*, Appendix ii.

5. Donald Menzel to H.P. Robertson, April, 16, 1958. Menzel Collection, APS.

6. Ibid.

7. Donald Quarles, "Department of Defense Release 1053-55," 10/25/1955, *www.theufochronicles.com/2009_05_01_ archive.html.*

8. Hall, Richard "US Air Force Censorship of UFOs Stirred Controversy in 1958," *www.nicap.org/armstrong.htm.*

9. Ibid.

10. Grant Cameron, "Disney, UFOs and Disclosure," *www. rense.com/general27/dis.htm.*

11. Quintanilla, *UFOs: An Air Force Dilemma*, p. 53.

12. Ibid., p. 55.

13. Ibid., p. 56.

14. Ibid., p. 59.

15. Ibid.

16. Ibid., p. 78.

17. Ibid., p. 22.

18. Menzel letter to Seamans, January 5, 1970, APS.

19. Ibid.

20. Letter from Robert Low to Philip Klass, February 27, 1969, Klass Collection, APS.

21. Letter from Robert Low to Philip Klass, May 6, 1969, Klass Collection, APS.

22. Letter from Condon to Klass, October 31, 1969, Klass Collection, APS.

23. Letter from Menzel to Klass, August 20, 1968, Klass Collection, APS.

Chapter 7

1. FBI document on the Lonnie Zamora, Socorro, NM UFO sighting, *www.nicap.org/docs/640424zamora_fbi_docs.pdf.*

2. Allen Hynek's Project Blue Book Report, p. 2, Project Blue Book files, *www.nicap.org/docs/640424socorro_docs51-75.pdf.*

3. Klass, *UFOs—Identified*, p. 220.

4. Druffel, *Firestorm*, McDonald's notes, "Socorro Landing Report," p. 217.

5. Klass, *UFOs—Identified*, p. 198.

6. Allen Hynek, "Report on Trip to Socorro-Albuquerque-Socorro," March 12–13, 1965, *www.nicap.org/docs/640424socorro_docs26-50.pdf,* p. 16.

7. Project Blue Book Report, *www.nicap.org/docs/640424socorro_docs51-75.pdf,* p. 19.

8. Hector Quintanilla, Project Blue Book Files, "Studies in Intelligence," 1966.

9. Philip Klass to James Moseley, July 31, 1987, Klass Correspondence files, APS.

10. Hynek, "Report on Trip."

11. C.E. Gilson's polygraph exam report, Walton's investigation files supplied to Marden by The Mutual UFO Network.

12. C.E. Gilson's letter to Sheriff Gilespie, November 13, 1975, *Wikimedia.org/Wikipedia/commons/a/a2/ TravisWalton.*

13. Philip Klass, "New Evidence that the Walton UFO Abduction is a Hoax," June 20, 1976, p. 7.

14. Ibid.

15. Letter from William Spaulding to Philip Klass, February 18, 1985, Klass's Walton Collection, APS.

16. Letter from James Lorenzen to Philip Klass, November 5, 1976, Klass's Walton Collection. APS.

17. Harder's response to a question asked at the UFO Congress in Chicago, Klass's Walton file, APS, June 24, 1977.

18. Klass's transcript of his conversation with Lorenzen on March 21, 1976, Klass's Walton Collection, APS.

19. George J. Pfeiffer, Jr.'s report on Duane Walton's polygraph exam, February 9, 1976, Klass's Walton Collection, APS.

20. George J. Pfeiffer, Jr., report on Travis Walton's polygraph exam, February 9, 1976, Klass's Walton Collection.

21. Klass, "New Evidence," p. p. 15.

22. Mike Rogers's letter to Philip J. Klass, September 18, 1976, Klass's Walton Collection, APS.

23. Mike Rogers's letter to Philip J. Klass, December 12m 1976, Klass's Walton Collection, APS.

24. Klass's transcript of his teleconference with Gonsalves, May 21, 1976, Klass's Walton Collection, APS.

25. Mike Rogers to Phil Klass, Klass's teleconference with Rogers, July 11 1976, APS files.

Chapter 8

1. Klass's comment in his "White Paper" on the Travis Walton case.

2. Bergstrom AFB interview with Cash, and Landrum, *www.cufon.org/cufon/cashlani2.htm#top*; and John Schuessler, "Cash-Landrum Case Investigation by U.S. Army Inspector General," p. 8.

3. Letter to Philip Klass from Peter Rank, MD, March 23, 1982, Klass's Cash-Landrum Files. APS.

4. Ibid.

5. Gary Posner, MD to Peter Rank, MD, April 5, 1982, Klass's Cash-Landrum Files, APS.

6. Ibid.

7. George Sarran, Memorandum of Division Chief, DAIG, no date, *www.blueblurrylines.com/2013/11/the-daig-investigation-of-cash-landrum.html*, p. 2.

8. Private correspondence between Marden and Schuessler, November 22, 2015.

9. Billy Cox, "Klass Act: No Principles," *Sarasota Herald Tribune*, February 20, 2012, *http://devoid.blogs.heraldtribune.com/12797/klass-act-no-principles*.

10. Ibid.

Chapter 9

1. Lee Spiegel, "Lord Martin Rees: Aliens Fascinate Everyone: But Only Kooks See UFOS," September 19,

Notes

2012, *www.huffingtonpost.com/2012/09/19/lord-martin-rees- aliens-ufos_n_1892005.html.*

2. Merriam Webster Dictionary, *www.merriam-webster.com/dictionary/anecdote.*

3. James McDonald, "RB-47 Case Report for the AIAA," *Astronautics and Aeronautics*, July 1971.

4. Seth Shostak, *Confessions of an Alien Hunter* (Washington: National Geographic Society, 2009), p. 135.

5. Ibid.

6. Ibid.

7. Ibid.

8. Don Lincoln, *Alien Universe: Extraterrestrial Life in our Minds and in the Cosmos* (Baltimore, Md.: Johns Hopkins University Press, 2013), p. 33.

9. Ibid.

10. Ibid., p. 35.

11. Ibid.

12. Ibid., p. 36.

13. Michael Sainato, "Dr. Michio Kaku on Why Aliens May Exist but Aren't Landing on the White House Lawn," *The Guardian Observer*, November 4, 2016, p. 8.

14. Marcel Kuijsten, "The Development of the Transistor and the Integrated Circuit: Exploring Col. Corso's Claims of Extraterrestrial Reverse Engineering," 2015.

15. Philip J. Corso, and William J. Birnes, *The Day After Roswell* (New York: Pocket Books, 1997), Foreword p. X.

16. Philip Corso's military records, *www.cufon.org/cufon/corso_da66.htm.*

Chapter 10

1. The Shulman Files at *www.youtube.com/ watch?v=6P2qXq_WnmQ. 12/24/2015.*
2. Ibid.
3. Ibid.
4. Ibid.
5. "I Had Sex With an Alien," Mentorn Productions for Discovery Canada, March 1, 2006, Marden's Collection.
6. Fox News, "Watter's World," *http://video.foxnews. com/v/4790830458001/watters-world-ufo-edition/#sp=show-clips*, February 2016.
7. John Quinn letter to Philip Klass, February 14, 1978, Klass Correspondence files, APS.
8. John Quinn letter to Philip Klass, July 20, 1978, Klass Correspondence files, APS.

Chapter 11

1. Bolender Memo, October 20, 1969.
2. Ibid.
3. Emily Calandrelli, "SETI Scientist Explains Why We Haven't Found Aliens Yet," *Tech Crunch*, February 4, 2016, *http://techcrunch.com/2016/02/04/seti-scientist-explains- why-we-havent-found-aliens-yet/?ncid=rss# .symxod8:s6vq.*
4. Nicholas Kristoff, "Are We Getting Nicer?" *New York Times*, November 23, 2011, *www.nytimes.com/2011/11/24/ opinion/kristof-are-we-getting-nicer.html?_r=1.*
5. "List of Religious Populations," *https://en.wikipedia.org/ wiki/List_of_religious_populations.*
6. Dr. Shabir Ally, "What Does Islam Say on UFO Aliens Disclosure," Educating Humanity, *www*

.educatinghumanity.com/2013/03/what-does-Islam-say-on-UFO-aliens-Disclosure.html.

7. "Chile: Declassification Begins," Educating Humanity, *www.educatinghumanity.com/2011/02/declassification-begins-in-chile-of-ufo.html.*

8. "Air Force Order on Saucers Cited," *New York Times*, February 27, 1960, p. L30, *www.wanttoknow.info/600228nytimes.*

9. Ottawa, CA, PRWEB, November 24, 2005, *http://rense.com/general68/eurdo.htm*, accessed February 3, 2016.

10. Interview with Paul Hellyer by RT news in Toronto with Moscow, *www.youtube.com/watch?v=Pg6VTzacb9I.*

11. Complete letter at *www.ufoevidence.org/news/article161.htm.*

12. George Filer, Filer's Files, February 12, 2016.

13. Micah Hanks, "Poll Position: UFOs and the Enigma of Public Opinion," July 3, 2012, *http://mysteriousuniverse.org/2012/07/poll-position-ufos-and-the-enigma-of-public-opinion/.*

Chapter 12

1. Hynek, *The UFO Experience*, p. 103.

2. Jerome Clark, *The UFO Book: Encyclopedia of the Extraterrestrial* (Canton, Mich.: Visible Ink Press, 1997), p. 459.

3. Erol Faruk, *The Compelling Scientific Evidence for UFOs* (Amazon Digital Services, July 2014), p. 64.

4. William Markowitz, "The Physics and Metaphysics of UFOs," *Science*, 15 September 1274, 1967.

5. Project Blue Book Special Report No. 14, October 25, 1955, p. 12.

6. Bolender's Memo, October 20, 1969.

BIBLIOGRAPHY

AFR.200-5. August 12, 1954, *www.cufon.org/cufon/4602smpl4.htm#top* (visited 10/15/2014).

AIAA UFO Subcommittee. "UFO an Appraisal of the Problem," *Astronautics and Aeronautics* August 1, 1970, p. 49. (Review of Condon Report).

AIAA UFO Subcommittee. "UFO: An Appraisal of the Problem," *Astronautics and Aeronautics* 8:11 (1970): 49. (Review of Condon Report).

"Air Force Order on Saucers Cited." *New York Times*, February 27, 1960, p. L30, *www.wanttoknow.info/600228nytimes* (visited 2/5/2016).

Air Force Regulation 200-2. August 1954, *www.cufon.org/cufon/afr200-2.htm* (visited 10/17/2014).

"The Alien Abduction Files: A Christian Perspective." *http:// endtimesaltandlight.com/wp-content/uploads/2016/01/ AlienAbductions_AResponse.pdf* (visited 1/23/2016).

Ally, Shabir. "Educating Humanity," *www.educatinghumanity .com/2013/03/what-does-Islam-say-on-UFO-aliens-Disclosure .html* (visited 2/12/2016).

Bartholomaus, Derek. "Strange Things Regarding the Billy Meier Hoax Case Timeline," *www.abovetopsecret.com/forum/thread336734/pg1* (visited 10/17/2015).

Bergstrom AFB interview with Cash and Landrum. August 17, 1981, *www.cufon.org/cufon/cashlan1.htm* and *www.cufon.org/cufon/ cashlan2.htm#top* (visited 11/18/2015).

Bernstein, Carl. "The CIA and the Media," *Rolling Stone*, October 20, 1977, *carlbernstein.com//magazine_cia_and_media.php* (visited 4/20/16).

Bertrand, Eugene, and David Hunt. Letter to Hector Quintanilla, December 23, 1965, *www.bluebookarchive.org/page. aspx?PageCode=MISC-PBB2-280* (visited 10/15/ 2015).

"Billy Meier UFO Case: The Timeline." *www.billymeierufocase .com/billymeiertimeline.html* (visited 10/17/2015).

Bolender Memo. USAF Brigadier General Carroll H. Bolender, October 20, 1969, "Unidentified Flying Objects," *www.nicap.org/Bolender_ Memo.htm* (visited 2/4/2015).

Bordon, Richard C., and Tirey K. Vickers. "A Preliminary Study of the Unidentified Targets Observed on Air Traffic Control Radars. May 1953," *www.cufon.org/cufon/wash_nat/wash_faa .htm* (visited 10/9/2014).

Calandrelli, Emily. "SETI Scientist Explains Why We Haven't Found Aliens Yet," *Tech Crunch*, February 4, 2016, *http://techcrunch. com/2016/02/04/seti-scientist-explains-why-we-havent-found-aliens- yet/?ncid=rss#.symxod8:s6vq* (visited 2/8/2016).

Cameron, Grant. "Disney, UFOs and Disclosure," *www.rense.com/ general27/dis.htm* (visited 1/4/2016).

Cash-Landrum medical files. *https://app.box.com/s/ zvelar3gubgiee5zwgi3* (visited 10/3/2015).

Charles Weiner's interview with Edward Condon. Boulder, Colorado, October 1967, *www.aip.org/history.ohilist/4497_1.html* (visited 2/27/2014).

"Chile: Declassification Begins." Educating Humanity Website, *www. educatinghumanity.com/2011/02/declassification-begins-in-chile-of-ufo.html* (visited 2/14/2016).

"Christianity Statistics." *http://christianity.about.com/od/ denominations/p/christiantoday.htm* (visited 2/13/2016).

Clark, Jerome. "Phil Klass vs. the UFO Promoters," *FATE Magazine*, February 1981. Also at *www.nicap.org/klassvufo.htm* (visited 5/25/2011).

———. "The Debunkers vs. the UFO Menace," 1992. Also at *www. nicap.org/ debunk1.htm, 5/25/2011* (visited 11/20/2015).

———. *The UFO Book: Encyclopedia of the Extraterrestrial* (Detroit, Mich.: Visible Ink, 1998).

———. *The UFO Encyclopedia, Vol 3. High Strangeness: UFOs from 1960 to 1979* (Detroit, Mich.: Omnigraphics, Inc., 1996).

"Common Side Effects of Radiation Therapy." American Cancer Society, June 30,2015, *www.cancer.org/treatment/ treatmentsandsideeffects/treatmenttypes/radiation/ understandingradiationtherapyaguideforpatientsandfamilies/ understanding-radiation-therapy-common-side-effects* (visited 11/21/2015).

Condon, Edward U., et al. *The Scientific Study of Unidentified Flying Objects* (New York: Bantam Books, 1969).

Cooper, Gordon. "Letter to Granada's Ambassador Griffith," *www. ufoevidence.org/news/article16.htm* (visited 3/14/2016).

Corso, Philip, and William J. Birnes. *The Day After Roswell* (New York: Pocket Books, 1997).

Cox, Billy. "Cash-Landrum: Gone With the Wind," *Sarasota Herald Tribune, http://devoid'blogs.heraldtribune.com/11457/cash-landrum-gone-with-the-wind/#* (visited 11/20/2015).

———. "Klass Act: No Pricniples," *Saratoga Herald Tribune*, February 20, 2012, *http://devoid.blogs.heraldtribune.com/12797/klass-act-no-principles* (visited 11/20/2015).

Cybulski, J. "3rd Commander's Conference. Ent AFB, Colorado," *www.cufon.org/cufon/4602smpl3.htm#topHq4602dAISS* (visited 10/15/2015).

Didymus, John Thomas. "Roswell Alien Photo Slides to Be Released: 'Smoking Gun' Evidence of 1947 UFO Crash?" *www.inquisitr.com/1816875/roswell-alien-photo-slides-to-be-released-smoking-gun-evidence-of-1947-ufo-crash* (visited 1/29/2016).

"Delbert Newhouse UFO Footage." Tremonton, Utah, July 2, 1952, *http://youtube/of3m8_LvUWs* (visited 10/12/2015).

Dolan, Richard M. "New Klass Letter Found," *keyholepublishing.com/New%20Klass%20Letter%20Found.htm* (visited 5/18/2011).

———. *UFOs and the National Security State* (Charlottesville, Va.: Hampton Roads, 2002).

Dolan, Richard M., and Bryce Zabel. *A.D.: After Disclosure* (Pompton Plains, N.J.: New Page Books, 2012).

"Donald Howard Menzel." *Complete Dictionary of Scientific Biography* (High Beam Research, Inc., 2014), *Encyclopedia.com/topic/Donald_Howard_Menzel.aspx* (visited 7/24/2014).

Downing, Barry. *The Bible and Flying Saucers* 2nd Edition (Boston, Mass.: Da Capo Press, 1997).

Druffle, Ann. *Firestorm Dr. James E.McDonalds Fight for UFO Science* (Columbus, N.C.: Wildflower Press, 2003).

Durant, Robert. "The Durant Report of the Robertson Panel," *www.cufon.org/cufon/robert.htm* (visited 10/14/2015).

Faruk, Erol. *The Compelling Scientific Evidence for UFOs* (Houston, Texas: Create Space Independent Publishing Platform, 2014).

FBI declassified document dated 5/11/76 from Director. FBI to SAC, Newark, *www.CUFON.org* (visited 5/24/2011).

FBI documents on the Lonnie Zamora, Socorro, New Mexico case. April 25, 1964, *www.nicap.org/docs/640424 zamora_fbi_docs.pdf* (visited 12/4/2014).

FBI Memorandum by Agent Heim, February 21, 1975, *www.cufon.org/cufon/Klass_FBI.pdf* (visited 4/20/2014).

Bibliography

Filer, George. "Filer's Files" (newsletter by subscription), February 12, 2016.

Friedman, Stanton, and Kathleen Marden. *Captured! The Betty and Barney Hill UFO Experience* (Franklin Lakes, N.J.: New Page Books, 2007).

———. *Science Was Wrong* (Pompton Plains, N.J.: New Page Books, 2010).

"From Their Own Lips: Betty, Vickie and Colby Tell Their Story." August 17, 1981, *www.blueblurrylines.com/2013/07/from-their-own-lips-betty-cash-colby.html* (visited 10/22/2015).

Fuller, John G. "Flying Saucer Fiasco," *LOOK* May 14, 1968, pp. 58–63.

———. *Incident at Exeter* (New York: G.B. Putnam's Sons, 1966).

———. *The Interrupted Journey* (New York: Dial Press, 1966).

"Function to Defense Command Combat Readiness Elements of Information by Overt Collection of Air Combat Intelligence in the Air Defense UNIDENTIFIED FLYING OBJECTS." Section 2 in a series of 7, June 1953, *www.cufon.org/cufon/4602smpl2.htm#top* (visited 10 /10/2015).

Gilson, C.E. Letter to Sheriff Gilespie. November 13, 1975, *Wikimedia.org/Wikipedia/commons/a/a2/TravisWalton* (visited 9/24/2010).

"Gordon Cooper." *https://en.wikipedia.org/wiki/Gordon_Cooper* (visited 3/14/2016).

Griffin, David H. "Project Blue Book Report," HQ817th Combat Support Group, Pease AFB, *www.bluebookarchive.org/page.aspx?PageCode=MISC-PBB2-303* (visited 4/17/2015).

"Hair Loss from Cancer Treatment." *www.emedicinehealth.com/hair_loss_from_cancer_treatment-health/article_em.htm* (visited 10/21/2015). Hall, Michael. "Project Blue Book 1951–1969," *www.nicap.org/bluebook/51-69.htm* (visited 3/3/2013).

Hall, Richard. *The UFO Evidence* Vol. 2 (Lanham, Md.: Scarecrow Press, 2001).

———. "US Air Force Censorship of UFOs Stirred Controversy in 1958," January 22, 1958, *www.nicap.org/armstrong.htm* (visited 12/22/2015).

Hanks, Micah. "Poll Position: UFOs and the Enigma of Public Opinion," July 3, 2012, *http://mysteriousuniverse.org/2012/07/poll-position-ufos-and-the-enigma-of-public-opinion/*. (visited 2/5/2016).

Hastings, Robert L. *UFOs and Nukes*, "Extraordinary Encounters at Nuclear Weapons Sites" (Bloomington, Ind.: Author House, 2008).

Hilton, John.L., John Luce, and A.S. Thompson. "Hypothetical Fusion Propulsion Vehicle," *Journal of Spacecraft* Vol. 1 (1964), p. 276.

Howe, Linda Moulton. "History and Background CHD 4-29." April 29, 2013, *http://disclosure.media/linda- moulton-howe-history-and-background-chd-4-29/#sthash.OITjiMiv.dpbs* (visited 10/22/2015).

Huessner, Ki Mae. "Steven Hawking: Alien Contact Could be Risky," April 26, 1010, *http://abcnews.go.com/Technology/Space/stephen-hawking-alien-contact-risky/story?id=10478157* (visited 2/10/2016).

Hynek, Allen. *The Hynek UFO Report* (New York: Dell Publishing, 1977).

———. "Report on Trip to Socorro-Albuquerque-Socorro," March 12, 1965, p. 16, *www.nicap.org/docs/640424socorro_docs26-50.pdf* (visited 10/13/2014).

———. *The UFO Experience: A Scientific Inquiry* (Chicago: Henry Regnery Co., 1972).

———. "The UFO Mystery," *FBI Law Enforcement Bulletin*, pp. 16–20, February 1975, *www.cufon.org/cufon/hynek-fbi-leb* (visited 4/20/2014).

Hynek, J. Allen. "Are Flying Saucers Real?" *Saturday Evening Post*, December 17, 1966, *www.ufoevidence.org/documents/doc364.htm* (visited 1/15/2015).

"I Had Sex With an Alien." DVD by Mentorn Productions for Discovery Canada, March 1, 2006.

Interdepartmental Memorandum from Mr. Moore to Mr. Heim. Klass's FBI file, February 21, 1975, *www.cufon.org/cufon/Klass_FBI.pdf* (visited 4/29/2013).

Interview with Hellyer by RT News in Toronto with Moscow. *www.youtube.com/watch?v=Pg6VTzacb9I* (visited 2/15/2016).

Bibliography

Jacobs, David. *The Threat: Revealing the Secret Alien Agenda* (New York: Fireside, 1998).

———. *Walking Among Us: The Alien Plan to Control Humanity* (San Francisco, Calif.: Disinformation Books, 2015).

Kelso, John. "US Test Gone Wild Brings Suit," *Austin American Statesman*, September 29, 1985.

Klass, Philip. *UFO Abductions: A Dangerous Game* (Buffalo, N.Y.: Prometheus Books, 1989).

———. *UFOs Identified* (New York: Random House, 1968).

———. *UFOs: The Public Deceived* (Buffalo, N.Y.: Prometheus Books, 1983).

———. White Paper, "New Evidence that the Walton UFO Abduction is a Hoax." Philadelphia, APS, June 20, 1976.

Kristoff, Nicholas. "Are We Getting Nicer?" *New York Times*, November 23, 2011, *www.nytimes.com/2011/11/24/opinion/kristof-are-we-getting-nicer.html?_r=1* (visited 2/8/2016).

Kuijsten, Marcel. "The Development of the Transistor and the Integrated Circuit; Exploring Col. Corso's Claims of Extraterrestrial Reverse Engineering," 2015.

Letter from Philip J. Klass to Clarence Kelly, FBI director, June 14, 1975. Klass's FBI File, *www.cufon.org/cufon/Klass_FBI.pdf* (visited 4/28/2013).

Lincoln, Don. *Alien Universe: Extraterrestrial Life in Our Minds and in the Cosmos* (Baltimore, Md.: John Hopkins University Press, 2013).

"List of Religious Populations." *https://en.wikipedia.org/wiki/List_of_religious_populations* (visited 2/12/2016).

Marden, Kathleen. "Psychological Studies on Abduction Experiencers," *www.kathleen-marden.com/psychological-studies.php* (visited 2/20/2016).

Marden, Kathleen, and Denise Stoner. *The Alien Abduction Files* (Pompton Plains, N.J.: New Page Books, 2013).

McDonald, James E. *UFOs and Science: The Collected Writings of Dr. James E. McDonald*, ed. by V. Vaughn (Mt. Rainier, Md.: One Reed Publications, the Fund for UFO Research, 1995).

McGilpin, William. USAF Headquarters document, *www.nicap.org/ reports/650903exeter_docs1.htm* (visited 2/13/2016).

McNiel, Legs. "Loving the Aliens," *Spin*, July 1987, p. 63, *https://books. google.com/books?id=sc9ijqDIbEgC&pg=PA63&lpg=PA63&dq=w endelle+stevens+prison&source=bl&ots=outDr9X2Vo&sig=H1IR HDhJUOhMWLVFnaUujFnpoVI&hl=en&ei=fGNTO34BoWCsQ- OUhr3BBA&sa=X&oi=book_result&ct=result&sqi=2#v=onepage&q= wendelle%20stevens%20prison&f=true* (visited 10/17/2015).

Menzel, Donald. "Prepared Statement by Donald H. Menzel, UFO: Fact of Fiction?" Presented to the Committee on Science and Astronautics of the U.S. House of Representatives, July 29, 1968, pp. 198–205, *www2.8newsnow.com/docs/1968_UFO.pdf* (visited 7/25/2015).

Merriam Webster Dictionary. *www.merriam-webster.com/dictionary/ anecdote.* (visited 10/26/2015).

Michaud, Michael A.G. *Contact With Alien Civilizations* (New York: Copernicus, 2007).

Morse, Philip M. "A Biographical Memoir of Edward Uhler Condon, March 2, 1904–March 26, 1974," National Academy of Sciences, 1974, *www.nasonline.org/publications/biographical-memoirs/ memoir-pdfs/condon-edward-u-1902-1974.pdf* (visited 1/27/2014).

Olive, Dick. "Most UFOs Explainable Says Scientist," *Star Gazette* (Elmira, N.Y.), January 26, 1967, *www.nicap.org/docs/HipplerLetters. pdf* (visited 1/26/2014).

Ottawa, CA, PRWEB. November 24, 2005, *http://rense.com/general68/ eurdo.htm* (visited 2/3/2016).

Philip Corso's military records. *www.cufon.org/cufon/corso_da66.htm* (visited 1/24/2016).

Posner, Gary. "Extraterrestrials May Be out There, but He Says They're Not Here," *Skeptic* 7:3, December 1999, *www.skeptic.com/reading_ room/extraterrestrials-may-be-out-there* (visited 9/16/2015).

"Potential Cultural Impact of Extraterrestrial Contact." *https:// en.wikipedia.org/wiki/Potential_cultural_impact_of_ extraterrestrial_contact* (visited 2/12/2016).

Project Blue Book Files on Refueling Mission. *www .bluebookarchive.org/page.aspx?PageCode=MISC-PBB2-267* (visited 2/16/2016).

Project Blue Book files on the Lonnie Zamora, Socorro, New Mexico UFO sighting. *www.nicap.org/docs/640424socorro_docs01-25.pdf* (visited 10/3/2014).

"Project Blue Book Report." Project Blue Book files, p. 2, *www .nicap.org/ docs/640424socorro_docs51-75.pdf* (visited 9/16/2014).

Project Blue Book Case 1661, 12W2, 18/5A, Bx 35, RG 341 Records of the USAF, Project Blue Book, "Washington National Sightings," July 1952, www.cufon.org/cufon/wash_nat/bb_1661.htm#Zero (visited 10/9/2014).Quarles, Donald. "Department of Defense Release 1053-55 Áir Force Releases Study of Unidentified Flying Objects," October 25, 1955, *www.theufochronicles.com/2009_05_01_archive. html* (visited 3/16/2016).

Quintanilla, Hector. *UFOs: An Air Force Dilemma* (1974), *http://ufologie. patrickgross. org/doc/quintanilla.pdf* (visited 3/12/2015).

Randle, Kevin. "UFOS: A Different Perspective," January 22, 2014, "Philip Corso and the Day After Roswell" again (visited 3/14/2016).

"Report of the Scientific Advisory Panel on Unidentified Flying Objects Convened by Office of Scientific Intelligence," CIA, January 14–18, 1953, *www.cufon.org/cufon/robert.htm* (visited 2/10/2015).

"Review of the University of Colorado Report on Unidentified Flying Objects by a Panel of the National Academy of Sciences." Attachment 2, Archival document, 1969.

Rojas, Alejandro. "Roswell Alien Slides Deciphered, Says it's a Dummy," May 19, 2015, *www.openminds.tv/roswell-alien-slides-placard-deciphered-says-it-is-a-mummy/33612* (visited 1/29/2016).

Roswell Daily Record, July 8, 1947, found at *www.roswellufomuseum. com/incident.html* (visited 2/21/2015).

Ruppelt, Edward J. *The Report on Unidentified Flying Objects* (Garden City, N.Y.: Doubleday and Co., Inc. 1956).

Sainato, Michael. "Dr. Michio Kaku on Why Aliens May Exist but Aren't Landing on the White House Lawn," *The Guardian Observer*, November 4, 2015.

Salas, Robert. *Unidentified: The UFO Phenomenon* (Wayne, N.J.: New Page Books, 2014).

Samford, John A. General Samford's Press Conference minutes. DOD, Minutes of Press Conference, July 29, 1952, *www.nicap.org/waves/pressconf_1952.htm* (visited 10/13/2014 and 5/23/2015).

Sarran, George. "Memorandum of Division Chief, DAIG." No date, 2, *www.blueblurrylines.com/2013/11/the-daig-investigation-of-cash-landrum.html* (visited 11/17/2015).

Saunders, David, and R. Roger Harkins. *UFOs? Yes!, Where the Condon Committee Went Wrong* (New York: Signet Books, 1968).

Schuessler, John, and Bob Pratt. *The Cash-Landrum Incident* (Houston, Texas: Create Space Independent Publishing Platform, 1998).

———. "UFO-Related Human Physiological Effects," *Journal of Scientific Investigation*, 1996.

Serling, Rod. *www.disclose.tv/action/viewvideo/90488/Rod_Serling_s__UFOs:ItHasBegun1976__Full/* (visited 2/14/2016).

Sheaffer, Robert. "Between Beer Joint and some kind of Highway Warning Sign: The Classic Cash-Landrum Case Unravels." *http://badufos.blogspot.com/2013/11/between-beer-joint-and-some-kind-of.html.* (visited 1.24/2015).

Shostak, Seth. *Confessions of an Alien Hunter* (Washington: National Geographic Society, 2009).

"The Shulman Files." www.youtube.com/watch?v=6P2qXq_WnmQ (visited 12/24/2015).

Spiegel, Lee. "Lord Martin Rees: Aliens Fascinate Everyone: But Only Kooks See UFOS," September 19, 2012, *www.huffingtonpost.com/2012/09/19/lord-martin-rees- aliens-ufos_n_1892005.html* (visited 10/26/2015).

Stein, Jennifer. *TRAVIS: The True Story of Travis Walton*, award-winning documentary, Onwinges Productions, 2015.

Sturrock, Peter. "Physical Evidence Related to UFO Reports: Physiological Effects on Witnesses," Sturrock Panel Report, *www.ufoevidence.org/documents/doc491.htm* (visited 1/26/2015).

Swords, Michael, Robert Powell, et al. *UFOs and the Government: A Historical Inquiry* (San Antonio, Texas: Anomalist Books, 2012).

Swords, Michael. "Project Sign: An Estimate of the Situation," *www. nicap.org/papers/swords_Sign_EOTS.html* (visited 2/26/2015), FOIA document on pp. 474–475. Appendix. *UFOs and Government: A Historical Inquiry.* Swords, Powell.

Top Secret Declassified USAF Document. *http://upload.wikimedia. org/wikipedia/commons/6/22/1948_top_secret_USAF_UFO_ extraterrestrial_document.png* (visited 2/29/2016).

Tough, Allen. "What Role will Extraterrestrials play in Humanity's Future?" *Journal of the British Interplanetary Society* Vol 39 (1986), pp. 491–498.

Truzzi, Marcello. "On Pseudo-Skepticism," *Zetetic Scholar* (1987) No. 12/13, 3–4. Also at *www.ufoskeptic.org* (visited 5/25/2011).

Twining, Nathan F. "AMC Opinion Concerning Flying Disks," September 23, 1947, *www.nicap.org/twining_letter_docs.htm* (visited 12/14/2015). Original document provided by Keith Chester.

USAF Fact Sheet 95-03. June 1, 2008, *www.cufon.org/cufon/malmstrom/ UFO_A.html* (visited 10/17/2015).

Walton, Travis. *Fire in the Sky: The Walton Experience* (New York: Marlowe and Co., 1996).

"Washington National Sightings." July 1952. 1661. *www.cufon.org/cufon/ wash_nat/bb* (visited 1/26/2015).

"Watter's World" News Segment. Fox TV, *http://video.foxnews. com/v/4790830458001/watters-world-ufo-edition/#sp=show-clips* (visited 3/2/2016).

Weiner, Charles. "The University of Colorado UFO Project: The Scientific Study of UFOs," *Journal of UFO Studies* Vol. 6 (Chicago, Ill.: CUFOS, 1995/1996), *www.cufos.org/condon_the_scientific_ study_of_ufoss.pdf* (visited 2/15/2014).

Weintraub, David A. *Religions and Extraterrestrial Life: How Will We Deal With It?* (New York: Springer, 2014).

Zimmer, Troy. "Belief in UFOs as Alternative Reality, Cultural Rejection or Disturbed Psyche," *Deviant Behavior* 6 (1985) 405–419.

INDEX

Index

ABOUT THE AUTHORS

Stanton T. Friedman is a nuclear physicist who worked on a wide variety of advanced, classified nuclear systems for major industrial companies. He has lectured about UFOs at more than 700 college and professional groups in 50 states, 10 provinces, and 18 countries. He began the civilian investigation of the Roswell Incident; wrote *Flying Saucers and Science* and *TOP SECRET/MAJIC*; and co-authored *Crash at Corona, Captured! The Betty and Barney Hill UFO Experience*, and *Science Was Wrong*. He has appeared on hundreds of radio and TV programs and has visited 20 archives. He resides in Fredericton, New Brunswick, Canada.

Kathleen Marden is a bestselling author and award-winning, scientifically trained UFO researcher who is passionate about archival research. She has lectured nationally and internationally, and is a frequent guest on radio shows. Her expert testimony has been heard on the History, Discovery, National Geographic, and Destination America channels, as well as several news segments. She is the coauthor of *Captured! The Betty and Barney Hill UFO Experience, Science Was Wrong,* and *The Alien Abduction Files.* She resides near Orlando, Florida.